TERROR IN AUSTRALIA
Workers' Paradise Lost

by
John Stapleton

ISBN: 978-0-9944-7911-2

Cover design by Jessica Bell

A catalogue record for this book is available from the National Library of Australia

NATIONAL LIBRARY OF AUSTRALIA

Australian jihadists:

- Adam Dahman, 18, from Melbourne, strapped a belt bomb to himself and detonated it in a busy marketplace near a Shi'ite mosque in Baghdad killing five people on 17 July, 2014.
- Abu Asma Al-Australi aka Ahmed Succarieh, 27, a family man from Brisbane and Australia's first suicide bomber; he detonated a truck loaded with 12 tonnes of explosives, killing 35 Syrian soldiers. Video shows him giving a speech on the back of the truck draped in the Islamic State flag prior to the martyrdom operation.
- Abdul Numan Haider, 18, killed by counter terrorism officers in Melbourne. Hailed by Islamic State as a martyr.
- Man Haron Monis, 50, died in Sydney in December, 2014, in the resolution of the Martin Place siege. Hailed by Islamic State as a martyr.
- Abdul Salaam Mahmoud, reportedly killed in Syria in March, 2015. A Sudanese born Australian.
- Abdul Mohamad Al-Ghaz'Zaoui, Australian born of Lebanese descent from Bankstown in Western Sydney. Reportedly killed in Syria Christmas of 2014.
- Ahmad Moussalli, Lebanese Australian killed in Syria, February 2014.
- Temel Caner, 22, killed in Syria, January 2014. Went AWOL from Brisbane army barracks.
- Irfaan Hussein, 19, killed in Syria, allegedly for attempting to return to Australia.
- Mustapha Al Majzoub, 30, killed by rocket attack in Syria, 2012. Sydney resident and former President of the Islamic Awareness Society.
- Sammy Salma, 22, killed in Aleppo in April, 2013. From Roxburgh Park, Melbourne.
- Suhan Rahman, 23, killed in Kobane, Syria. Sent messages to Australian Muslims urging them to spill blood. Former student, Melbourne University.
- Zakarayah Raad, 22, killed in an ambush in Syria, June, 2014. Appeared in Islamic State recruitment video There is No Life Without Jihad.
- Zia Abdul Haq, 33, former Brisbane City Council worker, killed October, 2014.
- Abu Nour al-Iraq appeared in a propaganda video for Islamic State. He was an Australian insurgent but his true identity remained in doubt.

- Yusef Ali, 22, from Redcliffe north of Brisbane, was found dead in a bullet-ridden house in Syria in January, 2014.
- Wife of Yusef Ali, former suburban Sea World staffer on the Gold Coast Amira Ali aka Amira Karroum was killed with her husband in Aleppo. Studied graphic design at Queensland University.
- Roger Abbas, 23, kickboxing champion from Melbourne, was killed near the Turkish border during a skirmish in October 2012.
- Yusuf Toprakkaya, killed in a sniper attack in Syria in December, 2012. He left behind a wife and son in Melbourne's northern suburbs.
- Mustapha Al Majzoub, of Bankstown, Sydney, killed in a rocket attack in Syria while fighting in Aleppo on behalf of terror group Jabhat al-Nusra.
- Former nightclub bouncer from Sydney's Kings Cross Ali Baryalei became a senior member of Islamic State in Turkey. Reportedly killed by drone attack in 2015.
- Sydney born Zakaryah Raad appeared in an Islamic State recruitment video calling Australians to jihad. He died a martyr following the filming.
- Preacher Ahmad Moussalli from Parramatta in Western Sydney, believed to have been killed in Syria.
- Former Australian soldier Caner Temel went AWOL from Brisbane army barracks in 2010 and died in Syria in January of 2015 while fighting for Islamic State.
- Sydney father of two Housam Abdul Razzak was killed in Lebanon in 2015.
- Melbourne party boy turned Muslim Mahmoud Abdullatif reportedly killed while fighting for Islamic State in Syria in January, 2015.
- Ahmed Mohammed Al-Ghazzawi, born in Lebanon and living in Bankstown in Western Sydney was killed by Syrian forces on Boxing Day, 2014.
- Jake Bilardi, 18, Melbourne. Died as part of a series of coordinated Islamic State suicide bombings in the Iraq city of Ramadi in which at least 17 people were killed and dozens injured. 12 March 2015.
- Mohamed Elomar, 29, reportedly killed June 2015. Notorious for social media posts. Drone attack.
- Khaled Sharrouf, father of five, unconfirmed reports killed June 2015, drone attack.
- Sharky Jama aka Abu Tawba Alsomalee, former male model from Melbourne killed in April, 2015 fighting in Syria for Islamic State.

CONTENTS

CONTENTS

SECTION ONE: A TERRIBLE BEAUTY IS BORN

IN THE SECOND decade of the 21st Century after Christ, or the year 1436 in the Muslim calendar, Australia's national security agencies were jumping out of their skins; sitting on a time bomb, the final countdown. Month after month, they had quelled one spot fire of terrorism after another, equally unable to trust themselves as they were their informants and their surveillance. The diversity employment programs aimed to make the security agencies reflective of the ethnic makeup of the population as a whole and to entice Arabic speakers meant that there were good people of the Islamic faith scattered throughout the security and police services. Nothing wrong with that; except that it was a factor converging into a time when the government had seriously misread and mishandled the country's security, and was participating in a morally indefensible war in Iraq, killing Muslims in foreign lands, thereby further radicalizing the local populations day by day.

Australia, by its support of its ally America, whose conduct in the Middle East many, not just Muslims, saw as beyond reprehensible, in its torture, its massacres, its bombings, its misguided invasion and destruction of a sovereign country Iraq, the "mother mistake" as the invasion was called, had torched a religious war.

Through its misguided rhetoric, the Australian government had demeaned and insulted Islam, stoked the fires of jihad across the nation and seriously imperiled the safety of the general population.

In 2015 the Australian Security and Intelligence Organisation (ASIO) predicted that another terrorist attack on home soil was almost inevitable.

The Australian government now faced The Rising, as the pre-Anzac Day counter terrorism operations had been so aptly badged, Operation Rising, The Rising of Islam.

You didn't have to be a genius, you barely had to be prescient, you barely had to be sentient, to realize that a terrorist attack in Australia was imminent.

The security forces had no idea which way to turn. They did not know where, they did not know when, but they knew, in their bones, in their hearts, in their calculating minds, the worst terror attack in Australian history was coming as sure as night followed day.

The authorities knew full well they could not thwart every last attack. And the authorities were riddled with those of the very faith they had so profoundly alienated, a faith that emphasized "my brother is my brother," that emphasized the unity of the Ummah, the body of believers, and who, just like those they were expected to target, believed in the literal words of their faith, that God was Great, Allah was the Lord of all the Worlds, the one who did not resemble the creations, that Muhammad was his Messenger and that the world was entering The End of Days, the Apocalypse of legend and prophecy.

The greatest terror of all was the unknown. Perilous, uncertain and contradictory times bred inward looking populations, and as the danger increased the Australian population fell ever deeper into a daze of soap operas, cooking shows, game shows, celebrity gossip and sporting events.

But the security agencies knew they did not know; and many of the most senior governmental figures were severely, savagely spooked thanks to the master propagandists within the jihad movement.

This terrible fact was due entirely to failed social, economic, immigration, border security and foreign policies of the past; the government had imperiled local populations by involving the nation in foreign wars of which it should have had no part, created a depressed, demoralized, divided and disaffected populace by misguided economic and social creeds, both the left and right side of politics had brought in large numbers of people of the Muslim faith on the theory that a bigger Australia was a better Australia, and thanks to the relentless activism of Australia's refugee lobby, in ideological lockstep with refugee lobbyists in other Western countries, many of the new arrivals had no identification papers. In other words, jihadists had been immigrating to Australia without barrier.

In both April and July of 2015 there were angry scenes as anti-Muslim protestors and anti-race demonstrators clashed in cities around Australia. In Melbourne 100 police were forced to stand between the two groups. The group Reclaim Australia, which organized the anti-Muslim protests, said it wanted to maintain Australia's traditional values, make Islamic law illegal in Australia, ban Halal certification, ban the teaching of Islam in public schools and the burqa. Their website declared: "We have had enough of minorities not fitting in and trying to change our Australian cultural identity." Five people were arrested at one protest in Sydney. One anti-racism organizer said: "We're trying to say that it is dangerous to allow hate speech to occur on the streets." [1]

Muslims were, by the very nature of their faith, opposed to capitalism and Western-style democracy. That their arrival in large numbers would prove problematic for traditional Australian society

---

[1] Anti-Islam demonstrations held across Australia, *The Guardian*, 4 April, 2015.

should have been self-evident to the social engineers holding sway over social and immigration policy.

Muslims knew that they had been cast into a society of unbelievers in order to transform the country of apostates in which they found themselves. With Australia conjoined with the crusaders America in invading Muslim lands and killing Muslims in the Middle East, and with much of Australian society in serious decay, what they saw around them in 2015 could only confirm their views.

They were in Australia, so far from their own ancestral lands, at the behest of a higher power, and there was no arguing with Allah.

Maintained within Islamic communities, Islamic radio, Islamic schools, Islamic friendly shops, unintegrated with broader Australian society, much of what they saw confirmed their worst beliefs: that they had landed amid the infidels, in a sick and Godless society. That there was a desperate need to change Australian society was evidenced everywhere they looked.

"Rapists, paedophiles, killers, wife beaters and baby bashers cleared to work with children," screamed a front page headline of *The Sunday Telegraph* in mid-2015.

The story began: "A woman on parole for a bashing murder. A man convicted of incest against his 14-year-old daughter. A swimming coach who fondled boys in a public toilet.

"These are some of the convicted criminals, including rapists, paedophiles and killers, who have been awarded a Working With Children Check over the past 12 months, despite being deemed unsafe to work with children by the NSW Office of the Children's Guardian.

"After being rejected by the Children's Guardian, the disqualified applicants took their cases to the NSW Civil and Administrative Tribunal, which overturned their cases on appeal." [2]

In September, 2014, the month the Australian government announced it was sending troops to Iraq yet again, Christians invading Muslim Lands, Australian authorities ramped up the terror alert index to High. The only place left to go on the index was Extreme.

Assisting with the invasion of Muslim lands aka Iraq and Syria inflamed the half-million strong Muslim minority within Australia and escalated the domestic terror threat to unprecedented levels.

Set against the backdrop of a rising Islamic State caliphate gaining rapidly in power across the world, having seized territory the size of Great Britain and Iraq and Syria, threatening the historic capitals of Damascus and Baghdad, militants in places as far removed from one

---

[2] Rapists, paedophiles, killers, wife beaters and baby bashers cleared to work with children, Yoni Bashan, *The Sunday Telegraph*, 7 June, 2015.

another as Nigeria, Pakistan, and Yemen, and in Libya Islamic State had acquired an airbase at Sirte, the hometown of former leader Muammar Qaddafi.

The circumstances were without historical precedence, and the decision to take Australia to war in these circumstances was sheer, irresponsible lunacy.

Or a welcome entrée into the Sharia, as substantial sections of the country's Muslim minority saw it. Islam, just like Christianity, was a faith riddled with end time prophecies, and for the good Muslims of Australia, they truly believed they were entering The End of Days. Armageddon, the Final Battle.

Until the arrival of the monotheistic religions, all of them spawned from one single individual, Abraham, Earth had been a place full of shamans and mystics, spirits and magic, a place in the cosmos full of ancient souls and mysteries that passed all understanding; where its peoples accepted the divine in everything, animals, plants, stones, ancestors, the sky above and the earth beneath; in each other.

Just as industrialization, globalization, the spawning of secular creeds and the rise of the internet and multiple accompanying technologies would transform the 20th and 21st Centuries, so the belief in one true God, alien to the ancient tribes, had transformed humanity's spiritual understandings.

Chronology was the simplest way to tell any story; but in many ways this was a story which defied chronology, which began with the origins of the monotheistic religions, Judaism, Christianity, Islam, the invention of fanaticism as some writers saw it. The three religions which began with Abraham became known as the Abrahamic faiths.

The world's monotheistic faiths had all been born amid the desert sands, the oases, the crowded markets and spectacular landscapes of the Middle East; and from their earliest days they were in conflict, and there followed century upon century of martyrdom, massacres and wars; all of this violent history spewing through into the 21st Century and America's disastrous involvement in the Middle East, the West's incubation of Islamic State.

Abraham, history told, put those who did not believe in a one true God to the sword, along with those who worshipped his creations rather than himself, a tradition which would continue.

Australia was a country literally on the other side of the Earth. And courtesy of its indigenous inhabitants it was gifted with a spirituality entirely separate to the Abrahamic faiths; a spirituality rooted in a sense of place, the spirits of place, in the intrinsic power of singularity, of the land itself, the phantasmagorical night skies wheeling above, the roar of the core beneath, arms reached out to Heaven and to Earth. The

Western invaders had always considered the indigenous to be simple people; lost in their own myths, without technology. They had been anything but simple. The invaders had desecrated the sacred lands and destroyed their holy peoples more quickly, in more terrible ways than even the ancient souls, fluid in time, could ever have imagined. It was a tragedy beyond anything a Western mind could grasp.

And now these ancient lands were embroiled in The Age of Terror; and in the blink of time in which the Westerners had been there, it was entirely the invader's fault.

Hundreds had already gone to fight in Syria or Iraq, or were contemplating doing so. Some thirty or so Australians had already died in the Middle East.

The announcement in September of 2014 that Australia was once again entering the arena of Iraq in coalition with the Americans had radicalized local Islamic populations; and the troops dispatched with so much ballyhoo were, within months, caught perilously close to Islamic State territory.

There were thousands of those of the Islamic faith with jihadist sympathies within Australia.

Any country ignores its best minds at its peril, and one of the many bizarre things about the situation Australia found itself in in 2015 was that the government, led by staunch Jesuit trained Roman Catholic Tony Abbott, appeared, on the face of it, to have ignored all the professional advice available to it; military, social, on terror messaging, on relations with the Islamic community.

One of the world's leading counter terrorism experts David Kilcullen also happened to be an Australian. From 2005 to 2006, he was Chief Strategist at the US State Department, later a senior advisor to General David Petraeus and later still to US Secretary of State Condoleezza Rice, as well as to the British and Australian governments. He was the author of three acclaimed books: *The Accidental Guerrilla, Counterinsurgency* and *Out of the Mountains*.

It was a pity the Australian government hadn't taken his advice.

Kilcullen described the original decision to invade Iraq as "the mother mistake." A mistake in which Australia had been a member of the so-called Coalition of the Willing.

He was once quoted as saying the invasion of Iraq was "fucking stupid." Forced to make a retraction by his then boss US Secretary of State Condolezza Rice he said: "I can categorically state that the word 'fucking' was said off the record." Another phone call from his boss.

David Kilcullen had a gift rarely found in academics, the ability to communicate.

In the opening riff of his seminal essay Blood Year: Terror and the Islamic State, published in *The Quarterly Essay*, Kilcullen said that that amongst senior international political figures and advisers there was a dazed sense of the world unraveling. In the northern summer of 2014, over roughly one hundred days, ISIS launched its blitzkrieg in Iraq, Libya's government collapsed, civil war engulfed Yemen, Abu Bakr al-Baghdadi declared himself Caliph and the United States and its allies, including Australia, sent aircraft and troops back to Iraq. At the same time Iran continued its push for nuclear weapons.

As the disastrous year closed, nine million Syrians languished in miserable, freezing mountain camps, with little prospect of going home.

"Across the increasingly irrelevant border with Iraq, thousands of people had been displaced, sold into sexual slavery, decapitated, shot in the street or crucified for minor infractions of sharia law – as idiosyncratically interpreted by whatever local ISIS thug happened to make it his business," Kilcullen wrote.

"Panic pervaded Baghdad.

"ISIS provinces appeared in Libya, Afghanistan, Pakistan and Egypt, and extremists in Indonesia and Nigeria swore allegiance to the Islamic State caliphate. Attacks by ISIS inspired terrorists hit Europe, America, Africa, the Middle East and Australia.

"Thirteen years, thousands of lives, and billions upon billions of dollars after 9/11, any gains against terrorism had seemingly been swept away in a matter of weeks. " [3]

By mid-2015 Syria and Iraq were in flames, western bombs rained down as Islamic State continued to expand its territory; while news and vision of ever more violent massacres and ritualized executions, including hundreds of murders of men, women and children in the ancient cities of Palmyra and Ramada, came by the day. Western democracies and traditional nation states were under threat, including Australia. The Islamic State and its affiliates were on the move from Yemen to Afghanistan, while the number of terror attacks escalated. Government statistics, questioned by some as an underestimate, suggested that more than 120 Australians were fighting in the Middle East, and almost 40 may have already died.

Not many months before the American President dismissed Islamic State as being akin to a minor baseball team while the Prime Minister of Australia Tony Abbott called them a "death cult."

Talk of the fall of Baghdad and Damascus was everywhere in the wind. As Middle East analyst Jonathan Spyer wrote, "The Islamic State

---

[3] Blood Year: Terror and the Islamic State, David Kilcullen, *The Quarterly Essay*, May, 2015.

threat pervades everything here. It is there in the muscular armed men deployed outside the luxury hotels. In the barbed-wire fences and heavy iron gates protecting the residences of the remaining foreigners. In the quick and suspicious glances passing between strangers.

"Islamic State is surely already organising in the city, unseen. As it did in Ramadi and in Mosul, in Fallujah and all the way to Raqqa far to the west long before that. The mysterious explosions have already begun."

Two upmarket hotels in central Baghdad, Cristal and Babi, frequented by foreign journalists, were the subject of terror attacks in May, with 15 dead and 42 injured.

Illustrating the utterly confused state of the war in Iraq, Spyer travelled with a militia group to the frontline. He quoted a number of the fighters claiming that America was helping Islamic State: "We are trying to fight them, but the Americans come and bomb us and that allows ISIS to run away. I've seen it with my own eyes. They parachute aid, weapons and clothing and they drop it to ISIS. America is not fighting ISIS. America is helping ISIS." [4]

American and Australian drones killed fighters and civilians, the mujahedeen tweeted pictures of homosexuals being pushed off buildings and adulterers being stoned to death. "Beheaded Corpses line Palmyra," ran one headline, referring to the ancient Syrian city. The Yazidi, a religious minority in the north of Iraq seen as devil worshippers by Islamic State, were massacred in their hundreds and enslaved in their thousands. Ethiopian Christians crossing Libya to seek a better life in Europe were caught; and ritually massacred, vision of their slaughter being prominently placed on websites around the globe.

Online, high production value videos overlaid with jihadi chants, accessible within less than a second to anyone in Australia with a decent internet connection, showed the wide eyed shock of the beheaded as their open necks stained the sea red.

"Let volcanoes of jihad erupt everywhere," the leader of Islamic State Baghdadi declared following a massacre in a Saudi mosque.

In June of 2015 an Islamic State spokesman urged jihadists to turn the holy month of Ramadan into a time of calamity for the infidels: "Be keen to conquer in this holy month and to become exposed to martyrdom. Obama and your defeated army, we promise you in the future setback after setback and surprise after surprise." [5]

And so, in that winter in the Southern Hemisphere, it came to pass.

---

[4] Iraq falls apart, Jonathan Spyer, *The Australian*, 4-5 July, 2015.

[5] ISIS urges followers to escalate attacks, Reuters, 24 June, 2015.

In the opening days of Ramadan, the month of fasting and fighting, there was a massacre, with 38 dead in a seaside resort of Tripoli; where elderly tourists on their sunbeds were shot. A French factory boss was decapitated and his head placed on a the fence outside the factory, with his body and head desecrated with Arabic writing. Kobane saw the largest massacre in its history. And in Kuwait at least 27 were killed and more than 200 injured in a massacre in a Shi'ite mosque.

"Terror on three continents," ran the headlines.

In response to the latest round of massacres, the Australian Prime Minister Tony Abbott ramped up the rhetoric: "Again Australians have woken up to news of horrific terrorist attacks overseas overnight.

"This illustrates yet again, as far as the Da'esh death cult is concerned, they're coming after us. We may not feel like we are at war with them, but they are certainly at war with us. It seems one of the other attacks was inspired by Da'esh. The death cult is regularly admonishing its supporters and sympathisers around the world to kill.

"Regrettably, as we saw in France, all you need for terrorism these days is a knife, a flag, a camera phone and a victim.

"This is the grim reality that the world faces now. This is why it is so important – it is so important – that the message get out there that what is being done by Da'esh has nothing to do with God, it has nothing to do with religion, it has nothing to do with building a better world.

"Under these circumstances it is more important than ever that we maintain our level of vigilance and that we do everything that we reasonably can to disrupt, degrade and ultimately destroy this death cult at home and abroad." [6]

The use of the confusing term Da'esh instead of Islamic State was an attempt to calm rising ethnic tensions.

It was a loose acronym for al-Dawla al-Islamiya al-Iraq al-Sham, the Arabic for the Islamic State of Iraq and the Levant. The name was commonly used by enemies of ISIS, and it also had many negative undertones.

UK Prime Minister David Cameron described Islamic State as the greatest existential threat to the West in history.

The headlines just kept coming. All up, some 3,000 people had been executed in Syria, including 74 children. In Turkey 32 people attending a youth conference were killed; while in a wave of retaliatory attacks 35 militants were killed in one air strike alone.

One hundred years before, Australia saw its first jihad attacks, against New Year's Day picnickers in Broken Hill, NSW. On New Year's Day,

---

[6] Doorstop Interview, Melbourne, The Prime Minister of Australia, 27 June, 2015.

1915, two Muslim men shot and killed four people and wounded several others before finally being killed by police. Their intention was to die for the faith "in obedience to the Sultan's order" following an Ottoman fatwa that declared it was a religious duty "for all the Muslims in all countries, whether young or old, infantry or cavalry, to resort to jihad with all their properties and lives." [7]

Following a National Security Meeting in the first days of Ramadan Immigration Minister Peter Dutton cautioned that the risk of extremist violence was "as great as it's ever been" and was "only going to get worse in the foreseeable future" as Islamic State gained territory in the Middle East and supporters around the world: "Obviously instructions have been issued by leaders within that terrorist group to conduct attacks and it seems that that's what's happened.

"The fact that 23 people have been charged with terrorism-related offences since last September really shows how significant and how this threat has ramped up in recent months and over the last couple of years. My judgment is this will get much worse before it gets much better."

Dawood Elmir, a former Melbourne man fighting with Islamic State in the Middle East, tweeted: "Blessed attacks begin in France this Ramadan."

Within Australia an Islamic State supporter posted: "So many victories in this month already, many more to come." [8]

****

Alex, a pseudonym for the author, was a "retired" news reporter blessed with a sardonic tilt of phrase. As an old journalist with a career spanning decades, he had literally dived in and out of thousands people's lives, recording triumphs and tragedies and passing fads, trends and price fluctuations, and there were days in 2015, with the world spiraling out of control, when, after such a life, he really did feel halfway to God, whatever that term might mean.

News stories, books, journalism, were linear forms in a not very linear world. And of all the many thousands of stories Alex had written across his lifetime, this was perhaps the least linear of all.

He had never attended a journalism course, did not graduate in media studies, wandered into newspapers because he liked to write; and did not always approach stories in the same way as most of his colleagues. He looked at what was happening on the ground, saw how people felt,

---

[7] Terror Australis, Ely Karmon, AIJAC.

[8] Terror Threat Will Get Much Worse: Peter Dutton, Jared Owens and Mark Schliebs, *The Australian*, 29 June, 2015.

and only belatedly consulted the experts. If there was one quote from writers across the ages he most particularly liked it was the words of W.B. Yeats two years before his death: "Don't speak to me of originality or I will turn on you with rage. I am a crowd, I am a lonely man, I am nothing."

His favorite line? "A terrible beauty is born."

From Easter 1916, a poem about the massacres of the Irish during an uprising against the British:

All changed, changed utterly:
A terrible beauty is born.

This wasn't a poetry lesson, but there were times when those lines, in an era when more information was available than ever before, the greatest of writers and artists a mere click away, when the consciousness of mankind had changed in an instant, when old Alex walked the now haunted Sydney streets in the early hours and could hear vividly in his head: "Changed, changed utterly, A terrible beauty is born."

And equally he could hear the lines from Islamic State: "We will kill you. We will kill the artists. We will kill the writers."

The entire devolving security situation was set against a rapid collapse in Australian society, which had seen a once proud, optimistic, larrikin country become impoverished, dispirited, and broken.

Alex had always treated the streets of Sydney like his own back yard, from the days when the city was more like Amsterdam by the Pacific than the place that it became. Restless in the early hours, as he had always been, in 2015 he walked through the same interlocking network of inner-city streets which he had known so well almost half a century before.

In the 1960s those streets connected what had once been the major entertainment districts but which were now largely desolate: Kings Cross, Darlinghurst, Rushcutters Bay. There were no longer 24-hour coffee shops and late night clubs; the streets were no longer full of raffish intrigue. Now they were more like walking through a Dead Zone set or a Mad Max movie than a major city, the only difference being the black crows were replaced by squawking seagulls from the nearby beaches; just as eerie, just as apocalyptic in their mournful cries.

Even as he arrived in the early hours at his office, an ice dealer sat in a small car outside the building, checking his phone constantly before suddenly roaring off to service the local brothels and renegades.

There were few remnants of the Kings Cross that he had fallen so passionately in love with as a 24/7 wild child almost half a century before.

What did remain as a reminder of a more bohemian, artistic, colorful and happier period, in front of empty shops, down-at-heel sex shops and sad looking clip joints, were embedded in the form of plaques into the street.

There was a quote, for instance, from the internationally famous Australian actor Peter Finch, who had said in 1954: "Kings Cross was a wonderful place. Nothing since then, London, Paris, Hollywood or New York, has been quite so wonderful. And although I lived on the edge of destitution, I had never been happier in my life."

Finch went on to star in numerous films, including *The Power and the Glory* and *Far From the Madding Crowd*. He died in Hollywood in 1977 after suffering a heart attack in the Beverly Hills Hotel.

He would not have believed the Kings Cross that came to be in 2015.

As Alex walked past shuttered shops, toothless prostitutes, ravaged ice addicts, the city's underclass more desperate than he had ever seen them, he kept having those same freeze frame moments of impending calamity W.B. Yeats had written so well about:

From cloud to tumbling cloud,
Minute by minute change.
A shadow of cloud on the stream
Changes minute by minute;
A horse-hoof slides on the brim;
And a horse plashes within it
Where long-legged moor-hens dive
And hens to moor-cocks call;
Minute by minute they live...

Changed, changed utterly.

A terrible beauty is born.

There was a price to pay for bottom-up journalism, for a fascination with the underclass, for paying heed to the translucent clairvoyance of street people, for his own passing delinquencies of mind. Never mind. Mercy came in many forms.

But in this case, often enough it seemed he was just writing a peon to a lost world; every writer he had ever admired, Jean Genet, Malcolm Lowry, Paul Bowles, Patrick White, David Malouf, Ursula le Guin, Flannery O'Connor, Helen Garner, Dylan Thomas, William Burroughs and many in between, Andre Gide, D.H. Laurence, Philip K. Dick, all under the sharia would have been stoned to death, beheaded, crucified on crosses, set alight while still alive, shoved off tall buildings; along with virtually all the friends he had ever known or the people he had ever been intimate with.

That was the world that was being ushered in; a world without rock music, a world without film, without the multiple flavors, the high camp hilarity and low camp tragedies of the demimondaines he had once so loved to explore; all of it lost.

As one commentator put it: "Within the narrow bounds of its theology, the Islamic State hums with energy, even creativity. Outside those bounds, it could hardly be more arid and silent: a vision of life as obedience, order, and destiny." [9]

Australians who spoke out, including prominent cartoonists Larry Pickering and Bill Leak, were threatened; as had Islamic State critics around the world.

Pickering said he was offered police protection after he drew a cartoon of the prophet Muhammad as a pit-roasted pig skewered on a pencil. One of his major targets since he left full time work had been Islam.

After the Charlie Hebdo killings in Paris he condemned political leaders, including the Australian Prime Minister Tony Abbott, for saying the terrorist attacks had nothing to do with the religion of Islam. "To see the beautiful city of Paris self destruct is depressing," Pickering wrote. "To hear French President Hollande say Islamic terrorism has nothing to do with Islam is distressing. It's sickening that our leaders resolutely refuse to identify an evil enemy within." [10]

In the wake of the Hebdo attacks *The Australian* newspaper published a cartoon by Bill Leak of Jesus Christ and Muhammad sitting together in heaven. Jesus is holding the Koran, telling Muhammad that it "needs a sequel," just as the Bible has an Old and New Testament. Muhammad responds by showing a newspaper with the headline "World at War" and saying that he cannot return to earth because he would be "crucified." The cartoon was captioned with the line: "Let Us Pray."

In a statement the newspaper said the cartoon was meant to send a message about not being afraid to criticize any person or group. One of the most damaging aspects of the Charlie Hebdo attack was "that it hit our civilisation in a place already shaping as our Achilles Heel — a spineless and growing penchant for political correctness. Over recent years, in the face of the perpetually outraged, our pluralistic, democratic

---

[9] Graeme Wood, What ISIS Really Wants, *The Atlantic*, March, 2015.

[10] Larry Pickering says police offered him protection due to Muhammad cartoon, Amanda Meade, *The Guardian*, 13 January, 2015.

and free societies have gradually been yielding on our hard-won freedom of expression." [11]

There were threats online of a *Charlie Hebdo* repeat in Australia.

YouTube, once the domain of rock stars, pop artists, cute videos about pets, tributes to the collectors of eccentric paraphernalia and earnest documentaries suddenly became filled with Islamic propaganda: "The one who does not believe in God will be punished for sure"; "The caliphate will last until the end of the world"; "My brothers in the ISIL, I swear our most honourable wish is to meet Allah, We must use all means at our disposal to terrorise. Terrorism is a precept of our religion." Documents with titles like: "ISIS: World's Richest Terror Army."

By 2015, every day the news got worse, or better if you were a supporter of Islamic State.

Thousands of tanks paid for by American taxpayers were seized by IS from fleeing Iraqi forces. Jihadists threatened attacks in Australia, America and Europe.

Saudi Arabia, a country which Australia was supposedly in alliance with in the Middle East, pressured Pakistan, claiming its nuclear bomb was for all the Islamic World.

Islamic State claimed it could afford to buy a nuclear weapon from Pakistan, fly it to Mexico and smuggle it across the border into the US and create havoc. The agitation of fear. Other stories reported Islamic State was seeking chemical weapons and dirty bombs.

Iraq and Syria were named as the first social media wars. Islamic State were pumping out more than 100,000 pieces of propaganda a day.

In April of 2015 Islamic State released an 11-minute high production video called "We Will Burn America," with an accompanying hashtag #WeWillBurnUSAgain.[12]

The video threatened 9/11 style attacks and warned: "America thinks it's safe because of the geographical location. Thus you see it invades the Muslim lands, and it thinks that the army of the Jihad won't reach in their lands. But the dream of the American to have safety became a mirage. Today there is no safety for any American on the globe. By Allah's willing, the fear will spread among them again soon. Here it is America now losing billions still to make sure their country is safe. But today, it's time for payback." [13]

---

[11] Mohammad cartoons published worldwide, *Inquistr*, 10 January, 2015.

[12] ISIS threatens another 9/11 style attack on social media, *NY Post*, 13 April, 2015.

[13] Sickening new ISIS video warns 'we will burn America,' Anthony Bond, *Mirror*, 13 April, 2015.

News stories declared 2015 the worst year in history for refugees and revealed that the US President Barack Obama was liaising with the Muslim Brotherhood, the progenitor of Islamic State, while popular culture, including the latest masterful Mad Max movie, reflected the apocalyptic feel of the age, The End of Days. Mosul, Palmyra, Ramadi, Raqqa, fell. Towns in Libya fell. After the loss of so many lives, the Afghan Parliament came under Taliban attack. "ISIS Cuts off 4 Kids Hands; One for Stealing Toy," went one headline. "Islamic State hang two boys for not fasting on Ramadan." "Islamic State committing atrocities on an industrial scale, says UN." "Christian Boy Set On Fire Succumbs." "ISIS opens a new front on Europe's Doorstep." "Another day, another act of depravity."

The brutal, mind numbing chant just went on. The worst that man was capable of.

****

The United States President Barack Obama, the Australian Prime Minister Tony Abbott and numerous other politicians across the Western world, in an effort to calm tensions which would never be calmed as long as their respective militaries were killing and maiming Muslims, had claimed Islamic State was un-Islamic.

A failure to understand the idea of Islamic State, and the theology behind the movement, had led to many miscalculations of which Australia was a part.

As that superbly intellectually gifted journalist Graeme Wood wrote in *The Atlantic*, the beheadings, the slavery, the crucifixions, the subjection of Jews and Christians, all were part of a medieval Islamic tradition. The laws of war passed down through the Koran and in the narrations of the Prophet's rule had been calibrated in the initial instant to fit a violent and turbulent time. In 2015 the fighters of Islamic State were authentic throwbacks to early Islam and were faithfully reproducing its norms of war; and precipitating the so-called End of Days prophesied in Islamic texts 1400 years before.

Wood argued that because military intervention drove recruitment and inflamed Muslim sentiment worldwide, the biggest proponent of an American invasion was Islamic State itself. The West had played straight into their hands: "The United States and its allies have reacted to Islamic State in an apparent daze."

Islamic doctrine required believers to live under the caliphate.

The Australian government policy of canceling passports and blocking Muslim fighters before they left the country frustrated the ambitions of jihadists leaving their country to fight in the Middle East and to fulfill their religious duty to live inside the caliphate. With nowhere else to go, they were nonetheless compelled to follow their calling to commit and celebrate jihad. They would kill the unbeliever where they lived, where they slept.

Sydney Muslim community leader Jamal Rifi repeatedly warned that thwarting the travel of extremists and keeping them in Australia with no passport was a recipe for disaster because they become "ticking time-bombs." He said Australia had narrowly averted several terror plots planned by extremists who wanted to travel overseas but had their passports cancelled.

Clive Williams, an adjunct professor with the Department of Policing, Intelligence and Counter Terrorism at the Australian National University said the cancellation of the passports of Australians suspected of extremist links had increased the chance of an attack on home soil.

"The policy of stopping extremists from traveling overseas and fighting in Syria or Iraq has resulted in a large pool of frustrated people," he said. "They are a large risk to us and more of a threat than Australian jihadists who are already in the Middle East and may decide to come back one day."

The security situation in Australia, just as it was in America, was self-created, a profound miscalculation. And it had never been worse.

Wood argued that Islamic State differed from nearly every other jihadist movement in believing that it was written into God's script as a central character.

The Islamic State might have had its share of worldly concerns in the areas which it controlled, collecting garbage and keeping the water running, but the End of Days was a leitmotif of its propaganda.

The Islamic State was no mere collection of psychopaths, Wood argued, but a religious group with carefully considered beliefs, among them that it was a key agent in the coming apocalypse. Pretending that it wasn't actually a religious, millenarian group, with theology that had to be understood to be combated, had already led the United States to underestimate it and back foolish schemes to counter it. Virtually every major decision and law promulgated by the Islamic State adhered to what it called 'the Prophetic methodology,' which meant following the prophecy and example of Muhammad, in punctilious detail.

"We'll need to get acquainted with the Islamic State's intellectual genealogy if we are to react in a way that will not strengthen it, but instead help it self-immolate in its own excessive zeal," Wood wrote.

"Islamic State rejects peace as a matter of principle; hungers for genocide; its religious views make it constitutionally incapable of certain types of change, even if that change might ensure its survival; and it considers itself a harbinger of—and headline player in—the

15

imminent end of the world. The reality is that the Islamic State is Islamic. Very Islamic." [14]

****

In an era where a medieval-style holy war was also raging, the dangers inherent in the rapid evolution of technology in the 21st Century were all too painfully evident. High-tech agents for mass slaughter were increasingly at hand; readily available to even the smallest of militant groups.

The Future of Violence: Robots and Germs, Hackers and Drones, Confronting A New Age of Threat, by security experts Benjamin Wittes and Gabriella Blum of the Brookings Institute and Harvard University Law School respectively, dramatically demonstrated the escalating dangers faced by non-believers in the West.

With the creation of everything from microdot surveillance instruments to swarm cameras to insect sized flying robotic weapons to viruses which could be manipulated by ordinary citizens and unleashed on entire cities, the times were increasingly perilous. Artificial intelligence was being increasingly realized. Goggles, due to be in commercial production by the end of 2015, would allow a single individual to be able to see in real time what was happening anywhere from the top of Mount Everest to Times Square. Multiple on location cameras combined with computer wizardry would provide a genuine sense of actually being in the location, sounds, wind, the scudding sky, the honk of taxis and flashing neon; there were obvious military applications.

It was a world where the gift of anarchy was not the sole domain of nation states but of any individual or political group. Violence had been democratized, where many Little Brothers were as menacing as any Big Brother. The miniaturization and automation of weapons weakened national boundaries as effective lines of defense; just as front doors also became less safe. Relatively small, non-state groups could now wage conflicts against powerful states. The trend threatened to give every individual with a modest education and a certain level of technical proficiency the power to create catastrophe.

Wittes and Blum wrote in *The Future of Violence* that traditional ways of thinking about national security were now out of date: "As a thought experiment imagine a world composed of billions of people walking around with nuclear weapons in their pockets. Governments

---

[14] What ISIS Really Wants, Graeme Wood, *The Atlantic*, March, 2015.

must contemplate the possibility of ever smaller groups of people undertaking what has are traditionally understood as acts of war." [15]

****

Terrorist attacks in Australia made news headlines around the world; but in a very real sense the story began on the streets. The hapless state of the Australian economy and thereby Australian society was everywhere visible. A once vibrant and optimistic country had lost its way.

Australian democracy was in collapse. A country once proud of its own story, of its tough convict origins and rough bush legends, a prosperous country which held its head high in the world with a brazen, laissez faire anti-establishment attitude, had been in retreat for years.

Now it had reached the Dead Zone. Defeat.

On Oxford Street in Central Sydney the homeless were moved on; rough sleepers hidden from public view.

By 2015 Australia had risen to 12th in the list of the world's largest economies, but much of the population felt, and were, poor. There was little disposable income; and the phrase "the working poor" acquired new depth with each passing year.

Australians still liked to hear that they were the greatest country on Earth, but it had never been true and in recent years many so-called developing countries had leapfrogged over the great Southern land, leaving a quiet, over-regulated, over-governed country on the edge of a great, dramatically beautiful, sparsely populated interior; with the wild southern oceans stretching down to the Antarctic and dramatic desert landscapes at its heart.

Australians themselves were increasingly critical of their own country, often describing it as a police or nanny state.

The crowded, flickering patterns of market stalls and multiple enterprises which made so much of the world so dynamic were largely absent in Australia, a pale form of capitalism where businesses too often just furled and died, seen off by ridiculous levels of regulation, heavy compliance burdens and brutal levels of tax. The population were being asked to make sacrifices through high levels of taxation on a socialist ideal of fairness; but there was nothing fair about any of it.

Drunks, wayward, schizophrenics, Sydney's lost and troubled, those who heard voices and slept rough, had long washed up along a

---

[15] *The Future of Violence: Robots and Germs, Hackers and Drones, Confronting A New Age of Threat*, Benjamin Wittes and Gabriella Blum, Basic Books, 2015.

particular stretch or corridor of what was known as Oxford Street. The thoroughfare stretched for several kilometers from the formalities of Hyde Park and the War Memorial. It passed up through Paddington, once a working class suburb and student lair whose terraces now sold for well over a million dollars each.

But when people referred to "Oxford Street"; they usually meant just the bottom of the stretch, a six lane road which sloped upwards from the park to an intersection known as Taylor Square. It was a strip of about one kilometer. On either side there was a motley dribble of small, shabby businesses, fast food outlets, restaurants, cafes, a few bars, a diminishing number of sex shops, and, in a sign of the times, numerous empty stores.

In decades gone by Taylor Square had been a busy but poorly lit, atmospheric square; a kind of alternative center of the city to the business district's Martin Place. At its heart had been a mound of pounded earth colloquially known as Gilligan's Island, where the city's drunks instinctively gathered each day as if it was a sacred site. Men in suits gathered at Martin Place, men in rags gathered at Gilligan's Island.

Back then, when he had been a news reporter for the city's major newspaper The Sydney Morning Herald, Alex had done a story on the last night of Taylor Square's newspaper vendor. The stand had been known throughout the city as the first place it was possible to get an Early Edition.

Job seekers, late-night workers, collectors competing for bargains amongst the classified ads, young journalists who, like his younger self had excitedly lined up to buy a copy of the paper so they could see what their stories looked like in print, all had lined up to buy in those pregnant, possibility filled minutes before midnight. Queues of taxis would form, waiting, waiting for that glorious smell of fresh ink.

There had been a lot of calls the next morning after that story: people who wanted to tell their own anecdotes about the newspaper vendor, how their whole lives had changed as a result of a purchase there; how they had been the first to answer an advertisement for a job in New Guinea, met their wife or lifetime partner there, now had grandchildren, whatever the circumstance was.

The newspaper vendor, the coin filled aprons, the piles of first editions dumped fresh from the delivery trucks, had long since disappeared into the city's history.

As had Gilligan's Island.

What had once been such character crowded part of Sydney had long been vanquished by a corporate makeover; the dead hand of the modern day Sydney City Council everywhere.

A dreary "contemporary" water sculpture and a neatly grassed mound replaced Gilligan's Island; and while ratbags and the just plain ratty still wandered from the nearby hostel for the homeless, Edgar Hoover Lodge and the neighboring Sydney City Mission, the transformation was more or less complete.

Along with the rest of the city, Taylor Square had been dragged into deathly shallows of the 21st Century, and was no better for it.

It may have been dying when he arrived, but in the six months that Alex lived at the bottom of the strip, the first half of 2015, it turned up its feet and died.

When Alex had arrived for the Christmas of 2014, there had still been a few spasmodic signs of life: late night clubbers, suburban adventurers, cruising rat packs, groups of women out for a night, gangsters and aspiring gangsters aiming for one of the city's only early morning drinking clubs. The club was soon to close. The suburban adventurers gave up all hope of finding entertainment. The wanton lads of the gay demimonde stayed home and watched television.

Yet some signs of character still persisted. The area continued to attract the odd and the unformed, the fallen angels, those whose grasp on the terrain was very weak indeed.

Curiously, as if spilling down from a central source, a random, small and shifting cast of the homeless still kept trying to make their rudimentary camps along Oxford Street, usually a blanket on the pavement, perhaps a bag, those little nests that man had made since the beginning of the species. They slept in the doorways of Oxford Street for a few days; and then disappeared.

In decades gone by their equally troubled forebears, gathering ritualistically each day, had found refuge, solace, drinking companions in these very same places, their madness seemingly less extreme in the company of others, a black humor all pervasive. Sting, a mixture of orange cordial and methylated spirits, could always be shared. There was always a hiding place somewhere, even on an open street.

Just at the top of Oxford Street, next to Taylor Square, lay what was once Darlinghurst Jail, a place where one of Australia's greatest poets and storytellers, Henry Lawson, was frequently incarcerated for drunkenness. During Lawson's time bridging into the 20th Century he had seen the area from high and low; as a nationally famous writer and author; and as a hapless, disregarded derelict.

The entire block was now an Art School.

Henry Lawson was one of those repeatedly attracted to the areas of Sydney's inner-city demimonde, those exact same streets Alex often traversed, from Kings Cross to Taylor's Square and many an alley in between.

Alex often wondered as he walked those same streets what Henry Lawson would have made of Sydney in 2015, what he would have written.

Lawson may have been haunted by his own ghosts, but Sydney was now full of ghosts.

It was during his periodic dives into alcoholism that Lawson found himself drifting with the very same people that drifted on Oxford Street still; the lost and the deranged.

The new immigrants knew nothing of the country's vagabond, literary past; and the new creatures of the bourgeoisie cashed up from the property boom would have dismissed Lawson in an instant as nothing but a drunken scumbag sleeping on the street.

But it was Lawson who would be remembered long after they were gone as one of Australia's greatest writers; and the poem he wrote from Darlinghurst Jail, adjacent to Taylors Square, One hundred and three, after the number he was given in prison:

A criminal face is rare in jail, where everything else is ripe
It is higher up in the social scale that you will find the criminal type.
But the kindness of man to man is great when penned in a sandstone pen
The public call us the 'criminal class,' but the warders call us 'the men.'

The clever scoundrels are all outside, and the moneyless mugs in jail
Men do twelve months for a mad wife's lies or Life for a strumpet's tale.
If the people knew what the warders know, and felt as the prisoners feel
If the people knew, they would storm the jails as they stormed the old Bastille.

A century after the poem was written Australia's social justice system was just as bad as the world Lawson knew, the society just as hypocritical, the laws as barbaric and ill-informed.

While the homeless and the alcoholic were regularly moved on, the soulless grip of the authorities worse than ever, on Oxford Street the drift of fallen angels persisted.

It was as if something, some powerful comforting force, had once occupied the place when it had all been tribal lands. As if, long before English brutality had paved the way for bitumen streets and Western jails, this place had drawn the wayward spirits of an ancient tribe, and now, in another century, there were residual compass affects; spiritual harmonics which had chimed down the centuries.

Even though the bodies to which the old spirits had been attached had long since passed on, the place still attracted the disturbed, weather vane personalities of street people who appeared, for whatever reason, to find in the otherwise unremarkable strip of road a place which was the closest they could come to stability, mental or otherwise, in the chaos and often enough agony of their own collapsing life stories.

Unlike days of yore, the homeless were now an untidy inconvenience unbefitting the twee image the Council wanted to portray and were inevitably moved on.

Despite all the local, state and federal rhetoric about the poor and the vulnerable in the community, the bleeding heart planks from which so many expensive and more often than not counterproductive bureaucracies had been built, there was no room in Sydney's heart for the soulful or the unsuccessful.

But whether anyone cared or not, they still gathered in much the same places; exhibited their deranged behaviors for a few hours or a few days before an uncomprehending and uncaring audience; and waited for the authorities to hose them down and out, away from public view. Off to rehab, off to homeless shelters, off to psych wards, off to some terrible, sober confrontation with their own worst selves.

As the sun came up over Oxford Street early one summer morning a van of police pulled up for coffees outside the Swiss Cafe, a couple of hundred meters down from Taylor Square. Two men, two women, a gender balance only the elderly might think worthy of comment, disembarked from the police vehicle.

Sitting on the park bench with a man who was just out of jail and a few other assorted, the old man, whose adopted name for the purposes was Alex, took in the scene. Next to the 7/11 was the bright yellow and black signage of a pawn shop: "MONEY$LENT"; parked out front a shopping trolley full of old clothes and makeshift bedding. On the downhill side there was a dilapidated string of establishments catering to base instincts: The Den, VIP Lounge, Toolshed.

"This is Australia," the old man said, apropos of nothing.

Council workers swept the streets of the evening's litter and by 8am the yellow flack jacketed parking patrols were already out, searching for that easiest of targets, a citizen looking for a parking spot.

The Sydney City Council made some $70 million out of parking meters and extortionate fines; and had no motive whatsoever to solve one of the problems which made Sydney such an unpleasant and expensive place to live, the absence of anywhere to park.

On the sidewalk there was a not unusual sight: an over-excited man, his arms jerking, his eyes bulging, moving erratically in front of the early opening cafes and shops, shouting fragments of sense. The country, disintegrating at the seams, was in the midst of an ice epidemic. Another consequence of prohibition, of idiot laws by self-serving politicians always ready to whip up moral panic around law and order for the sake of a vote, was that the drug was being regularly cut or substituted with a cheaper alternative known as "jump"; and much of the bug-eyed madness of the loosely integrated that was now a common feature of street scenes was due not to the drug itself but to the garbage with which it was being cut.

As they waited for their coffees from the Swiss Cafe and bought odd things from the neighboring 7/11, the police appeared to decide they might as well do some work at the same time, and pulled the over-excited man aside, one part aboriginal, nine parts lost.

A minor assortment of that morning's vagrants watched on as the police went about their "duty"; including a tribal man from the Pitjantjatjara Lands of Central Australia, one of the world's most truly beautiful stretches of desert. Pissed for sure, but wreathed in a kind of elder statesman's dignity, he was almost three thousand kilometers from home. On that bench, at the bottom of the ladder, drunk in the dawn, everybody was kind to each other.

The police donned the demeaning occupational health and safety rubber gloves which had become standard for body searches since the grim reaper fear of AIDS and needles. The gloves gave the distinct impression the authorities were afraid of being contaminated by the poor; that they weren't dealing with fellow humans but with some diseased, leprous underclass.

The police made the man spread his legs, turn around and put his arms up against the shop front.

It was a humiliating stance, but the police, friendly enough in a place which sooner or later saw more than enough of the comic, cosmic and bizarre, also combed through his possessions, a carry bag of dirty clothes, the sandshoes he had kicked off. It was ridiculous. If the man had anything significant to hide beyond personality problems it was unlikely he would have been wandering the street in such a deranged state.

With their search finding nothing the police told him to wait while they checked if he had any "out-standings," warrants from the past that might not have been complied with, which would then have justified taking him into custody.

The man, already upset at being frisked on a public street, wasn't going to stand for any of that, and headed off down the street without shoes, making odd shouts, weaving wildly.

The police made as if to follow him, but then just watched as he disappeared down Oxford Street, in between the mixing shifts of people heading home or people heading to work; the office workers replacing the night denizens. Nothing the police could do was going to make any difference.

The news came through, there were no outstanding warrants, making the man of even less interest.

His shoes and his bag, his haphazard collection which barely classified as "belongings," remained in a small pile by the shop front.

As they climbed back into their vehicle, the police packed them neatly next to the garbage bin.

A man who had almost nothing now genuinely had nothing.

Soon enough the over-excited man would be someone else's problem. Almost inevitably he would be jailed again for some minor infraction; re-incarcerated into a prison system which, thanks to mistaken policies of the past, was overloaded with the mentally ill.

Wealth, mental stability, sobriety, a stable temperament, a loving and preferably powerful family, a lack of the alcoholic gene, a lifetime of achievement and high social status, they all bought protection from the harassment of authorities.

On the other hand street alcoholics had always been easy prey.

Fleeing harassment, or avoiding incarceration, the wild-eyed man gave a final jag at the bottom of the street and disappeared into the early morning traffic.

****

At 8.33am on the morning of the 15th of December 2014 Man Haron Monis walked into the Lindt Café in Martin Place, Sydney's central business square.

At 9.44am Monis rose from where he had been sitting with a bag at his feet, drew a gun and told customers to stand with their hands up. He shouted that he was a representative of Islamic State and this was a terrorist attack.

While Australia had been party to the Iraq Wars, this was the country's first major experience of a terrorist attack on home soil. There had been numerous other plots, but until this point in time all had been foiled.

Man Haron Monis, 49, was an immigrant from Iran, a self-styled sheikh with known extremist views. In taking 18 people hostage, he was responding to the Islamic State's calls for lone wolf attacks on Western targets; and was hailed by them as a martyr.

Two hostages and Monis died in the bullet sprayed closing scenes of the siege at 2am the next morning.

At the time of the incident Monis's security and police files already ran to several hundred thousand pages. But somehow or other, he had fallen off the security agency watch lists. Eighteen calls to a security hotline in the previous days had failed to raise alarm bells. Despite a long list of criminal activity, and known extremist views, an assessment by the Australian Security and Intelligence Organisation in 2009 concluded that Monis was not a threat to public safety. Monis was reassessed by ASIO in late 2014 and found he fell well outside the threshold to be included in the top 400 high priority counter terrorism investigations. He was only one of thousands of potential security concern. A government review released in February of 2015 found that government agencies had acted reasonably and concluded that only modest changes to the laws were required.

He had previously come to public attention after sending offensive letters to soldiers returning from Afghanistan. He was out on bail over allegations he was an accomplice to burning his wife to death at his front gate.

Iranian officials had provided information to the Australian government about his criminal record and mental state; duly ignored. Iran's Chief of Police Brigadier General Esmail Ahmadi Moqadam said Monis fled Iran after stealing more than $200,000 dollars from customers of his travel agency and had a "dark and long history of violent crime and fraud."

The Islamic Republic News Agency was critical of the poor perception of Iran and Iranians Australian authorities had generated as a result of their mishandling of the case: "The western media tend to ignore the fact that the Islamic Republic of Iran for over two decades has been asking Australian officials via Interpol to hand over the culprit to the Iranian police but eventually met with the decision of the Australian government to grant asylum to him. Even after his involvement in a murder case, the Sydney police let him free." [16]

That Monis was not under any security watch at all at the time of the attack defied belief.

With a long history of activism and online extremism, there could hardly have been a jihadist in the whole of Australia who had not done more to attract attention than Man Haron Monis.

---

[16] Analyst derides Australian Government, Islamic Republic News Agency, 16 December, 2014.

Monis used a one month business visa to enter Australia in 1996, after which he sought a protection visa. From 1997 to 2000 he held a security guard license.

Between 2008 and 2009 Monis was on the National Security Watch List run by the Australian Security Intelligence Organisation, ASIO.

With the country in a state of high terror alert, Abbott had channeled more than a billion dollars of extra funding into the security services. Exactly how well that money was being spent, and on exactly what measures, would remain forever a subject hidden from the taxpayer.

"I don't know why he was dropped off the watch list in those days, I really don't," Prime Minister Abbott said. "What we do know is that the perpetrator was well known to State and Commonwealth authorities. He had a long history of violent crime, infatuation with extremism and mental instability. We know that he sent offensive letters to the families of Australian soldiers killed in Afghanistan and was found guilty of offences related to this. We also know that he posted graphic extremist material online. As the siege unfolded yesterday, he sought to cloak his actions with the symbolism of the ISIL death cult.

"We particularly need to know how someone with such a long record of violence and such a long record of mental instability was out on bail after his involvement in a particularly horrific crime. And we do need to know how he seemed to have fallen off our security agency's watch list back in about 2009." [17]

Clear answers never came.

At the time of the Sydney siege Monis was out on bail for alleged involvement in the murder of his ex-wife, who was stabbed 18 times and set alight at his front gate. Monis's then partner was charged with the murder.

Monis also had more than 50 sexual assault and related charges. Included on his charge sheet were 22 counts of aggravated sexual assault, 14 counts of aggravated indecent assault, one count of aggravated act of indecency, one count of sexual assault and two counts of assault with act of indecency.

In a country gripped by bureaucratically fueled domestic violence concerns, where a separated father could be sent to jail for sending a Christmas card to his children, as the history books showed, that Monis, with such a long history of sexual assaults, was still walking free stood out as a trail of special pleading.

As an old newspaper reporter, Alex had seen numerous Australians sentenced to jail for minor offenses, including having a fight outside a

---

[17] Sydney Siege, Man Behind Martin Place stand-off, ABC, 16 December, 2014.

hotel. Often recovering from the influence of alcohol, the men, almost always men, blinked in confusion at being sentenced to jail over an event they could not recall and for which there was little damage but a black eye and a hangover.

Sniffer dogs patrolled railway stations and busted the hapless and the hopeless, the young and the naive, for minuscule amounts of marijuana. In the Australia of 2015, more than half a century after the sixties, the authorities used archaic and demonstrably counterproductive drug laws to harass, survey and criminalize significant sections of the public; justify their own jobs and curtail civil liberties. There was, as far as Alex was concerned, no freedom, no compassion, no common decency in any of it.

The incident he remembered most vividly for whatever reason was in the old sandstone Local Court in Liverpool Street. An aboriginal woman, 22, mother of two young children, had been charged with stealing two Mars Bars and cake from a store, thereby breaking her bail conditions.

Her Legal Aid lawyer gave a moving defense, speaking passionately about how her client had two young children to care for, had been an enthusiastic participant in twelve-step rehabilitation meetings in jail, had reformed her life, and was deeply regretful of the incident which led her to be in the dock.

"You may see hope for your client," the magistrate thundered at the lawyer. "I see no hope at all."

Bang, two years in jail. For a couple of Mars Bars and a packaged slice of cake.

That was the Australia of the 21st Century, one law for the rich, one for the poor.

Like convict days of yore, when the starving underclass of Britain were sentenced to deportation and years of imprisonment for stealing a loaf of bread, loaded on to ships and sent to the other side of the world. Australia.

Unfortunately, the English brought their dire judicial system with them; the lash, their brutal indifference to the suffering and circumstances of others.

In 2013 Monis was sentenced to 300 hours community service and placed on a good behavior bond on 12 counts of misusing the Australian postal service to cause offense.

He, together with his partner Amirah Droudis, undertook a campaign of sending letters to the families of the 41 soldiers killed in Afghanistan. The letters protested the presence of Australian troops in Afghanistan and called the soldiers murderers. He urged the grieving families to petition the government to remove its troops from Afghanistan.

The campaign of what the presiding judge described as "grossly offensive" letters to the families of seven soldiers killed in Afghanistan between 2007 and 2009. The letters called the bodies of the soldiers "contaminated" and referred to them as "the dirty body of a pig." They also equated the fallen soldiers as inferior in moral merit to Hitler. In one letter Monis said the deceased soldier was going to hell.

In a two-person operation, Monis and Droudis would call family members of deceased soldiers asking for their address so Mr Monis could send "sympathy letters," what he was later to call "flowers of advice."

They found contact details from the public telephone directory, known in Australia as the White Pages.

Soon after, the duo began sending more than just letters.

In a video sent to a funeral home, which held a service for an Australia soldier killed in battle, a widow was told her husband was a murderer.

"Our troops unjustly have gone to other countries and we just can't ignore this and we shouldn't be honouring them as we don't honour Hitler's soldiers," Amirah Droudis said in the video. "I feel sorry for you but not him. I do not honour the soldiers who go to unjust wars. I do not feel for murderers."

Monis also wrote to the family of the Australian trade official Craig Senger, who was killed in the 2009 Marriott Hotel bombing in Jakarta. Three of the seven victims in that attack had been Australians. Fifty people were also injured in the suicide bombings. The two bombers had checked into the hotel several days before.

Senger's mother Joan Senger said when she received Monis's letter she was not in a mental state to cope. "That's why it was such a serious thing," she told reporters outside one of the numerous court appearances which Monis made.

Mrs Senger said she hoped the sentence of community service, although laughably light by any measure, would help deter others and prevent something similar happening again. It did nothing of the kind.

Of Monis she said: "I just think he doesn't think like normal people think."

Also at the time of his sentencing Bree Till, widow of Sergeant Brett Till, killed while defusing a bomb on March 12, 2009, said: "We sat reading these letters [which] made out to be something supportive but then the juxtaposition of this man accusing my husband of being a child-killer while dictating how I should raise my children. It was scary."

One of the families harassed was that of Lance Corporal Jason Marks, who

had been 27 years old when he died in Southern Afghanistan. Four other soldiers were seriously injured in the incident.

Marks was survived by his wife and two children.

In an official statement, the Australian Department of Defence announced the news "with great sadness." The statement said Lance Corporal Marks had died when Australian soldiers were engaged by Taliban extremists using small arms fire and rocket-propelled grenades: "Jason was a strong character who was determined to be the best he could be, striving for perfection and living for every moment. His memory was honoured in a memorial service held as friends, family and comrades recounted tales of his steadfastness, determination and humour."

His wife Cassandra Marks said: "There are no words to express how we are feeling. Our family is devastated at the tragic loss. Jason was a devoted father to our two beautiful children and a loving husband to me. All Jason ever wanted to do was join the Army. He was the type of man who knew what he wanted, even from the age of 12, all Jason ever wanted to be was a soldier.

"Becoming a Commando was a dream of Jason's, he was proud of who he was and proud of what he did. Jason loved to be active, whether it was through playing union, league or rock climbing. He even became a combat fitness leader in the Army he loved it so much. Jason always strived to be the best he could be, he loved the Army, he loved his mates and he loved his family."

Monis also harassed the grieving family of Private Luke Worsley, who was killed by small arms fire while participating in an attack by Australian forces against Taliban leaders and their supporters.

He was 26 years old when he died in Afghanistan in 2007.

Monis' targeting of the family began when he rang Luke's father, John Worsley, on the evening after the family learned of their son's death, saying he wanted to send a condolence letter.

What followed were three diatribes calling Luke a "killer of innocents" and "a nasty piece of work."

His mother Marjorie said she never felt safe again.

In a letter delivered to the family and posted on the internet Monis wrote:

"Dear Mr Worsley,

"It is painful but we should be proud when we loose (sic) our dear kids for defending our country while we are unjustly attacked by another country.

"But it is more painful and we can't be proud when we loose our dear kids for defending our country while we are unjustly attacked by another country.

"We loose our dear kids for nothing if we unjustly attack to another country and our kids are killed while the other country is defending itself."

Private Worsley's father John Worsley said they were very hurt by the letter: "We're very proud of our boy."

After this the family got another letter from Monis expressing puzzlement that they should be offended: "John, why did this hurt you? Was it this word? Was it this word?"

Authorities at the time assured the Worsley family that Monis was a self-styled preacher, more of a talker than a violent actor.

His mother Marjorie said: "I was worried: 'Gee, our house has been on television, he knows what it looks like, he knows where we live.' And they say, 'No, he's not that sort ... He's more verbal than action.' But there you are."

Speaking to the media as the drama unfolded she said she felt desperately sorry for the families and the Martin Place siege could have been prevented had Monis not been free on bail. "It's a husband, or a mother and father, or a child that isn't going home," she said. "He's not a nice person. How do you let someone like that out?" [18]

Private Worsley enlisted in the Australian Regular Army in 2001, deployed with the Delta Commando Company Group to Afghanistan in 2006 and redeployed in 2007. For his services in East Timor and Afghanistan Private Worsley received numerous commendations, including the Unit Citation for Gallantry.

In a statement released through the Defense Department his parents said: "Our family is devastated at the tragic loss of our son, Luke, in Afghanistan. He was a special service commando and very proud to be a soldier and to be doing his duty. We are extremely proud of our boy and we know that we lost him doing a job he was trained for and loved doing.

"Luke leaves behind a loving mother and father, three sisters and a brother, two brothers-in-law, two nieces, two nephews and a wonderful girl who adored him.

"When he was growing up, we would never have thought of Luke as a soldier, but he loved the Army, its discipline, training and spirit. Luke had strength of mind, body, character and will. The Army was the life Luke wanted and he was happy.

---

[18] Mother of killed soldier never felt safe after being harassed by Man Haron Monis, *The Sydney Morning Herald*, 16 December, 2015.

"Our son chose his profession and as fate would have it, he paid the ultimate sacrifice."

Each year his comrades continued to visit the family on the anniversary of his death.

Just as Australians had adopted an English poem for its chief poem of remembrance, a poem read at Worsley's funeral, The Final Inspection, was written by an American soldier Sergeant Joshua Helterbran. It rapidly gained currency around the world:

The soldier stood and faced God,
Which must always come to pass,
He hoped his shoes were shining,
Just as brightly as his brass.
"Step forward now, you soldier,
How shall I deal with you?
Have you always turned the other cheek?
To My Church have you been true?"
The soldier squared his shoulders and
said, "No, Lord, I guess I ain't,
Because those of us who carry guns,
Can't always be a saint."

Monis was told by NSW Police he would receive a seven year jail term if he penned another letter.

NSW court documents revealed his response: "I don't care about seven years imprisonment when it comes to the security and interests of the country."

Less than two months after being warned, Monis wrote to another grieving family. He would write to two further families before he was finally arrested by NSW Police.

When interviewed, Monis protested his innocence and said he never meant to offend any of the families.

"Someone from the family has passed away, of course I don't want to hurt that person but maybe some part of my English has not been good enough that someone has take it wrong." [19]

By March 2009, Australian Federal Police were advising families of fallen Australian soldiers not to open letters with "Australian Muslim Cleric" signage on the envelope.

After being found guilty of misusing the Australian Postal Service Monis stepped up his campaign, claiming it was the duty of everyone to advise people not to kill innocent people.

[19] Australian soldiers akin to Nazis, Nine MSN, 23 December, 2014.

Gate crashing a funeral of an Australian soldier, Monis and his partner accosted his pregnant widow before being intercepted by a member of the Australian Defence Force.

Monis's partner Droudis received a two year good-behavior bond, in effect a non-sentence, for assisting Monis in sending the letters. She appealed the sentence, the lightness of which would have delighted any offender, but on 12 March 2015, after the Martin Place siege, Droudis dropped her appeal.

Forty one Australians serving with the Australian Defence Force had died in Afghanistan since 2001. The last, Lance Corporal Todd Chidgey, died in 2014. Seven soldiers died in 2012. Loss of life, loss of treasure. Politicians from both sides of the political divide eulogized the fallen soldiers.

By 2015 their legacy, the legacy of those dead soldiers, cause for which they died, was, sadly, in serious question.

Dissident Army officer Bernard Gaynor wrote that despite an expenditure of $7.5 billion the situation in Afghanistan was hopeless: "The unfortunate reality is that the Islamic State will have more say over Afghanistan's future than we will. That means Australia's most lasting legacy in Afghanistan may well be that the mosque we built in Oruzgan is used to rally jihadis to conduct attacks on our home soil."

Gaynor, a clean cut family man and staunch Christian with conservative social values, was drummed out of the army afte her had made himself extremely unpopular with the powers-that-be by stating what others considered obvious, that the courting by the defense and security apparatus of the Muslim community and their employment in large numbers constituted a significant non sequitur; that hiring people whose faith propelled them to agitate for the overthrow of the very government they served in favor of an Islamic caliphate made no sense at all.

As far as he was concerned the issue of national security and the state creed of multiculturalism were in direct conflict.

He claimed that any Australian Defence Force officer who stated the obvious and dared to deviate from a politically correct line was purged.

Gaynor told a Reclaim Australia Rally in mid-2015: "The Australian Defence Force is under attack. It is being weakened from within. Recently, the federal government decreed that the Australian Defence Force should have an imam to encourage Islamic recruitment. And so they appointed one just last month. I am telling you now, this means that your tax dollars spent on the defence of this nation will instead be used to build mosques on military bases. And you should know what these mosques will preach.

"There is an Islamic organisation called Hizb ut-Tahrir. The Lindt Café terrorist, Man Haron Monis, attended Hizb ut-Tahrir events. Hizb ut-Tahrir has called for an Islamic army in Australia to impose Sharia law. And the Islamic community rallied earlier this year to defend Hizb ut Tahrir. It put out a statement saying, in part: 'We strongly oppose Prime Minster Abbott's politically convenient threats to 'tackle' and 'crack down' on Islamic groups such as Hizb ut-Tahrir...'

"And guess what. The new imam of the Australian Defence Force signed that statement. He has defended Hizb ut-Tahrir publicly before and now he has the chance to do it in uniform. This is the kind of idea that is now going to be promoted in mosques in the Australian Defence Force.

"I am telling you that these ideas are going to result in the death of Australian soldiers. Not in Iraq or Afghanistan, but here at home. These ideas are bringing the war to our door."

Gaynor said many of the terrorist attacks thwarted in Australia over the previous decade had focused on military bases.

"The ideas being pushed through the Australian Defence Force make these attacks more likely, especially when you consider this fact: more Muslims from Australia have signed up for the Islamic State than the Australian Defence Force," he said. "These ideas put our uniform on the enemy and patriotic Australian families will suffer as a result... Our Australian Defence Force is under siege from the politically correct protection of Islam." [20]

On the question of Iraq and Afghanistan, Gaynor claimed the moral cowardice of the defence force leadership would inevitably lead to the complete waste of the services and sacrifices made by thousands of Australian personnel. He said there had been a triumph of bureaucratic administration over battlefield considerations: "In a nutshell, the Australian military and Western governments in general do not understand the enemy. That is why the war in Iraq was a failure, and was always going to lead to disaster for Iraq. Furthermore, the rise to power of violent Islamists in Iraq today is a window into the future of Afghanistan. Despite the hard work, bravery and sacrifice of Australian and Coalition soldiers, these wars have not made the West safer, nor have they improved conditions for those living in Iraq and Afghanistan, or the wider Middle East. I used to think and hope that it was otherwise. But wishful thinking does not equal the truth." [21]

---

[20] Bernard Gaynor website, Reclaim Australia speech, 20 July, 2015.
[21] Australia's efforts in Afghanistan begin to fall apart, Bernard Gaynor website, 2 June, 2015.

Of Gaynor's forced resignation from the military Fairfax columnist Paul Sheehan wrote: "Gone, too, regrettably, is the credibility of Australia's military missions in Iraq and Afghanistan. The army will need to confront the reasons for this abject waste of blood and money, given that jihad against the West and western liberalism, being waged by militant Islamists, has a long, long way to run." [22]

Journalist Louise O'Shea, in words hard to dispute, wrote that the chaotic reality of Afghanistan stood in stark contrast to the self-congratulatory rhetoric of the Australian government: "The war and occupation of Afghanistan have been the most expensive and longest running military operation in Australian history. The triumphalist bombast that accompanied the mission and the troops' departure has likewise evaporated into the political ether. The pronouncements from Tony Abbott that Australia could 'look back on with pride' a mission that had 'helped to pacify, stabilise and improve Afghanistan' have been quietly buried, so out of kilter are they with the reality of Afghanistan today."

O'Shea estimated that 50,000 Afghans, including children, lost their lives as a result of Australia's intervention. [23]

On the opposite side of the conflict, the Australian government reported that 30 Australians travelled to Afghanistan to link up with the Taliban and engage in jihad. Of those 30, 25 returned to Australia. 'Of those 25, 19 were involved in preparing and planning mass casualty terrorist attacks in Australian and of those 19, eight were actually prosecuted and convicted. [24]

In the legal proceedings which resulted from his harassment of the families of the soldiers who died in Afghanistan, Man Haron Monis took full advantage of Australia's Legal Aid system; an inequitable distribution of money away from workers to the professional classes, and towards cases which the government's senior lawyers, bureaucrats and government officials deemed worthy. It was a kind of welfare system for lawyers, and propped up many cases through the court system which should never have been there. It routinely distorted the judicial process; and as only one side of a dispute could be funded, was chronically misused. Legal Aid chose the winners and losers based on

---

[22] Christian army officer Bernie Gaynor pays the price, Paul Sheehan, *The Sydney Morning Herald*, 10 July, 2014.

[23] Australia's crimes in Afghanistan, Louise O'Shea, *Red Flag*, 24 July, 2015.

[24] ASIO concerns over returned jihadists grow, David Wroe, *The Sydney Morning Herald*, 16 July, 2014.

the fashionable social agendas of the day and the biases and of administrative cliques.

Depending on their victim of choice, Legal Aid would often back murderers against the police in protracted court cases which consumed resources and took officers away from frontline duties, thereby, it could be argued, making the streets less safe. It also routinely backed mothers against fathers in custody cases and unfairly favored the victim of choice at any one time in Australia's social history; and the victims of choice in the 21st Century were refugees and asylum seekers.

Hence Monis had access to legal assistance all but the wealthiest of Australians could only dream of. A Legal Aid barrister in court, supported by at least one lawyer and a legal assistant, costs the taxpayers of Australia thousands of dollars per day.

Unrepentant over being found guilty of misusing the Australian postal service, just three days before the Martin Place siege Monis lost his second appeal to the High Court of Australia against the charges.

As a newspaper reporter Alex had watched all too many dreams of determined litigants crash and die in the padded labyrinth of the Law Courts complex just up the road from where Monis held his hostages.

To get as far as Monis did in Australia's legal system required an obsessive perseverance. And plenty of money.

According to a government inquiry, Monis had received eight grants of Legal Aid between 2010 and 2014 for the criminal charges relating to his abuse of the Australian postal services, including High Court challenges, as well as his murder and sexual offense charges.

In the opening hours of the siege Monis's demands included speaking to the Prime Minister and the delivery of an Islamic State flag.

News management in a crisis or terrorist attack was always an issue.

As an old journalist it was sometimes this aspect of unfolding stories, as much as the substance of unfolding disaster which interested Alex the most.

And in the Martin Place siege the media coverage itself was in lock down; as reporters and news editors censored themselves, reporting the drip diet of news from official sources.

Over the more than two decades Alex had worked as a general news reporter in Sydney, the police media unit had become less and less informative.

And as events unfolded around the Lint Cafe, the control of public information was never more evident.

Particularly in this case; where the gunman put his demands up on YouTube for the world to see, but the city's radio, television and newspaper outlets were obliged to stick to the official version of events.

Knowing that there were people who had been delighted by the Twin Towers attacks, Alex had always been surprised that there had not been a major terrorist attack in Sydney before; that the Sydney Harbour Bridge, the Opera House, the crowds gathered for the fireworks on New Year's Eve, had not been enveloped in smoke and blood, dismembered limbs and screaming survivors and a kind of sick horror.

In the wake of all that vivid imagery of the collapsing World Trade Centre, as a general reporter for the national newspaper, Alex had been sent out on numerous false anthrax alarms, mischief makers, malfunctioning horns in multistory car parks, unfocused tension, a general, seeping distrust.

Senior editorial staff had all been brief on protocols for a major assault.

But the terror attack Alex had always expected never came.

Until now, when it came as no surprise to find that in December of 2014 the city was suddenly, finally, in lock down.

For varying reasons the year had been a difficult one for many, if not most, and on the whole Australians, including Alex, were glad to see the end of it.

As *The Guardian* newspaper reported, there had been little news about that particular day, on the crest of the holiday season; some terror raids in north-west Sydney which, because of their frequency and the fact they did not affect the average person, were, in a sense, unremarkable. But other than that, most news lists were dull; a report making the business case for the East-West tollway in Melbourne, the release of a financial report from the Federal Treasurer Joe Hockey: "Monday was a typical summer day – hazy, warm and soporific, made for skipping off work early, lazy lunches, Christmas shopping or drinks with friends.

"Then, at 9.44am, it all changed." [25]

Inside the Lindt cafe was the usual random assortment of people: an 83-year old former Wimbledon tennis player, a 50-year old woman and her 70-year old mother, both of whom lived outside Sydney and had come to the cafe as a Christmas treat, two Indian software engineers working for a nearby bank.

Mother of three Katrina Dawson, a former head girl at one of Sydney's most elite high schools and later a student leader at Sydney University's prestigious Women's College, a high achiever throughout her life, worked as a barrister at the nearby Eight Selbourne chambers. She went to the Lindt Cafe each morning for a hot chocolate. That Monday morning she was there with several of her colleagues.

---

[25] Sydney Siege Timeline, *The Guardian*, 20 December, 2015.

The doors of the cafe were locked and the hostages forced to stand with their hands in the air.

News of an unusual situation, possibly an armed hold-up, was first broadcast to the wider world by a tweet from *The Australian* newspaper's political columnist Chris Kenny at 9.52am. It said: "Scary situation Martin place – cops clearing area – woman says man may have shotgun."

Guardian reporters checked the information with NSW police, who replied a "police operation was ongoing."

Kenny added more detail, saying there were hostages with their arms against the window in the Lindt coffee shop. He had gone in for a takeaway coffee and narrowly missed being caught inside.

Popular television station Channel Seven had put their studios behind glass directly opposite the Lindt Cafe and fronting onto Martin Place in 2004; a promotional ploy which allowed passersby to watch well known presenters going about their work.

It was a strategy that paid off in full on that Monday morning; as they were directly on top of the scene. Morning Show hosts were on air as armed police began to gather in the background of their shot.

Within minutes of the siege beginning the news had gone around the globe.

Martin Place and surrounding shops and offices were evacuated and a police cordon placed around the cafe. Black-clad police huddled against the Lindt cafe walls. Westpac Bank, who had some of its staff trapped inside, closed all of its 12 Central Business District branches.

At around 10am, barely a quarter of an hour after the siege began, terrified hostages appeared at the window, pressing a jihadist flag against the window; above the gold colored lettering: "Lindt Cafe MERRY CHRISTMAS."

The black flag being pressed against the window was not the official Islamic State flag but the Shahadah, the Islamic creed rendered in calligraphic Arabic: "There is no god but God, Muhammad is the messenger of God." The message appeared on the flag of Saudi Arabia, the al-Qaida linked group Jabhat al-Nusra, and the jihadist group Hizb ut-Tahrir.

Alex had had first become fully aware of the jihad movement brewing in the Australian suburbs after covering town hall events of the Hizb back in the early years of the new millennium.

He would never forget those lines, delivered in a powerful mix of Arabic and English: "Ask yourself my brothers, why, why has Allah been so cruel as to cast you amongst the unbelievers?"

These people weren't in Australia happily practicing their faith in a multicultural paradise as so many pundits would have it.

They were living amidst the infidels, and horrified at what they saw.

"If you believe in everything, you believe in nothing."

The sooner a caliphate was installed, the sooner they would have fulfilled their manifest destiny.

Members of Katrina Dawson's family were trying to contact her by text, without success.

With Australia experiencing its first major terrorist attack, the question of the place of the Muslim minority in Australian society and the success or otherwise of the nation's multicultural policies came instantly to the fore.

Some critics suggested mismanagement of Australia's immigration policies, the subject of billions of dollars of taxpayer funded propaganda over decades, including the oft repeated but by no means always true claim that Australia was a proud multicultural society, had led inexorably to this moment.

The virtues of having people from 200 nationalities co-existing in the one city were self-evident to some, harmony in diversity as the mantra went. As, too, were the opposite views to a different cohort, with anti-Muslim demonstrations a characteristic of the year.

****

The factors shaping events, including the rise of Islamic State, was a world away from the traditional history of the country but a world equally distant from its recent colonial history and equally distant, in a shorter time frame, from what had once been seen as a workers' paradise.

In 2015 Australia ranked 12th in the list of the world's largest economies on the back of mining exports. But the money, creamed off by multinationals and next in line the managers and shareholders, followed closely by hordes of bureaucrats, never filtered down to ordinary people.

Much of the population, taxed into submission, felt poor. There was little disposable income; and the phrase "the working poor" fitted all too well. Shop after shop was shuttered. Most of those that survived were struggling. Country towns looked like they hadn't seen a lick of paint since before the last Great Depression in the 1930s.

The democratic contract was broken. Australian politicians frequently boasted theirs was the greatest country on Earth. It simply wasn't true. The hapless state of telecommunications, including the some of the world's costliest and slowest internet, most expensive electricity, highest costs of living and expensive housing anywhere on the planet, with little national pride or social cohesion and communal identity, all made for a disillusioned population.

The traditional cheerful self-reliant, irreverent character of Australians had disappeared; and a population which, despite, or some would argue because of decades of "progressive policies," was schismatic, ill at peace with itself; no longer united in its belief of Australia as a land of opportunity and with little faith in notions of the larger good; and zero faith that commonsense would triumph.

There were days when people were friendly in the sunshine, smiled to themselves and each other, laughed easily, but optimism, like money, was unevenly spread.

In the capital cities there were enclaves of the rich, where late-model four-wheel drives, BMWs, Mercedes, and the wank tank of the moment Audis were easily spotted, but the wealth was not evenly distributed; in Australia, after decades of wealth redistribution and policies aimed at benefiting lower socioeconomic groups, disparities of income and social status were more marked than ever.

Step by step, individual freedoms grew forever less. Without public consultation, and with zero pretense of acting in the public interest, the NSW government introduced demerit points on licenses for unpaid parking fines; further empowering the rapacious gouging of Sydney motorists by money hungry local councils. "They want us down here and them up there," the builder outside his office said; as the speed camera flashed yet again on the downhill slope of William Street, at a point where motorists had to brake to be under the limit; each flash hundreds of more dollars to the state; another worker who might as well have stayed home that day.

Another fine, another demerit point, another increase in prices, they might have seemed small moves barely worthy of comment in a world where Islamic State was beheading, stoning and crucifying the "kafir," the unbeliever; but the entire decay of Australia had occurred in incremental steps, an extra speed camera here, another regulation there. Dogs by law had to have harnesses. Cafes were not allowed to put chairs out on the streets. On June 6th, tobacco in prisons was banned while on the outside smokers could be charged for smoking near a pedestrian crossing. Step by step.

So multiple were the imposts and regularity impositions on businesses, a distrust of commerce so interwoven into the overlaying levels of local, state and federal governance, that many natural markets were closed. Weekend markets were now virtually a thing of the past, thanks to insurance and compliance costs imposed on even the smallest of traders. The crowded, flickering patterns of stalls and multiple enterprises which made so much of the world so dynamic were largely absent in Australia, a pale form of capitalism where businesses too often just furled and died, the closure of every last enterprise a dream destroyed.

There were few nightclub and red light areas even in the capital cities.

With the Muslim ban on entertainment coming into force by default and absurd over regulation of alcohol consumption, Sydney's entertainment districts were in their death throes. The demimonde, the bars, clubs, cafes and street scenes he had once so loved were no more.

Community fury over the desolate state of Sydney's once vibrant inner-city finally found a focus in mid-2015 with some well calculated condemnations of the desolate disaster Sydney had become.

"Why are there no rooftop bars?" asked journalist Jenni Ryal. "Why is there nowhere to go after midnight? Why is the city a dead zone? Why do the police keep turning up when friends are visiting after 10 p.m.? Where is the culture, Sydney? Those are the unanswered questions of a generation." [26]

Founder of one of the world's trendiest magazines *Wallpaper*, Tyler Brûlé, said Australia was fast becoming "the world's dumbest nation" because of nanny state rules and restrictions, ridiculous liquor laws, excessive council regulation, restrictions on al fresco dining and mollycoddling occupational health and safety regulation.

"If you want to be globally attractive, you do need to have bars open until whatever hour of the day," he told a seminar to cheers from the audience.

"And I need to be able to open a pop-up shop in Surry Hills and walk on the pavement with my wine glass. To me that's actually important. It is not going to bring about the collapse of society because you do that."

They were the same complaints that Alex heard from Australians constantly, at home or abroad, that the country was a nanny state, a police state, grotesquely, absurdly over-regulated, that it had become a joke, and a very unpleasant place to live. It was more than just the Dead Hand of Socialism, it was the Dead Hand of Everything.

"You could wipe out 90% of what governments, local, state and federal do in this country and we would all be better off," Alex often enough thought. There was no evidence to contradict his views.

---

[26] Sydney, it's not me, it's you: The fight against the 'nanny state,' Jenni Ryall, Mashable, 26 June, 2015.

According to the City of Sydney council's website, venues wishing to serve alcohol in outdoor dining areas need to propose a "plan of management." The plan was required to address issues such as operating hours, capacity, security, waste management and crowd and noise control.

Venues were required to ensure that their *alfresco* activities had "no adverse impact on the amenity of the neighborhood." Premises whose applications were approved were then put on a period of probation. [27]

"If you want to be globally attractive, you do need to have bars open until whatever hour of the day," Brûlé said. "We're forgetting the value of what a city is supposed to be," he said. "Humanity is about noise and dirt and mistakes. And yet we want to sanitise our cities."

Urban designer Matt Golan also had a go in his piece Sydney Could You Chill the Fuck Out With The Nanny State Vibes: "How on earth did we, Sydneysiders, become so bloody conservative? How did we become so fearful of breaking rules, challenging social norms, and being innovative? When did we decide that politicians should decide what 'fun' is and that it should be legislated? When did we lose all common sense and decide to be told how to live in our cities?

"Megalomaniac politicians, over regulation and our subsequent fear of consequence has culminated in a big grey shit storm that has drowned out any cultural vibrancy, innovation, or sense of community that this city once had.

"You only have to set foot outside of a popular Sydney pub with a wine glass in hand to be reminded that rules and restrictions are suffocating Sydney more than ever. Whilst it's easy to point the finger at our governments for the excessive 'do's' and 'don'ts,' I think that we are part of the problem.

"We don't make the laws, but we have accepted them as if we were sheep being herded into a grassier paddock. Idiocy, at an authoritative and political level, is at an all-time high in Sydney at the moment. With this in mind, every progressive, innovative, community driven idea aimed at improving city life that is struck down by the law, and publicised, will serve to highlight to the public just how far we're setting ourselves back in the global climate.

"Great cities need to relax planning laws and accept that noise is part in parcel of any great city… and that the centre of a city should be a place that's full of life, buzz and excitement."

Golan said whether they realized it or not, people had themselves become walking, talking nanny-state advocates, thoughtlessly

---

[27] Nanny state rules making Australia 'world's dumbest nation': Tyler Brûlé, *The Sydney Morning Herald*, 27 May, 2015.

regurgitating tripe fed to them by politicians, consent authorities, and police.

"I heard a rumour that following on from Gold Coast trials, Police in Sydney will soon have the power to breath test patrons inside licensed venues and issue fines based on their level of intoxication. Good God, this is starting to feel like Demolition Man or Brave New World." [28]

The city was a mess.

And on a broader stage, the government wailed over the size of the welfare budget; but sat astride a system so clogged with regulation that almost no one could go out and create themselves a job or a business; no one could fulfill their restive dreams. Workers donned fluorescent council safety jackets and went to work for their local councils; or they starved. Public money, public jobs.

A patina of age had settled over many urban and rural areas. Many parts of the country had seen no sign of development in decades. Many suburban shopping centres and many patches of the inner-city were full of empty shops; and had become little more than a conglomeration of ailing businesses, a hot bread shop, a newsagent if they were lucky, a grocery store, sometimes with half its shelves empty, a florist which survived on funerals. Against the law, many shops sold single cigarettes for a dollar each. Just as with petrol, much of the cost was government taxes. The political class had gifted themselves heavy taxing big spending governments; and the country was now paying the price.

One of the only businesses to survive was the American hamburger chain McDonald's, whose economies of scale meant they could push all the local enterprises out of work, destroying local businesses en masse along with the health of the population. The nation's eating habits had changed for the worse; and in 2015 the obesity levels were at their worst ever.

Once upon a time you could once buy decent food at any suburban milk bar.

Now all you could find open in many places was McDonald's. Coca Cola and chips. Alex had done enough stories on the disadvantaged areas of Sydney to know perfectly well that was the breakfast plenty of children had before school, as their harried, scratching mother sat in the car park and yelled at her children to hurry up.

The country, having sowed the seeds of its own destruction, was now destroying itself.

---

[28] Sydney Could You Please Chill The Fuck Out, Matt Golan, Stony Road, 24 June, 2015.

****

The minute they passed they seemed to be far off, those last days of May, as the days grew shorter and the nights colder, in that place so distant from the Middle East where the monotheistic religions had originated, Islam, Christianity, Judaism and where much of the trouble had originated.

While the rest of the country had been whimpered into submission by excessive regulation, that the good Muslims of Australia had been paying little attention to the local ordinances became clear with the release of the annual Organised Crime in Australia Report.

The report showed that crime gangs were using sophisticated funds transactions and complex business structures to launder money overseas.

The ice epidemic, evident on the streets wherever Alex walked, had spread rapidly through Australia for the simple reason that there was no social cohesion and little employment; a direct result of a disaffected and disengaged population. Demand had never been higher. The lawyers made money. The prisons remained full. The police justified their existence. Politicians got their votes. And traffickers made their fortunes.

In 2015 came official confirmation that the same crime gangs empowered by the drug trade were funneling hundreds of millions of dollars directly to terror networks.

Dan Box, despite his comparative youth, was an old-style journalist, and one of the most gifted reporters *The Australian* had; possessed of a very good sense for news.

Alex had grown fond of him over the years they worked together on the news floor.

His inset story on the front page didn't mince words. The headline read: "From street to the frontline; drug trade funding terrorists."

"International terrorists are profiting from millions of dollars sent overseas by Australian crime gangs seeking to launder money from selling drugs and other illegal activities, the head of the Australian Crime Commission warns.

"Many of these gangs use a network of informal transfers, including Hawala brokers across the Middle East, to move their money, in order to prevent it being traced by the police.

"The transfers are often coordinated by intermediary groups that have links to organised criminals and they have links to terrorist groups."[29]

---

[29] From street to the frontline; drug trade funding terrorists, Dan Box, The Australian, 21 May, 2015.

Hawala is an Arabic word meaning transfer and is a system of money brokerage primarily based in the Middle East, North Africa, the Horn of Africa and the Indian Subcontinent.

Head of the Crime Commission Chris Dawson said: "The intermediaries launder the money, which is ultimately returned to the crime gang in Australia, while retaining a cut that may be passed on to terrorist groups that had been proscribed by the government. Whether they are direct supporters, sympathisers or are in it for their own profit-making, they are methods that are subject ... to ongoing investigation."

The Organised Crime in Australia report observed: "Of particular significance in 2015 is the continuing threat of terrorism. The problem of Australians going abroad to fight is an emerging area of complexity for this country. As counter-terrorism efforts throughout Australia are enhanced, the linkages between terrorism and the broader organised crime and volume crime environments are being identified. These linkages include, but are not limited to, Australians who advance terrorist activities, Australians who leave Australia to support terrorist causes, and who may return to Australia with the intent of inciting harm on the Australian community, or may be recruited by organised crime groups seeking the specialist skill sets they developed in foreign conflicts."

In some fine sounding rhetoric the Government had previously declared its intention to detect and disrupt terrorism financing in Australia and take action against people who provided support to terrorist organizations.

It announced that as part of the Government's $630 million counter-terrorism package, $20 million was being provided to AUSTRAC to improve detection and disruption of terrorism financing. Additional funds had also been provided to the Australian Federal Police, Australian Security Intelligence Organisation, Australian Secret Intelligence Service, Customs and Border Protection and other agencies.

The report continued: "Terrorist groups need both material and financial support to carry out their operations. Anyone who chooses to support terrorists is playing a direct part in the atrocious and violent acts they commit, and is putting Australian lives at risk. The consequences of participating in terrorism financing are severe and penalties of up to life imprisonment can be imposed on those found guilty."

To the politicians, it didn't seem to matter how many drug policy experts were quoted; how many rational arguments brought to the table. Short term gain, long term pain. Alex had lived long enough to see it all come to pass; while the perpetrators of this debacle on Australian society collected their plush parliamentary salaries and spread hysteria.

It was a stupidity in public policy which was greatly debilitating the nation's security services as it played cops and robbers with drug importers rather than concentrating on the single greatest threat to the country, terrorism.

As Johann Unrig put it so beautifully in his book *Chasing the Scream*, it was the bored, the unemployed, the disengaged and the unloved who took drugs in a manner which created personal and social problems; and presented in the street, just as alcoholics had done in the past, unwashed, deranged, dirty, desperate, unable to live inside themselves. Mistaken social polices of the past had created the Age of Loneliness.

As *Chasing The Scream* so amply demonstrated, the citizens of happy, industrious, socially inclusive cultures did not take drugs; at least not in ways which caused major problems to the individual or to the community. January 2015 marked 100 years since drugs were first banned in the United States. Millions of lives had been destroyed and entire neighborhoods turned into war zones, the opposite of the intended effect. The book put the lie to the right wing view that addiction was a moralistic failing resulting from too much hedonistic partying; and the left wing view it was a disease taking place in a chemically hijacked brain.

In fact addiction directly related to the cage, or society, in which the individuals found themselves.

The Australia of 2015 was a cage, not a culture.

As far as Alex was concerned, politicians should have followed the advice of experts they had been receiving for decades, develop social policies which created a cohesive and engaged community, take off the vast web of regulatory codes imposed on small business and individual enterprise, stop taxing everyone into submission, stop perpetuating a failed legal system wasting vast sums on enforcement which demonstrably did not work was feeding a terrorist underground. And once again create a country where Australian citizens could be proud of themselves and their individual enterprises, and proud of their country.

****

In 2009, the same year he dropped off the national security watch list, Man Haron Monis told a packed pray meeting in Western Sydney: "Your intelligence service is not working properly. If you are not aware there is criminal activity happening in your country, leave the position that you have. You are incompetent.

"The core of an Islamic society is justice, social justice. Society should behave in an Islamic manner and there should be justice." [30]

---

[30] Taped Granville lectures give glimpse inside the crazed mind of Sydney terrorist Man Haron Monis, *The Daily Telegraph*, 2 January, 2015.

He urged those present to use a religious occasion as "the day to say no to the idea of having more than one God.

"Yesterday they used to say that the power who controls the world in Britain, and today they say it is Russia and China and America. No, Koran says that the God is the controlling power of the world, and the determinant of the fate of any nation is that nation itself, peace be upon Mohammad."

He added: "You have to stand up and say no to polytheism."

Monis planned to establish a political party called Hezbollah Australia and once converted a large Campsie warehouse into a prayer hall where Muslim leaders issued Fatwas. He attended a number of mosques in Sydney, including the Nabi Akram Islamic Center, in Granville, where his religious lectures were delivered.

"He never said where his money came from, he was mysterious," said refugee advocate and Hizb spokesman Jamal Daoud. "He seemed to infiltrate everyone, Sunni and Shi'ah. He knew a lot about everybody, they knew nothing about him. This was high professionalism."

At the time, and in the months following the Martin Place siege, Australian governments local, state and federal attempted to paint Monis as a lone extremist, a bewildered individual, a violent, deranged and mentally ill person who had nothing to do with the peaceful religion of Islam and who was not connected with Islamic State, or any mainstream Muslim association.

But the Martin Place attack would throw into sharp relief the multiple problems Australia faced in 2015.

The pointedly acerbic Fairfax columnist Paul Sheehan, one of the few journalists to escape the orthodoxies which had settled over the industry, wrote: "Now for the cover-up. Australians are entitled to know, but are highly unlikely to be told, who were the lawyers and officials who advocated that Man Haron Monis be allowed to live in Australia, and then granted citizenship, despite red flag after red flag that he was trouble.

"Magistrates, lawyers and police prosecutors collectively decided that Monis, with a long history of harassing behaviour, with links to the brutal murder of his former wife, with charges for sexual assaults of multiple women, with a history of extreme political views, with convictions for writing threatening letters, and with an open record of support for jihad, was deemed no threat to society.

"Right at the start, in 1996, when Monis claimed political asylum, the Iranian authorities made it clear that he had been charged with multiple counts of theft that had nothing to do with either political persecution or capital crimes.

"Monis is a classic case study of why Australia needs to have probationary conditions applied to the residence status and then citizenship granted to immigrants, refugees and asylum-seekers. To cover for mistakes, this probationary status needs to be rigorous and lengthy."

Exactly as Sheehan had predicted, lawyers at a subsequent inquest painted Monis as schizophrenic, an isolated and deluded man with delusions of grandeur who suffered from paranoia and believed the authorities were watching him all the time. If they weren't watching they weren't doing their job.

During the inquest one supremely arrogant barrister, typical of his class, commented on Monis's style of Middle Eastern garb and sniffed that he was of low intelligence and his political views shallow.

Monis was intelligent enough to acquire a passable literacy in a second language, in a country where the vast majority of the population had few language skills at all. He was intelligent enough to dodge the security agencies of his homeland Iran and the security agencies of Australia, he was intelligent enough to milk the Australian welfare system and to utilize its Legal Aid system to mount protracted and expensive court cases denied to almost all locally born citizens. He was intelligent enough to be walking around on bail after a string of allegations against him, at the same time as many Australians were dispatched to jail for the most minor of misdemeanors.

In the end, all that mattered was that Man Haron Monis heard the call from Islamic State.

And if Islamic State had anything to do with it, many more would follow.

Sheehan concluded: "The instability through the Muslim world is growing worse. Thousands of Muslims are killing thousands of Muslims, leaving millions of Muslims displaced. The murder of more than 100 school children in Pakistan . . . is the latest numbing installment of the butchery being carried out in the name of Islam in Syria, Iraq, Afghanistan, Nigeria, Libya, Pakistan, Somalia, Yemen, Chad and Kenya. Egypt is under martial law. Iran is a theocracy. Numerous outbreaks of jihad-inspired violence have taken place in Western Europe, Russia, Canada, the United States and Australia.

"With instability growing in the Muslim world, the tacit policy of open borders, advocated by the Greens and the churches, would have seen the 50,000 people who bypassed Australian immigration under Labor grow exponentially. No one in the Greens or the churches offers structures setting limits, not 100,000 undocumented arrivals, or 200,000, or 500,000. Only compassion without limits. No limits were placed on Man Haron Monis." [31]

---

[31] Monis proves we need to sort out our immigration mistakes, Paul Sheehan, *The Sydney Morning Herald*, 18 December, 2014.

Populist tabloid *The Daily Telegraph* screamed on their front page: "SYDNEY SIEGE FALLOUT: Man Monis was not rated in the nation's top 400 jihadi suspects when he launched NSW's first Islamic terror attack. We now know that among us today there are thousands. WHAT ARE THEY UP TO?"

Expanding the theme under an inside headline spread across two tabloid pages "Hordes of hate lurk in our midst" the paper reported: "SYDNEY siege terrorist Man Haron Monis was deemed such a small risk by spy and policing agencies that he didn't even rate among the top 400 people in Australia identified as being potential national security threats. Even more alarming is the admission in the Commonwealth and NSW government review of the Martin Place siege that there are several thousand people in Australia who are now classified as a 'security concern.'" [32]

The joint Commonwealth NSW report on which the story was based concluded: "Australia currently faces a concerning security environment due to the challenge and volatility of threats from terrorism, clandestine activity by foreign powers, and self-motivated malicious insiders abusing privileged access to government information." [33]

At the end of the siege, virtually the first words out of Sydney Lord Mayor Clover Moore to the media were to declare Sydney a vibrant, multicultural society; as if it was a time for ideology.

With the assistance of her public relations team Clover Moore issued the following statement: "I want to express my sorrow to the families who have lost loved ones and empathy for the hostages who have had such a terrifying ordeal and appreciation for the bravery of our police. But this tragic incident doesn't change who we are – a welcoming, inclusive, harmonious and multicultural community.

"This was a one-off, isolated incident involving someone with a violent background and we need to unite as we deal with the aftermath of this tragic event and not let this change who we are – proud of our diversity.

"I encourage everyone to return to the city."

The woman knew no shame.

The bodies were still warm.

The police reported that there were no outbreaks of retribution against Sydney's mosques.

But other people were asking questions; about how all the high-flying ideals spawned in the 1970s had gone so badly wrong; why the

---

[32] Hordes of hate lurk in our midst, Simon Benson, *The Daily Telegraph*, 23 February, 2015.

[33] Martin Place Joint Commonwealth New South Wales review, January, 2015.

ceaseless preaching of open-mindedness and tolerance had led to a massive security bill just to monitor Muslim jihadists.

****

Three weeks after the Martin Place attacks, in Paris, on the 7th of January, there was a famous attack on the offices of the satirical magazine *Charlie Hebdo* in which eleven staff were killed and eleven injured inside the building.

In France there was a rally of national unity in Paris which drew two million people, while there were demonstrations around Australia in support of *Charlie Hebdo* and its staff.

With it being illegal under the 1970s legislation the Racial Discrimination Act to insult or cause offense, the entire point of *Charlie Hebdo*, the magazine could never have been published in Australia.

In counter to other rallies, Hizb Australia organized a demonstration of more than a thousand people named "We Will Not Abandon Our Prophet" in the western suburb of Lakemba, a Muslim stronghold.

Protestors waved placards such as "Mercy To The World Greatest Statesman" and "Insult to One Prophet is an Insult to all Prophets."

Hizb representative Sufyan Badar said: "An attack on the prophet is indeed an attack on all Muslims. It is unacceptable for Muslims to remain silent when an attack comes against our prophet. We need to defend him. Should we turn the other cheek?"

Turning the other cheek would not be Allah's will, he said, and claimed Muslims should not accept or embrace the freedom of speech preached by the West.

A cartoon distributed to the crowd showed a dog urinating on the grave of Charlie Hebdo. A chant rang out: "What they say is all in vain, Muhammad's name will remain. Our prophet we will protect."

As the first speech concluded riot police moved in to remove to anti-Muslim demonstrators. [34]

Hizb ut-Tahrir put up a statement on their website: "It seems some in Australia are arrogantly and irresponsibly heedless of the fact that provoking and insulting a people's core beliefs is a matter that can only end in acrimony for everyone concerned. If that wasn't enough, the biggest criminals of the world like Obama and Netanyahu are already seeking to exploit the events of last week for their predictable but nefarious purposes, despite the dust not settling and facts yet to be confirmed."

---

[34] Sydney's Muslim community rallies in Lakemba, *The Daily Telegraph*, 24 January, 2015.

To European politicians they declared: "The scale and tenor of the political response to the Charlie Hebdo incident reinforces Europe's desire to intensify its constant pressure on Muslims. In a manner unprecedented in recent times, European powers have responded with an outpouring expressly encouraged by the political class, including the largest demonstrations in recent times sanctioned by officialdom, suggesting a callous and calculated exploitation of events witnessed last week."

To Australians they said: "Muslims do not need to be lectured about the sanctity of human life. We especially do not need to be lectured by the greatest criminals of the modern age. There are some that question the apparent hesitance to condemn attacks such as those carried out at Charlie Hebdo. But the fact is that this reluctance is a conscious or subconscious desire to resist a vile, racist and narcissistic worldview that highlights and humanises European life but dehumanises and makes invisible non-European life. Our refusal to succumb to the woeful moral ambivalence of the West should be a cause for celebration, not a cause for condemnation." [35]

****

In February of 2015 there were two attacks in Copenhagen. One man was killed when a cafe hosting an event where a cartoonist who had caricatured the Prophet Mohammad was speaking was sprayed with bullets; and another fatally shot in the head just hours later at the city's main synagogue. Three police officers were hurt in the cafe shooting, and another two wounded in the second attack. Another man was later killed after he opened fire on police at a train station.

Australian Prime Minister Tony Abbott condemned the shootings in Denmark as an affront to free speech, and flagged further efforts aimed at securing Australia's borders amid growing concerns about the threat of terrorism attacks on home soil.

In a statement he said the thoughts of Australians were with the Danish people: "As with the Charlie Hebdo atrocity in Paris, the Copenhagen attack is an affront to one of our most fundamental values — freedom of speech. We stand with the people and government of Denmark in confronting this cynical attempt to undermine that fundamental right." [36]

---

[35] We Will Not Abandon Our Prophet, Hizb ut-Tahrir Australia, 11 January, 2015.

[36] Tony Abbott signals crackdown on borders amid terror threat, AAP, 15 February, 2015.

Not everyone thought the same; or cast the blame in one direction.

"The Danes have methodically built an underclass, a polyglot immigrant, welfare-dependent, high-unemployment, crime afflicted subculture," wrote Fairfax columnist Sheehan. "This subculture has become a petri dish for incubating social alienation expressed as radical Islam.

"As a result of large scale and poorly defined immigration and refugee intakes, in a country of a million people 4 per cent of Denmark's population is now Muslim and the Muslim population is significantly over-represented in crime and welfare dependence.

"Denmark's policy-makers will never admit they created an underclass through naive, complacent, ideological utopianism. They can't even admit that Muslim terrorism has been incubated in Denmark, let alone admit that it is a by-product of government stupidity." [37]

Australians, too, had methodically built an underclass, a polyglot immigrant, welfare-dependent, high-unemployment, crime afflicted subculture, a perfect petri dish for jihadists. Nor would there be any acknowledgment of fault.

Running a story on its front page in a manner that much of the nation's left-leaning media would not dare, a *Daily Telegraph* headline read: "Welfare Warriors: Jihadis on taxpayer dollar."

Senior News Limited journalist Simon Benson reported that nearly all the Australians who had gone to join Islamic State in Iraq or Syria were on the dole or other welfare payments when they left the country. In other words, average Australians workers were spending their days in tedious, poorly remunerated jobs and paying very high levels of tax in order that others could wage war against the West; to support people who would happily see them dead. Ninety six per cent of the jihadis had been on welfare when they left for the Middle East, and most had continued to collect payments from Australian taxpayers while training to become terrorists.

A federal investigation had captured the records of 57 Australians who had left the country before October, 2014, and of that number 55 had been confirmed to have been on welfare payments. Since then, at least 50 more Australians had joined Islamic State in the Middle East; most claiming some form of benefit, including unemployment, sickness, youth and carer's allowances, as well as the Disability Support Pension.

Abbott told *The Telegraph*: "As a nation, we were repulsed when images started appearing in the media last year of Australian members of the Islamist death cult gloating over the corpses of their victims and

[37] Murder in Denmark shows what happens when you create an underclass, Paul Sheehan, *The Sydney Morning Herald*, 18 February, 2015.

brandishing severed heads. I was equally appalled when I was briefed last September that 55 out of 57 Australians then believed to be fighting in Syria and Iraq with ISIL and other terrorist groups had been on some form of welfare." [38]

Drought gripped much of rural Australia.

And within the country, the grip of the state simply grew ever stronger; and the freedoms of Australians forever less.

While all the economic grace notes were bad, a falling dollar, rising unemployment, a budget out of control.

****

The escalating jihad threat within Australia in 2015 had all been known, had all been written about before.

It had come with ample warning that there were radical Islamic preachers stirring up jihad in the Australian suburbs; that just as with Afghanistan the invasion of Iraq would inflame the Muslim population and increase the country's domestic terror threat; that Australia was already a prime target for terrorist attacks.

Before he went on to a broader canvas, Australia had been gifted with one of the supreme journalists working in the field, Alex's former colleague at *The Australian* Martin Chulov. His 2006 book *Jihad Australia: The battle against terrorism from within and without* was the most comprehensive record ever compiled on the early development of the jihadist threat within Australia.

Old Alex had been doing some 4pm to midnight shifts on *The Australian* when the book was first published. They weren't exactly high status shifts, but when the day Chief of Staff went home at around 7pm he became the only reporter on at the heart of the headquarters of the national newspaper. He was expected to take over the Chief of Staff's chair, directly outside the Editor in Chiefs office. He had an eagle eye view across the news floor and down through the central turret of the building to the ground floor.

Occasionally there was a story or a crisis on; but mostly the processes were mechanical, checking in with police media, coordinating any late flowing copy, answering the odd call, arranging a job for the morning reporter. Occasionally a story broke, and there would be a flurry of fingers across the keyboard: "Come on mate, it's not a monthly magazine."

---

[38] Aussie jihadists were on the dole, Simon Benson, *The Daily Telegraph*, 21 February, 2015.

The shift suited him, when he didn't have care of the kids, because he was mostly his own boss. By that hour he was the only reporter on the paper at the Sydney headquarters; almost all the star turns having gone home, with the exception of Martin. Chulov had always been a smart operator, with superb contacts in the country's intelligence and police communities, and too clever by half to be contained within the journalistic culture of *The Australian*. Alex admired him; for his ability to break stories, and for his dedication. In Britain, in 2015, he won the Orwell Prize for Journalism.

Chulov had been enormously proud of *Australian Jihad*, and signed a copy for him as Alex sat at that desk; under the fluorescent lights; in the silently busy, mostly indifferent if not treacherous calm at the center of the headquarters of the national newspaper; as the subs processed copy and he checked the wires.

Australian Jihad was withdrawn shortly after publication and pulped without any proper public explanation.

The book was a masterful reprise of material which had to a large extent already been published in *The Australian*. As it was written by one of the paper's star turns, the book was not being launched into the world without careful legal review.

The crushing of the book smelt of deliberate government suppression. A number of orders limiting the media's coverage of one of the cases in the book had been issued by the Victorian Supreme Court, orders which would not be lifted for a number of years.

The Christians had engaged in book burning, just as had the Muslims.

As had the secularists.

The publishers Pan Macmillan ignored a request for information as to whether or not they came under any government pressure to withdraw the book from sale.

But it was still possible to find a few copies of *Australian Jihad*. You just had to know where to look.

In the end, the truth would out. Failure to confront always created bigger problems in the end. As the expression went, a problem turned and faced will disappear, a problem ignored will follow you forever.

With all the strands of the early development of the terrorist threat in Australia pulled together into one place, what *Australian Jihad* demonstrated more than anything else was: the politicians of Australia had been lying to the people all along about the threat the religious beliefs of the Muslim minority posed to the country's traditionally easy going way of life.

Alex wasn't normally in the habit of quoting back cover book blurbs, but in the case of *Australian Jihad* the blurb said much: "In the global war on terror, just how much of a target is Australia? In this gripping and disturbing book, Martin Chulov lays bare the threat posed to us by the rise of the Islamists since the early 1990s. Far from being on the periphery of radical Islam's priorities, we have slowly moved towards the centre of their sights. Australia is now seen unambiguously as a key player in the Crusader alliance. Homegrown radical Islam is on the rise, and so too are attempts to target us by the global band of jihadis that form a virtual Terror Inc.

"*Australian Jihad* reveals details of key plots against the nation and its people abroad; discloses a shocking highly emotional sequel to the first Bali bombings; uncovers how the decade of developments shaped the very real threat from within; and outlines how Australia's spies are desperately trying to evolve from easy beats to contenders able to take on their new adversary. Detailing the trailblazing visits to Australia of the global jihad pioneers; the clandestine mission of Frenchman Willie Brigitte; the trials and tribulations of the troubled wayfarers David Hicks, Mamdouh Habib, Jack Thomas and Mathew Stewart; and the 2005 counter terrorism arrests of 22 Australians accused of preparing a catastrophic strike against their countrymen, the book chronicles a growing menace.

"With unparalleled access to security sources both here and overseas, Chulov gives us the real stories behind the headlines, and in doing so has proved that the truth is often scarier than even the most frenzied conjecture. As compellingly written as any thriller, *Australian Jihad* is a vital investigation into just how secure our national security really is."

Why on Earth was a book like that not available for sale?

Why on Earth was a book like that not compulsory reading?

Any Australian politician who had not read the book was not doing their job.

"We have been far more central to radical Islamists' priorities than we ever recognised — and the radicalism they are peddling took root in Australian society more than a decade ago," Chulov wrote. "The lightning rod of Afghanistan has to a large extent been replaced by Iraq, which continues to have a profound impact on radicalised Muslims in Australia and Southeast Asia. Home-grown radicals are drawing strength from what they see as the anger and suffering of their brethren abroad. Existing radical groups are mutating. Others are mushrooming.

"A strategic defeat for the US-led coalition, or even a tactical withdrawal, would embolden the movement for decades to come. The Australian government can no longer disassociate itself from the perceived Crusader alliance. Since it was first legitimised as a target in November 2001 (when Osama bin Laden issued threats against the country), Australia has been nominated more than a dozen times... Stopping terror at its source is now just as important in Australia as it is in the Islamic nations from where the jihadi mindset hails." [39]

In other words the Prime Minister of Australia Tony Abbott already knew or most certainly should have known when he announced on 15 September, 2014 that Australia was heading back into war in Iraq the decision would further radicalize the local Muslim population, significantly increase the domestic terror threat and particularly with the use of discredited drone attacks would in all likelihood, as turned out to be the case, drive jihadi recruitment and strengthen the power of Islamic State.

All the while putting the lives of Australian soldiers at risk.

****

Fanned by government incompetence and poor decision making, the security situation in Australia deteriorated throughout 2014 and 2015.

The Ninth Edition of Dabiq, titled "They Plot and Allah Plots," the Islamic State praised two Australians who had sacrificed their lives and urged others to follow their example.

The cover was underlined with a quote from Abu Mus'ab az-Zarqawi, the militant Muslim from Jordan who ran a paramilitary training camp in Afghanistan and was a key Al-Qaeda figure and one of the ideological founders of Islamic State: "The spark has been lit here in Iraq, and its heat will continue to intensify - by Allah's permission - until it burns the crusader armies in Dabiq."

In an address from the leader of the Islamic State caliphate Abu Bakr al-Baghdadi, titled "March Forth Whether Light or Heavy," he warned against the attitude that led many of the militant factions into apostatizing and allying with unbelievers, and that is their willingness to compromise and hope for permanent peace with the crusaders.

Referring to the words of the Prophet Muhammad, Baghdadi declared: "O Muslims! Whoever thinks that it is within his capacity to conciliate with the Jews, Christians, and other unbelievers, and for them to conciliate with him, such that he coexists with them and they coexist with him while he is upon his religion and upon tawhid (an Arabic word meaning the oneness of God), then he has belied the explicit statement of his Lord."

He also said, "O Muslims, Islam was never for a day the religion of peace. Islam is the religion of war. Your Prophet (peace be upon him) was dispatched with the sword as a mercy to the creation. He was ordered with war until Allah is worshipped alone. He (peace be upon him) said to

[39] *Australian Jihad*, Martin Chulov, Pan MacMillan, 2006.

the mushrikin (the polytheist, believers in Gods other than Allah) other of his people, 'I came to you with slaughter.' He fought both the Arabs and non-Arabs in all their various colors. He himself left to fight and took part in dozens of battles. He never for a day grew tired of war...

"His companions after him and their followers carried on similarly. They did not soften nor abandon war, until they possessed the Earth, conquered the East and the West, the nations submitted to them, and the lands yielded to them, by the edge of the sword. And similarly, this will remain the condition of those who follow them until the Day of Recompense. Our Prophet (peace be upon him) has informed us of the Malahim (the final battle, Armageddon) near the end of time. He gave us good tidings and promised us that we would be victorious in these battles. He is the truthful and trustworthy, peace be upon him. And here we are today seeing the signs of those Malahim and we feel the winds of victory within them.

"And if the Crusaders (Christians) today have begun to trouble the Muslims who continue to live in the lands of the cross by monitoring them, arresting them, and questioning them, then soon they will begin to displace them and take them away either dead, imprisoned, or homeless. It is but the war of the people of faith against the people of kufr (those who deny Islam), so march forth to your war O Muslims. March forth everywhere, for it is an obligation upon every Muslim who is accountable before Allah...

Baghdadi then expounded on the obligation upon the Muslims during these Wars Before the Hour: "O Muslims! Do not think the war that we are waging is the Islamic State's war alone. Rather, it is the Muslims' war altogether. It is the war of every Muslim in every place . . . he must attack the crusaders, their allies . . . and their apostate forces, wherever he might be with any means available to him, and he should not hesitate in doing so, nor consult any supposed 'scholar' on this obligation. And he will find an excellent example in the shuhada' of the Islamic State including Numan Haider and Man Haron Monis..."

Numan Haider and Man Haron Monis were the two Australian Muslims who had up until that point, at least as they saw it, died on Australian soil in the service of Islamic State.

This was the propaganda so readily available.

In September of 2014 Numan Haider, 18, was killed after stabbing two counter terrorism officers outside a Melbourne police station, where he had been called to discuss the status of his passport. His grieving family remembered him as a quiet, well behaved boy.

An inquest heard that police had called Haider into the Endeavour Hills Police Station to talk about the cancellation of his passport. When met by two counter terrorism police he pulled a knife, stabbed the Victorian police officer in the face and then the AFP officer in the face, chest and shoulder. When the Federal Police officer fell to the ground Haider climbed on top of him and continued to stab him. The inquest heard the Victorian officer shouted at him to stop before shooting Haider once in the head. [40]

Haider was believed to have been heavily influenced by online Islamic State propaganda.

Jihad songs for teenagers were nothing but a click away.

Across increasing swathes of the Middle East, the Islamic State chanted their hymn:

> My Ummah, Dawn has appeared, so await the expected victory,
> The Islamic State has arisen by the blood of the righteous,
> The Islamic State has arisen by the jihad of the pious,
> They have offered their souls in righteousness with constancy and conviction,
> So that the religion may be established, in which there is the law of the Lord of the Worlds.

> My Ummah, accept the good news, and don't despair: victory is near.
> The Islamic State has arisen and the dreaded might has begun.
> It has arisen tracing out glory, and the period of setting has ended,
> By faithful men who do not fear warfare.
> They have created eternal glory that will not perish or disappear.

---

[40] Terror suspect Abdul Numan Haider continued to stab fallen officer: Inquest, ABC, 4 October, 2014.

SECTION TWO: BURN THE WORLD

JUST DOWN FROM the Lindt Cafe, also in Martin Place, lay the Sydney Cenotaph, completed in 1927, a 20 tonne monolithic granite block with the words "Lest We Forget" and "To Our Glorious Dead" on its flanks, and statues of a soldier and a sailor guarding it at either end.

But there could hardly have been two greater symbols of the polarization of Australian society than the terror site of the Lindt Cafe, one a comfortable pleasure dome run by an openly gay manager who was to lose his life during the siege, a tribute to the joys of chocolate, of life, of safety in numbers; the other a somber tribute to the lives of fallen soldiers, young Australians swept up in waves of nationalistic fervor. They had sacrificed their own futures at the behest of the country's political caste; and died for what they had been convinced was a noble cause, their country.

Australian governments had always appealed to nationalism in their aggressive drives to recruit young men to war. World War One posters included: "Under Which Flag Will You Live? Enlist Now"; "The Trumpet Calls"; "The Boys In The Trenches Vote Yes"; and "It Is More Serious Than You Think, The barbarian is almost at your gates, He Violates, Plunders, Murders, Don't let him get a footing on British soil, Help To Repel The Invasion By Enlisting Now."

Those young soldiers who marched with such pride, such joy, from family farms and scattered townships across Australia, if they had still been alive, would not have recognized the country they had fought and died for; would have dismissed with contempt the politicians eulogizing on their behalf, and would have been inconceivably grief stricken at the loss of their friends; and even, to a less formulated degree, at the loss of their own lives and loves, the children never born. Men with their whole lives in front of them died at the behest of Generals in London; and the obsequious political class in far off Australia. Good of heart, strong of limb. They would never grow old.

Base appeals to nationalism would still be a part of the justification for war and the manipulation of public opinion a century later.

As the center for the Anzac Day Dawn Services, every 25th of April crowds gathered in Martin Place in the hushed darkness before the dawn. Anzac Day was originally a time for returned soldiers to remember their fallen comrades; and became a day in honor of all the country's fallen soldiers. ANZAC was an acronym for the Australian and New Zealand Army Corps, whose soldiers were known as Anzacs.

The date marked the anniversary of the beginning of the first campaign in World War One, which led to major casualties, the attempt to capture the Gallipoli Peninsula in 1915.

The objective had been to take Constantinople, as Istanbul was then known, the capital of the Ottoman Empire, the largest Islamic empire in history. Turkey, as it came to be known, had sided with the Germans during the War; thus placing Australia, with its historical links to Britain, on the opposite side of the conflict.

Contrary to expectation, as 20th Century wars retreated into history and Australia transposed into a multiethnic society the crowds attending Anzac Day ceremonies had been growing in the years to 2015; the first signs of dawn silhouetting dense, reverential crowds, including the ancestors of those who fought and died, emotional in acknowledgment of the debt they owed their forebears.

Each year the dignitaries, politicians, and the profundity of the services added import to the Anzac Day ceremonies, ensuring Martin Place remained central to the Sydney's psyche as well as its business life.

Each year The Ode of Remembrance was heard, but only part of it was commonly read:

They went with songs to the battle, they were young.
Straight of limb, true of eyes, steady and aglow.
They were staunch to the end against odds uncounted,
They fell with their faces to the foe.
They shall grow not old, as we that are left grow old:
Age shall not weary them, nor the years condemn.
At the going down of the sun and in the morning,
We will remember them.

The Ode of Remembrance was not uniquely Australian. It was originally a poem by an Englishman, Laurence Binyon, who, overwhelmed by the carnage and loss of life by British and Allied forces, had penned one of the most moving war poems ever written, a tribute to the dead; originally published in *The Times* of England under the title For the Fallen.

As a young and somewhat idealistic general news reporter, out to make the world a better place, Alex had originally blanched when sent off by the News Desk of *The Sydney Morning Herald* in the 1980s to interview old soldiers. As one of the generation who had demonstrated ardently against the Vietnam War, he did not want to hear the glory stories.

In fact, to Alex's surprise, he discovered there was no one on Earth more anti-war than a returned soldier.

They marched in memory of their friends and comrades who had fallen in blood spattered agony into the mud and sands of foreign lands. They marched in utter sadness, out of respect for their fallen comrades, and each year, after the march, they got hopelessly drunk, maudlin and sentimental, made black jokes and were glad to see their surviving mates; and then were driven home in taxis, back into the fabric of their lives for another year.

They did not march in defense of or out of respect for those who had sent them to die.

They did not march in glorification of war.

Old foot soldiers, without a single exception that Alex ever found, had no respect for the senior military staff who so arrogantly sent them to their deaths, no fond memories of battle, no illusions of the glory and rightness of war; nothing but an enduring, terrible sense of grief and loss.

And above all they had no respect for the politicians who used their youthful enthusiasms for their country to send them to war; as politicians continued to do in the 21st Century.

In 2015, the same Australian political caste who had sent soldiers into conflicts spanning more than a century, including both World Wars and the Vietnam War, eulogized the legend of the Anzacs in ceremony after ceremony to mark the centenary of the Gallipoli Day massacres.

Those politicians who made such hay out of Anzac Day had never put their own lives on the line, never seen the smashed bodies of their friends falling into blood stained mud, never endured the repeated strains of military incompetence, had never been prepared to die for their country.

All they had ever been prepared to do was send others; and then to glorify their deaths as honorable.

Every single Australian of the 331,781 who went overseas during World War 1, was a volunteer. From the landing on Gallipoli onwards, the Australian troops were used as the spearhead of every attack carried out by the various British armies in which they served.

For this honor, they paid a terrible price: 59,258 were killed, 166,815 suffered wounds; 4,084 became prisoners; in a war half a world away.

At Gallipoli alone there had been 8,709 Australian casualties; and another 1,358 from New Zealand.

Total casualties suffered by troops of the British Empire during the First World War amounted to 35.8 per cent of the forces mobilized for war service. The total Australian casualties however, amounted to 68.5 per cent of their armed forces, the highest percentage of any nation engaged in the First World War.

The attempted invasion of Gallipoli was a military disaster coordinated from London with great discredit to the military leaders involved; but for Anglo-Saxon Australians, it had come to represent the forging of the national spirit, tough and cheerful in the face of adversity, self reliant, loyal to their comrades, determined to make the most of whatever dire circumstance the overlords dealt up to them, willing to make sacrifices for others and for their country.

Until 2015 Anzac Day singularly brought home the shock of the new to the body politic the day had been regarded as a day which brought the country together.

Many ethnic groupings encouraged to settle in the country since those early colonial wars had no relationship to Anzac Day, and saw it as little more than one of the quaint customs of their adopted country.

For Muslims who, equally as they saw it, had in recent and past years died fighting the aggressive colonial aggression of Western governments in places like Iraq, Syria, Turkey and other parts of the Islamic world, were not similarly honored. They saw Anzac Day as an offensive celebration of the invasion of the last caliphate, the Ottoman Empire.

The Anzac Day of 2015 would be different to any preceding year.

For a start, it was the anniversary of the Gallipoli conflict and the founding of the Anzac tradition; and as such was the subject of numerous national ceremonies; while the Prime Minister himself would travel to Gallipoli for the Dawn Service.

The Day was marked in ceremonies large and small, from neglected country town parks, to the grander ceremonies at war memorials in Sydney, Canberra and Melbourne.

But a day which was intended to bring the nation together highlighted instead its fundamental divisions.

A spokesman for the Muslim group Hizb ut-Tahrir said Muslims should not celebrate Anzac day because it was a "superficial, jingoistic" date that marked Australian colonial aggression against the Muslim world, an act it was now repeating with its invasion of Muslim lands in modern day Syria and Iraq.

In a press release issued to coincide with Anzac Day, the Hizb observed: "Anzac Day is commemorated with increasing fervor each year in Australia. The Australian Government goes out of its way to keep the 'Anzac spirit' alive. It seeks to impress the Anzac tradition as symbolic of the 'national character' of Australia and to impose the

Anzac history and concept on everyone, including Muslims living in Australia, as a universal Australian value."

Hizb ut-Tahrir Australia claimed the true legacy of the Anzac tradition was Australian involvement in the unjust invasions of Iraq and Afghanistan. Just as Australian troops were used for British imperial designs in WWI, so too were they used in Iraq and Afghanistan for American imperial and economic interests. The false pretext in both cases was the spurious claim of "fighting for our freedom," as if freedom could be predicated on the oppression of others.

"The truth is that Australia, as a former British colony in the past, and a modern independent sovereign state today, supports an international framework of deceit, exploitation and destruction led by the US and European powers. It is this ugly reality that is covered by superficial jingoistic celebrations based on crafted mythologies like the 'Anzac legend.'

"From the Muslim perspective, the Gallipoli campaign represents an aggression by Allied troops against the legitimate Islamic authority of the time, the Ottoman Caliphate. There is nothing for Muslims to celebrate about Australian's contribution to colonial aggression against the Muslim world.

"In the post- 9/11 and 7/7 context, the Government has impressed upon Islamic schools in Australia to introduce Anzac day commemorational activities. This is an imposition of foreign values and a foreign history on Muslims that is unacceptable. Will our children, in the near future, be made to observe one-minute silence and by lectured about the 'feats' of Australian troops in Iraq and Afghanistan too?

"We urge the people of Australia to rise above the lowliness of nationalistic sentiment to the higher plane of intellectual inquiry and to think deeply about the reality of Australian participation in war abroad, past and present. There are worthier ends than to live off the oppression of peoples abroad and worthier means than sacrificing the sons of this country at the altar of the economic and political interests of foreign powers like the United States and United Kingdom."

****

On April 20, 2015, a female Australian Islamic State (ISIS) member using the Twitter name Umm Abdullatif, the wife of Mahmoud Abdullatif, urged ISIS supporters in Australia to carry on with plans for an attack on Australian soil set for Saturday: "To the Muslims in Australia we say; CONTINUE what the brothers planned for Anzac Day. And your reward will be with Allah."

Melbourne man Mahmoud Abdullatif, described as a "party boy turned Muslim extremist," was reportedly killed in Syria in January of 2015. He had arrived in Raqqa around September of 2014 and immediately began sharing pictures of himself holding weapons. He came to the attention of Australian authorities after issuing calls for attacks against disbelievers in Australia. [41]

His wife, previously known as Zehra Duman, had flown to Syria to marry him in December. She was 21-years-old; and received a gun as part of her dowry. She claimed that her husband was now a "green bird," another term for martyr. She tweeted: "Till we reunite in Jannatul Firdaws my dearest husband. You won the race! Heart of a green bird insha'Allah habibi."

After his death his Australian jihad bride taunted authorities by telling them to "catch me if you can." Another of Umm Abdullatif's tweets declared: "Yous can say what all you want, but I know my husband is in Jannah bihnillah. Remember our dead are in Paradise, your dead are in hell fire." To a critic she said: "I can't hear you through all these isis victories." Another of her tweets declared: "The kuffar think that death to a Mujahid is a loss. NO, by Allah, martyrdom is a major reward and an honour! We will have victory either way."

Umm Abdullatif also used her Twitter account to encourage other jihad brides with comments like "The sunset here... it is something you need to see with your own eyes" and "Oh Muslims in the west, you are in great loss if you do not migrate." [42]

One of Abdullatif last posts read: "I got married today, alhumdolileh I made hijra and got married here man, insha Allah I receive a beautiful death as well."

****

Continue what the brothers planned.

Exactly what was planned, if successful, might well have changed Australia forever.

In Melbourne there was a spate of arrests as a plot to disrupt the Anzac Day March was uncovered.

Operation Rising, as it was so appropriately known, the Rising of Islam, resulted in the execution of seven search warrants in the South

---

[41] Melbourne man Mahmoud Abdullatif reportedly killed fighting for Islamic State in Syria, Andrea Hamblin and James Dowling, *Herald Sun*, 20 January, 2015.

[42] Australian ISIS widow tells girls 'lifestyle' in caliphate is 'amazing,' Breitbart, 2 April, 2015.

Eastern Metropolitan area of Melbourne, and the arrest of five men in pre-dawn raids across Melbourne.

Part of their alleged planning included targeting an ANZAC day ceremony. The men were alleged to be undertaking preparations for planning terrorist acts in Melbourne, including beheading a police officer, stealing his weapon and then committing acts of violence. Four of the men were 18 years old, the fifth 19 years old. [43]

Those arrested regularly attended the Al-Furqan Centre in Springvale South, subsequently shut down for promoting extremist ideas. Senior Islamic State recruiter Neil Prakash had also once been a regular.

The young men were associates of Numan Haider, the teenager who had died the previous September after stabbing two police officers in front of a police station. Some of those arrested in pre-dawn counter terrorism raids were with Haider before he attacked two officers with a knife outside the Endeavour Hills police station.

The Anzac Day attack plot allegedly involved killing a police officer and then using the officer's gun to go on a shooting rampage until the perpetrators themselves were killed. The plot was partly to seek revenge for Haider's death.

Police had originally become concerned that the men, whose passports had been cancelled, as had Haider's, frustrated in their desire to practice jihad in the Middle East, would turn their jihadi zeal towards Australians. Their fears were heightened by the emergence of a propaganda video in Prakash praised Haider's efforts.

Critics argued that the Australian government policy of confiscating passports of would-be jihadists was creating an increasing number of people with nowhere to go but home soil to fulfill what they saw as their religious obligation to practice jihad.

Sydney Muslim doctor and community leader Jamal Rifi said confiscating passports without any backup programs was nonsensical, leaving ticking time bombs in the community.

Dr Rifi, named as Australian of the Year by *The Australian* newspaper, warned: "All this does is keep these individuals in the local community. They're given a badge of honour to parade and thus in turn creating for them a fan base, without the availability for any pathways or programs for re-education.

"They have confiscated large numbers of passports. Some of them are already overseas, but in our area of Sydney there are at least 15 people roaming the streets who have had their passports taken away.

---

[43] AFP Media Releases, 18/20/30 April 2015.

"The type of people whose passports have been confiscated have been roaming the street and they are forming a fan base around them, taking the high moral ground, using intimidation strategies, and no one is engaging with them.

"It is a badge of honour for them. Their passport has been taken because they are a national security risk, but at the same time they pose a personal and family security risk to me. If they are so willing to go and help whom they call the oppressed people in Syria, give them their passport and I'll buy them a one-way ticket. Let them go."

Dr Rifi received death threats for his comments criticizing Islamic State and condemning one Australian jihadi posing with severed heads.[44]

An offer of a $1,000 was made for the supply of his home address. He was forced to step up security at both his home and surgery.

Former Immigration Minister Scott Morrison described as brave comments by Dr Rifi which could carry real consequences in the community.

So much for freedom of speech in a great pluralistic liberal democracy.

Former counter-terrorism officer Peter Moroney said cancelling the passports of radicals without any community back up measures was like "pulling the pin on a hand grenade and leaving it in a confined space."

Wissam Haddad, owner of the hardline Al-Risalah prayer center in Bankstown said would be jihadists should be allowed to leave the country and revoke their citizenship.

"You can't put a wild bird in a cage and just hope it's going to be domesticated," he said.

"Cancelling passports is not going to deter anyone from jihad. You can't kill an idea." [45]

The two 18-year-old youths retained in custody were Sevdet Ramden Besim and Harun Causevic.

In documents tendered in the Melbourne Magistrates Court police alleged Besim had been advised to practice decapitation on a "lonely person."

Besim allegedly received coaching on executing a terror attack from a 14-year-old British boy, and planned to sacrifice his life to fight the enemies of Allah.

---

[44] Australia takes passports away to keep terrorists at home, *The Irish Times*, 20 August, 2014.

[45] Cancelling passports of suspected Jihadists, Rachel Olding, *The Sydney Morning Herald*, 19 August, 2014.

Australian Federal Police agent Denis Scott told the court the 14-year-old, who also faced terror charges, wanted to attack on Anzac Day for maximum exposure.

In online conversations with the UK teen conducted through an encrypted program, Besim allegedly said he was thinking "a combo of knife and car" should be used in an Australian attack.

When Besim indicated he had access to a machete, the 14-year-old allegedly responded: "Sharpen that as hard as you can, then run police over and decapitate."

Besim allegedly replied: "That sounds like a plan."

The UK teen said Besim should break into a house to get his first taste of a beheading, a few hours before the operation.

"im (sic) talking a proper lonely person," the UK teen allegedly said.

Besim and Causevic had allegedly researched parade routes and possessed copies of a pledge of allegiance to the leader of Islamic State.

"25th is a good day coz its anzac day and this will mean they will remember this on that day every yr after," Besim allegedly told the UK teen.

"I can't wait now for the op. Like i said though id love to take out some cops ... I was gonna meet with them then take some heads ahaha." [46]

Another teen, Mehran Azami, 19, of Narre Warren, faced more than 20 weapons charges.

That there was no repentance was everywhere clear.

At a bail hearing Vehid Causevic's father claimed his son was innocent and had been the victim of a political conspiracy: "This is everything set up from government, from Prime Minister. This is political. This is message from Prime Minister to young Muslim go five times a day to mosque, be charged like terrorist. My son doesn't understand Islam, but he doesn't do nothing. If you find anyone in this country to say my son has done something bad I go in jail for all my life."

The court had earlier heard evidence that after a minor collision in a car park, his son had allegedly told the other driver: "Australia is shit and ISIS is going to kill this country."

Practice beheading on a lonely person.

****

[46] Anzac Day terror plot, *Herald Sun*, 8 May, 2015.

On April 21, 2015, four days before Anzac Day, the Islamic State via its official media arm Al-Hayat, released a video featuring Abu Khaled Al-Cambodi, 23, an Australian ISIS fighter of Cambodian origin.

Al-Cambodi, formerly known as Neil Prakash, travelled to Syria from Melbourne in early 2013. He was a former Buddhist who became Islamic State's senior recruiter in Australia.

Prakash provided an account of how he entered Islam and called for lone wolf attacks in Australia.

Al-Cambodi praised the terrorist attacks which had occurred in Australia in recent months, and called on Australian Muslims to join forces with ISIS and kill the disbelievers in their country. "You kill him [for] Allah has promised you a place in Paradise," he said. "Now Is The Time To Rise... Now Is The Time To Rush For That Reward That Allah Has Promised You."

In the 12-minute video, professionally produced and promoted by Islamic State, Prakash issued a call to arms to his "my brothers, my beloved brothers in Islam in Australia. Now is the time to rise, now is the time to wake up ... You must start attacking before they attack you.

"Look how much [sic] of your sisters have been violated. All I hear on the news in Australia is this sister was hurt ... her hijab was ripped off. But no, you see the brothers sitting.

"I ask you brothers, when are you going to to rise up and attack them, for them attacking you?

"I invite the Muslims to come here. I tell you that this is the land of life.

"The media has portrayed that we come here because we were social outcasts, because we had nobody we had to turn to Islam, because we were just trouble-makers in the past. This is far from the reality. We see people from all walks of life here." [47]

As part of the promotion al-Cambodi was featured in the April 2014 issue of the ISIS English-language magazine *Dabiq*.

While Prakash looked dashing in full military garb, the Forward quoted "Allah's messenger," the infamous Al-Qaeda fighter Abu Mus'ab az-Zarqawi, declaring: "We perform jihad so that Allah's word becomes supreme and that the religion becomes completely for Allah. Everyone who opposes this goal or stands in the path of this goal is an enemy for us and a target for our swords, whatever his name may be and whatever his lineage may be."

---

[47] Islamic State recruiter Neil Prakash calls for attacks in Australia in propaganda video, Marissa Calligeros, *The Age*, 22 April, 2015.

The Forward also quoted Abu Bakr al-Baghdadi: "O Muslims everywhere, glad tidings to you and expect good. Raise your heads high, for today – by Allah's grace – you have a state and khilafah, which will return your dignity, might, rights, and leadership. It is a state where the Arab and non-Arab, the white man and black man, the easterner and westerner are all brothers. It is a khilafah that gathered the Caucasian, Indian, Chinese, Shami, Iraqi, Yemeni, Egyptian, Maghribi (North African), American, French, German, and Australian. Allah brought their hearts together, and thus, they became brothers by His grace, loving each other for the sake of Allah, standing in a single trench, defending and guarding each other, and sacrificing themselves for one another.

"Their blood mixed and became one, under a single flag and goal, in one pavilion, enjoying this blessing, the blessing of faithful brotherhood. If kings were to taste this blessing, they would abandon their kingdoms and fight over this grace. All praise and thanks are due to Allah. Therefore, rush O Muslims to your state. Yes, it is your state. Rush, because Syria is not for the Syrians and Iraq is not for the Iraqis. The Earth is Allah's. The State is a state for all Muslims. The land is for the Muslims, all the Muslims."[48]

The next month Prakash wrought havoc on travel in the Middle East, forcing three major airlines to ground planes after a bomb hoax.

Etihad, Lufthansa and Turkish Airlines all had flights from Turkey and Egypt diverted or turned back after Prakash falsely claimed on social media that bombs had been placed on two planes.

The two flights he mentioned were Etihad's EY650 from Cairo to Abu Dhabi and "IST 1305."

IST is the code for Istanbul's international airport. Both Lufthansa and Turkish Airlines had flights numbered 1305 departing from that airport, and both were turned back shortly after departure. More than 450 passengers were directly affected, with delays at airports affecting many more. [49]

****

Speaking in Paris Australian Foreign Minister Julie Bishop said there would be an unprecedented level of security at Anzac Day ceremonies across Europe in the wake of terror threats.

---

[48] Dabiq, 1436, Jumada Al-Akhirah, Issue 8.

[49] Neil Prakash bomb tweets ground three planes, Mark Schliebs, *The Australian*, 14 May, 2015.

"I'm aware that terrorist attacks can take place at any place and any time," she said.

The countries hosting Anzac services, including the UK, Belgium, France and Turkey, were very conscious of the need to keep people safe, she said.

"There will be an unprecedented level of security across the globe for events such as this," she said. "Just as we do in Australia countries are doing that likewise overseas and those who are hosting Anzac ceremonies and similar ceremonies are taking steps to ensure that the security is appropriate.

"We will have representatives in London ... and I'm assured that the security will be as appropriate as it can be, as it will be here in France and in Belgium." [50]

Australian National University terrorism expert Clarke Jones said Anzac Day services were a "high risk" for terrorism threats: "It is a valuable target and it would be quite strategic for, say, Islamic State to launch something in Turkey. Gallipoli is a fair distance from the border of Syria and Iraq but distance is not big deal if they wanted to do it, especially given the porous border."

The 8000 Australians who had received tickets to the Dawn Service went through rigorous security screening before the event, six checks in all. There were some 4,000 Turkish police and paramilitary officers on duty. ASIO and Australian Federal Police also travelled to Gallipoli to assist with security arrangements. [51]

****

To begin at one kind of beginning. As one of the country's longest suffering general news reporters, having spent almost a quarter of a century as a staff member on some of the nation's most difficult, treacherous news floors, and more than 40 years as a journalist of one kind or another, Alex had covered many an ANZAC memorial service; standing with other reporters pad in hand in the predawn darkness of Martin Place or mingling, with pad in hand, among the dignitaries.

Alex had never hesitated to ignore all the usual bounds of official protocol or the roped off sections in which the media were supposed to contain themselves, and would sometimes find himself standing next to

[50] Security to be increased at Anzac Day Ceremonies Across Europe, Matt Miller, *The Sydney Morning Herald*, 21 April, 2015.
[51] Gallipoli ceremony terrorism risk, David Wroe, *The Sydney Morning Herald*, 17 April, 2015.

the State Premier of the day, the State Governor, past and present Prime Ministers, the Chief of the Armed Forces.

He regarded it as an essential tenet of journalism, talk to anyone, high or low.

One such story, written for *The Australian* newspaper in 2007, read: "Despite torrential downpours, thousands of people were crowded into Martin Place for 4am for the dawn service; many families brought their wide-eyed children. Amongst the crowd a were a few elderly diggers from the Second World War, fewer in number year by year."

Ronald Hanton, 87, said he wouldn't wish war on anyone: "I am one of the only survivors. Life is a wonderful experience, but I wouldn't want to send someone into the same situation I experienced."

Despite bouts of heavy rain, the atmosphere was hushed as state governor Marie Bashir read the dedication: "We who are gathered here think of those who went out to the battlefields of all wars, but did not return. We feel them near us in spirit."

Official guests who laid wreaths at the Cenotaph included NSW Premier Morris Iemma, state opposition leader Barry O'Farrell, federal Environment Minister Malcolm Turnbull representing the Prime Minister John Howard and Sydney Lord Mayor Clover Moore.

Eight years on Iemma had disappeared into the blighted history books of the state's Labor Party, O'Farrell had been and gone as State Premier, vanishing in scandal into the ignominy he deserved, Turnbull was cooling his heels as the nation's Communications Minister while plotting another tilt at the leadership; and John Howard had become only the second Prime Minister ever to lose his own seat at an election.

Only Clover Moore remained in the same role, hated by the city's business people, an enduring pestilence on the city; the person who, as far as Alex was concerned, had singularly, more than any other person in the city's history, destroyed the raffish charm and bohemian character of Sydney, bringing through grotesque levels of regulation and environmental zeal its once once vibrant inner-city life to a standstill.

Chaplain Murray Lund led prayers for peace around the world: "Raise up those who have courage and vision to work for a new world where children can grow up in peace and freedom."

As rain poured down a lone bugler played the last post, followed by a minute's silence.

Naval Commander of Australia, Rear Admiral Davyd Thomas, urged the crowd to remember the 3,500 Australian servicemen and women serving overseas and said the Anzac tradition continued through them: "Many of them were in harm's way this morning. Their service is still selfless, the mateship is as deep, the teamwork just as vital."

Like so many of his fellow countrymen caught up in another American quagmire and still suffering the consequences 40 years later, Ross Mangano, 67, who lost a leg in the Vietnam War, recalled a priest in an army field hospital trying to read him his last rites. "I shouted at him that I had never seen snow, I wasn't going to die," he recalled. "My platoon sergeant died in Vietnam, and I march for him and for all my mates who can't march. You can't go to war and not lose any soldiers. I am very proud to be Australian."

As part of those ceremonies, eight long years before, a special award was given to Wall Scott-Smith, the chief custodian of the Cenotaph for the previous 60 years. He never missed a dawn service in all that time.

"The crowds started increasing about seven years ago," he said as Alex had struggled to take down the words, in his own mix of shorthand and personal hieroglyphics, in the middle of the jam packed crowd, in the pouring rain. "At first it was teenagers, now it is mom, dad and the kids. The Dawn Service is very important, it means so much."

Many families had taken their children. Eight-year-old Claudia Cirillo from Manly, a beach suburb on the other side of the harbor, said of the service: "It might make little kids sad about the people who died in the war, but it is still important they come." Her mother Janette Cirillo said it was important to bring her children. "Anzac Day and the Dawn Service is part of our Australian heritage," she told him.

Scott Stanford, 37, dressed in full army regalia, said his great uncle Roy Stanford had been killed at Gallipoli: "I march so it is not forgotten about," he said. "I bring my young son, who is eight, with me every year. It is not about glorifying war, it is about ensuring it never happens again."

It would happen again.

****

After decades in journalism, there weren't too many things Alex hadn't written about.

He had also written a story about the world's last survivor of the Gallipoli campaign.

Several years before the old man's death Alex had been obliged to do a phone interview with Alec Campbell, on the occasion when Alec, due to having outlived everybody else, became the last surviving Gallipoli veteran.

Most people, particularly the elderly, are pretty chuffed if the national newspaper rings them up over one honour or another. Not Alec.

Given the assignment by the Chief of Staff, Alex went about his duties.

Unlike so many others, mortgage rates, interest rates, property prices, some dismal little demographic trend, something one of the editors had heard at a dinner party the previous evening, at least interviewing the oldest living survivor of the Gallipoli massacre had been a story worth doing.

In the first instance Alec's protective wife said she wasn't sure if he would feel like talking. An old carpenter, he was way down the backyard somewhere banging away at things, and didn't usually like to come to the phone.

Alec took his time, that was for sure. Alex hung on the phone for a good 15 minutes or more. Alec wasn't honored, he was grumpy that he had been disturbed doing whatever it was he had been doing, banging away at things as his wife put it.

Alex found him, well, taciturn; very unimpressed by politicians, proud of his union background, up the bosses, and contemptuous of the military commanders who sent his comrades to their deaths in their thousands, the terrible slaughter he had witnessed firsthand.

And, as had once been the traditional Australian way, utterly contemptuous of politicians.

He hadn't wanted to march on Anzac Day because he didn't want to glorify a lie: that war was a noble enterprise.

Alec Campbell had never sought fame for himself, never attended Anzac ceremonies until very late in life, thought the glorification of war was a complete crock and almost never spoke about his experiences at Gallipoli. There were better, more positive things in life.

He had worked many different jobs, as a stockman, carpenter, railway carriage builder and in his later years as a researcher and historian. He gained an economics degree at the age of 50. His love of life extended to an enthusiasm for sailing, and he circumnavigated Tasmania.

Like so many other young men deluded into thinking he was joining for a great cause and for an adventure worth having, he lied about his age to join up. He had been 16 when the horrific bloodbath that was Gallipoli occurred.

It was the boundlessly cheerful and the optimistic, as Alex had observed from interviewing countless people of all ages, who survived into old age; who did not let the injustices of life eat into their souls and kill them early. Campbell died in Tasmania at the age of 103. He was survived by nine children, 30 grandchildren and 32 great grandchildren.

The story Alex would subsequently write in May of 2002 on the occasion of Campbell's death was headlined "Tributes and praise pour in for an ordinary hero."

Then Prime Minister John Howard's media office had done a fine old job polishing up the Anzac myth for public consumption. Howard was the first cab off the rank to praise Alec Campbell: "On behalf of the nation I honour his life. Alec Campbell was typical of a generation of Australians who, through their sacrifice, bravery and decency, created a legacy that has resonated through subsequent decades and generations.

"All Australians will forever be in debt to the Anzacs, not only for what they did for us but for the legend, for the tradition, for the stoicism under fire, sense of mateship and all those other great ideals that, increasingly, young Australians see as part of their inheritance.

"The wonderful thing is that the spirit and the tradition is growing stronger as the years go by. It must have been a source of enormous comfort and reassurance and pride for somebody like Alec Campbell in his later years to see the warm embrace of Anzac by the young people of today as they walk the cliffs of Gallipoli."

Bullshit.

On his deathbed Campbell pleaded: "For God's sake, don't glorify Gallipoli — it was a terrible fiasco, a total failure and best forgotten." [52]

****

On the same day as the pre-Anzac Day threats, the 20th of April, 2015, Tony Abbott officially farewelled 330 troops deployed to Iraq at the army barracks in Brisbane. The ceremonies took place at the Gallipoli Barracks at Brisbane's Enoggera Defence Base. The troops were in addition to 200 Special Forces soldiers and 400 personnel already involved in the air mission against Islamic State. Australia had first joined the international effort to defeat IS militants in September after a direct request from US President Barack Obama. The contribution included six F/A18 fighter jets, a surveillance aircraft and a refueler.

The Prime Minister denied the provision of extra personnel was mission creep, claiming it was a continuation of "successful execution of the original mission."

---

[52] It's Anzac Day - not the Big Day Out, Jonathan King, *The Sydney Morning Herald*, 13 April, 2013.

The troops were embarking on a two year deployment, with most put to work training Iraqi soldiers. Defence officials asked the media not to identify the troops or their family members as a security precaution.

"The enemy we are facing has shown they are quite sophisticated," Colonel Matthew Galton said. "They have been able to exploit things like social media so we are just taking prudent precautions for the safety of the troops, but more so for the safety of their families back home."

Abbott told reporters: "Our build partner capacity mission is all about trying to ensure that the legitimate government of Iraq has a trained and disciplined and capable force that understands the rules of armed conflict at its disposal to retake ... the territory which is currently under the control of the death cult," Abbott told reporters. "Although Australian personnel will deploy to the building partner capacity mission in a non-combat role, they are fully aware that Iraq is a complex and dangerous environment in which to operate. Australian soldiers are among the finest in the world. We wish them all the best as they begin their mission and, importantly, we wish them a safe return to their families and friends."

Addressing the troops Abbott said it was fitting on the eve of the centenary of Anzac that this was yet again a partnership between Australia and New Zealand.

"Good luck, may God bless you, and we look forward to welcoming you back after your mission is accomplished. You are going abroad to a faraway country, to uphold our interests and our values, to keep us safe. You go abroad to support us." [53]

The rhetoric of the Australian government was hyperbolic.

To his critics the Prime Minister was imperiling the lives of the military men and women with whom he claimed to have so much empathy, involving the nation's taxpayers in a conflict the country could not win, and taking morally indefensible action in a far off religious war, thereby inflaming local Muslim sentiment and bringing the conflict straight on to the streets and into the homes of ordinary citizens.

Within the month those same soldiers being farewelled with such ballyhoo were camped perilously close to Islamic State, the massacres even more frequent, the security situation in Western countries increasingly perilous.

Australia, and Western, military intervention in Iraq had a long, expensive and disastrous history.

---

[53] Prime Minister Tony Abbott, Opposition Leader Bill Shorten farewell troops in Brisbane bound for Iraq, ABC, 21 April, 2015.

Why would this time be any different?

****

It was not just the Muslims who criticized Australia's involvement in the Iraq debacle.

As Tom Switzer, Alex's former colleague at *The Australian* turned political commentator and host of Between the Lines for the ABC's Radio National, a once staunch supporter of Tony Abbott, wrote: "It pains me to say it, but Abbott has learned nothing about Iraq. He's taken the Islamic State's bait."

One might expect the country's legions of left wing commentators to criticize the war.

But Switzer was unusual for being a warrior of the right, not of the left; in a generally left leaning profession.

Switzer prefaced his piece for *The Guardian* newspaper with one of Talleyrand's observations of the Bourbon monarchs: he has learnt nothing and forgotten nothing.

"At first glance, the new mission – to help train the Iraqi army to recapture the Sunni strongholds, such as Mosul, from Sunni insurgents – sounds like a noble cause. It is part of a US-led coalition effort to defeat the Islamic State (Isis) terrorists, who every sane person recognises as brutal barbarians. But the mission hardly serves the national interest of Australia or New Zealand, or for that matter the US; and it is bound to make a bad situation worse.

"For one thing, we've been there, done that. From 2003 to 2008, Australia helped the US government create and train an Iraqi army to the cost of US$25bn. This was, remember, the very same Iraqi army that disintegrated as soon as it faced Isis in north-west Iraq last June. The reason for that debacle had less to do with the might of the Sunni jihadists and more to do with the simmering sectarianism that has afflicted this arbitrarily created state for more than a decade."

The exact nature of the conflict in Iraq had always been difficult for the punter to follow, which was one reason politicians cloaked their justifications for military intervention in the rhetoric of a battle between good and evil.

"What is unfolding across Iraq, and indeed potentially the broader region, is a Shia-Sunni dispute," Switzer wrote. "By intervening (again), we are taking sides with Shia Muslims against Sunni Muslims in a sectarian conflict.

"If the Isis fanatics are indeed defeated, the likely winner would be Iran, a terrorist-sponsoring Shia power that wants to dominate the region."

Switzer echoed the warnings of Graeme Wood, the biggest proponent of an American invasion of Iraq is the Islamic State itself: "Those videos of carefully choreographed beheadings of western and Japanese hostages are designed to lure us into Iraq. They understandably shock our sensitivities. But in our outrage we are taking the terrorists' bait. In the calculations of Isis leader Abu Bakr al-Baghdadi, the US-led mission creep helps drive recruitment numbers, as well as give legitimacy to the perceived grievances of so many Sunnis in Iraq and elsewhere.

"Make no mistake: by intervening, we are helping radicalise young marginalised Sunnis in western nations and inadvertently encouraging them to join the jihadist cause, either at home or in the Middle East.

"The idea that air power – with some special forces and army instructors to train the grossly incompetent local army – can help regain Sunni strongholds from Sunni jihadists is fanciful. We should keep out of this mess and let the rival Sunni and Shia groups settle their differences and reach a settlement on their own terms. Our experience in Iraq shows Western powers are incapable of creating a durable peace." [54]

In May the US Consulate warned its citizens in Australia that a terrorist attack was likely. The warning suggested: "US citizens are reminded to be aware of your surroundings during this time of heightened alert, and report any suspicious individuals or items you may see." British, Canadian and New Zealand governments issued similar warnings for their citizens travelling in Australia. [55]

****

While there were some bouts of optimism, the price for insecurity was an ever deepening parochialism, a longing for the world to make sense, a squirrelling down into local circumstance. Just as Australians cared less and less for the vaudeville spread of bread and circuses, the handouts and public programs that had become the national government's primary way of bribing the public into voting for them, tired of grand social schemes and end of empire spending, by 2015 much of the population proudly expressed a total lack of knowledge of politics, and showed zero interest for the cultural and political debates of the day. They were returning to an untroubled place deep inside their

---

[54] It pains me to say it, but Abbott has learned nothing, Tom Switzer, *The Guardian*, 3 March, 2015.

[55] Terror alert: US warns citizens in Australia of 'likely attack,' *The Australian*, 15 May, 2015.

own hearts; and happy to see the years pass by watching soap operas and quiz shows without confrontation; in a vacuum cleaned of trouble.

Australian suburbs were quiet trammel places; people lived self-contained, often unprepossessing lives. Pretension was out of the question. Most people didn't know their neighbors very well, beyond noticing any obvious signs of wealth, a new car, an extra room, an overseas holiday. Concerns were narrow; the traffic, the cost of living, which celebrity was going out with which other celebrity, the behaviour of the various characters in their home and work lives, what was proving of interest in the wallpaper world of television: The Block, Who Wants to be a Millionaire? Million Dollar Minute, Master Chef Australia, Housos. Reruns of reruns. The Great British Bake Off. The Bachelor. The Bold and the Beautiful. Happy Days. Mash. Midsomer Murders. Antique Roadshow.

The private sector had shrunk. The public sector had expanded into every corner.

In any district the major employer was the local city council, easily spotted, because of the dearth of other activity, whiling away their days in slow work details; a terrifying lack of urgency.

Australia had once been known as a workers' paradise.

Everyone was on the up and up.

There was plenty of money washing through the economy; black and white, legitimate and illegitimate.

Perhaps it was a cliché; but it had lodged in his brain. The strapping builder briefly at home after work before dashing off to a cash-in-hand job; work which ensured the family was never short of money. The family car, a new utility, a truck, and the wife's car all parked in the garage, on the front lawn, or out in the street. The well-cared for kids all with new trikes or bikes.

In the evenings the family pored over plans for a holiday house, safe in the knowledge that not only was their own family home increasing in value, but they could afford additional investments. They were hard working, aspirational, cheerful. They knew their lives were getting better. All they had to do was keep on working.

Then Grinch won.

Work as much as you like in 2015, you could barely survive. The dream of home ownership was disappearing for an entire generation.

Where had the future gone?

The country had become an accountant's dream; every transaction monitored, every movement recorded. Form after form clogged every step.

Alex sometimes drove for hundreds of kilometers up the still incomplete Pacific Highway, through the 40, 50, 60, 70, 80, 90, 100 and 110 speed zones, under the average speed cameras and the red light cameras, past predatory high-tech police cars.

Not one new garage.

Not one single house with a fresh paint job.

Past rundown shacks and For Sale signs.

Past closed shops and bypassed towns.

Into an eternal impoverishment of the spirit; a highway dwindling into a goat track.

On his ceaseless walks, Alex passed a house in the Illawarra south of Sydney.

A woman sat on her veranda in her cheap dressing gown talking to two women at her gate.

"Ten dollars," one of the women said, waving a package. "I needed a new frypan. Only ten dollars. At Aldi. They were on special, half price. Ten dollars. I couldn't believe it. I needed a new frypan."

"Where?" the woman on the steps asked.

"Aldi, at Albion Park," one of the two women at the gate replied, repeating information she had already provided.

"Where?" came the question again, as if hard of hearing.

"Aldi, at Albion Park. Only ten dollars. I couldn't believe it. I needed a new frying pan."

It was like a scene from *Season at Sarsaparilla*, that 1962 play by Patrick White, one of the country's few Nobel Prize winners; and someone who had written evocatively about the spaces at the heart of Australian suburban life.

As reviewer Benedict Andrews wrote: "In *The Season at Sarsaparilla*, from such minutiae, White constructed a theatrical treatment of overlapping lives. In the brick boxes of expanding early 60's Sydney suburbia, he confronted The Great Australian Emptiness. His response was a savage attack on Australian ways of life. His suburbia is a nightmare. A conservative, monocultural hell of stultification and judgement. Peering into the homes . . . he saw cultural disease and spiritual sickness.

"The Season at Sarsaparilla is now a kind of ghost play, a theatrical séance. Like the 'great trees which continue to spread, never quite exorcised' over the back fences of Sarsaparilla, so the ghosts of a disappearing era return to haunt the onstage house."

****

Four days before the Martin Place siege brought terror to the front of the Australian consciousness, Alex's old colleague Martin Chulov published an utterly compelling piece of journalism in one of the world's best newspapers, *The Guardian*.

If Australia's political and military leaders had not yet come to grips with the Law of Unintended Consequence, it was about time they did. The piece demonstrated if nothing else exactly why Australia should have stayed as far away from the conflict in the Middle East as it possibly could.

It had been America and its allies, including Australia, which had incubated the world's most terrifying terrorist organization or most powerful religious and political movement, depending on your standpoint, Islamic State.

The hours before dawn were naturally Alex's own, before the hive minds of factories and offices, traffic jams and crowded streets took over. He could, or so it felt to him, hear them thinking, and he found it hard to concentrate in the buzz.

In the years he had lived in London on and off, every morning, in winter in the dark, in summer in the early light, Alex would walk down Tottenham Court Road through those freezing winter streets or magical summer mornings, to a newspaper vendor nearby. He was keen to avail himself of the world's best media, and bought copies of *The Times* and *The Guardian*, and on the weekends *The Sunday Times* and *The Observer*, while his lover of the time slept. It was an excitement of long ago, perhaps, but there were times when journalism could still excite.

Martin's *Guardian* story was slugged ISIS: The Inside Story, and centered around an interview with one of Islamic State's most senior commanders. The piece demonstrated exactly how America created Islamic State, how the American-run prisons of Iraq had proved the perfect incubator, allowing jihadists to coalesce, plot, and ultimately create the new caliphate.

Just as with the history of Islam itself, the piece presaged the evolution of Islamic State into a less violent, and therefore more broadly appealing, entity.

Chulov interviewed an Islamic State commander, who used the *nom de guerre* Abu Ahmed, an essential early member of the group and now a senior member of an organization spilling not just across the borders of Iraq and Syria, but across the world. Chulov recounted how, in the summer of 2004, as a nervous young jihadi, Abu Ahmed, shackled and in chains, walked for the first time through America's foreboding desert fortress prison Camp Bucca in southern Iraq: "I had feared Bucca all the way own on the plane. But when I got there, it was much better than I thought. In every way."

Abu Ahmed's recollected that the other prisoners had also been terrified of Bucca, but quickly realized that far from their worst fears, the US-run prison provided an extraordinary opportunity: "We could never have all got together like this in Baghdad, or anywhere else. It would have been impossibly dangerous. Here, we were not only safe, but we were only a few hundred metres away from the entire al-Qaida leadership."

It was at Camp Bucca that Abu Ahmed first met Abu Bakr al-Baghdadi, the yet-to-be Emir of Islamic State, the single most feared religious figure of 2015. Abu Ahmed recalled: "Even then, he was Abu Bakr. But none of us knew he would ever end up as leader."

His fellow prisoners saw Baghdadi as aloof and opaque, while their American captors saw him as conciliatory, turning to him to help resolve conflicts among the inmates.

"That was part of his act," Ahmed told *The Guardian*. "I got a feeling from him that he was hiding something inside, a darkness that he did not want to show other people. He was the opposite of other princes who were far easier to deal with. He was remote, far from us all. Baghdadi was a quiet person. He has a charisma. You could feel that he was someone important. But there were others who were more important. I honestly did not think he would get this far. But as time went on, every time there was a problem in the camp, he was at the centre of it.

"He was respected very much by the US army. If he wanted to visit people in another camp he could, but we couldn't. And all the while, a new strategy, which he was leading, was rising under their noses, and that was to build the Islamic State. If there was no American prison in Iraq, there would be no IS now. Bucca was a factory. It made us all. It built our ideology.

"We had so much time to sit and plan. It was the perfect environment. We all agreed to get together when we got out. The way to reconnect was easy. We wrote each other's details on the elastic of our boxer shorts. When we got out, we called. I cut the fabric from my boxers and all the numbers were there. Everyone who was important to me was written on white elastic. I had their phone numbers, their villages. We reconnected. And we got to work. It really was that simple. Boxers helped us win the war. By 2009, many of us were back doing what we did before we were caught. But this time we were doing it better." [56]

Ipso facto, by its military and diplomatic cooperation with the "crusaders," the so-called Coalition of the Willing, Australia had helped facilitate the creation of the Islamic State.

---

[56] ISIS: The Inside Story, Martin Chulov, *The Guardian*, 11 December, 2014.

Four days after the publication of Chulov's story, Man Haron Monis would heed their "lone wolf" calls.

****

Nothing illustrated the dismal ineptitude of the Abbott government's military intervention in Iraq more than the Kevin Andrews gaffe.

In a nationally broadcast interview, the Defence Minister was unable to even name the world's most famous spiritual leader, or most famous terrorist, depending on your point of view, the leader of Islamic State.

The interview with the Defence Minister Kevin Andrews was conducted by Leigh Sales. To the chattering right, who could be just as tedious in their certitudes as the chattering left, she was a journalist with bias. In reality she was one of the sharpest operators and best presenters the depleted stables of the Australian Broadcasting Corporation had to offer.

Although he had never met him, Alex disliked Kevin Andrews. To Alex, Andrews would have been better off as a priest in a fusty suburban church than as a senior politician. His appointment as Defence Minister four months previously had, as far as he was concerned, been just another signpost on the Abbott government's road to nowhere.

Australia, briefly, had been the first country in the world to legalize euthanasia, in the country's Northern Territory. The enlightened legislation had been decried by the then Prime Minister John Howard, concerned about the outcry from his conservative Christian base, and Kevin Andrews had been dispatched into the fray to solve the problem.

The law was overthrown by the Federal Government, using the status of the North as a Territory rather than a State to force the repeal of the legislation.

Who were these people to enact their moral agendas on the Australian people?

The excruciating interview for the ABC's 7.30 Report went thus:

Leigh Sales: At the start of the war on terror back after 9/11, the military campaign was heavily focused on the leadership of Al Qaeda and it remained so for a long time. When it comes to IS who is the top leader and what sort of focus is there on his capture?
Kevin Andrews: Well, there's a cadre of leaders in the ISIL forces and we're not just dealing with one organisation. There's fluidity between organisations and individuals who are involved.

LS: But there is a leader and a cabinet of IS, they run like a government.

KA: And that makes it more difficult in terms of the overall objective we're seeking to achieve here. But we will continue along the lines that we are.

LS: So just to be clear, who is the leader and what is the focus on his capture?

KA: I'm not going to go into operational matters obviously.

LS: Can you name the leader of IS?

KA: I'm not going to go into operational matters.

LS: I don't think it's operational, I think it's a matter of public record.

KA: I'm trying to answer your question as best as I can and that is ultimately our aim here is to degrade and to defeat ISIL. ISIL operates not just in Iraq but across Syria as well and there is fluidity between groups. There's not just one group involved and not one just group of individuals involved and so we have to counter that as best we can over the coming weeks and months.

LS: Minister, you're responsible for putting Australian men and women in harm's way in the cause of this mission, I'm surprised that you can't tell me the name of Islamic State's leader. The US State Department has a $10 million bounty on his head.

KA: As I said, ISIL is a combination of groups, Leigh, there is not just one individual involved in this. There are Australians involved in the senior leadership of ISIL or Daesh, and there is a fluidity between groups that we've seen over the past few months in that area. It's not just one person involved, there's a series of people involved and we must ultimately destroy all of them if we're going to degrade their operations in that area.

LS: The specific person who I have been referring is Abu Bakr al-Baghdadi. [57]

Trying to minimise the fallout from his public display of ignorance, Andrews later tweeted: "Focusing on individuals ignores the threat that extremist organisations present. We remain firm in our resolve to defeat Daesh."

This was the same man responsible for sending hundreds of his fellow countrymen into a dangerous conflict without end; thereby putting their lives at risk and ramping up the domestic terror threat.

In the same month the Prime Minister of New Zealand John Keys also distinguished himself in not being able to name Abu Bakr al-Baghdadi, despite having committed troops and significant resources in

---

[57] Islamic State leaders identity 'operational matter' says Defence Minister Kevin Andrews, ABC, 14 April, 2015.

the fight against Islamic State. When questioned in an interview for 3 News, he admitted he would get it wrong and said "it's al-Jaberi something but whatever." [58]

****

There were plenty of Australians who criticized Australia's involvement in foreign wars; questioned the loss of life, the morality, the enormous financial costs, questioned the motives, the negligent dishonesty of politicians and their loose patriotism, their calls for the working classes to make sacrifices they would never let their own sons and daughters make. There were plenty of people who questioned the jingoism employed as justification for war, academics, left-wing pundits and the silent majority without any means or desire to broadcast their views.

All these people just tended not to be Muslims.

And it was the Muslims who saw Gallipoli, and Anzac Day, not through the insincere nationalism of the politicians or the genuine emotion of descendants, but who saw Australia's past conflicts in terms of one faith against another, of Christians against Muslims, of a holy war; and Anzac Day as a celebration of an incursion into the Muslim lands.

Hizb ut-Tahrir Australia first publicly called on the country in 2013 to abandon Anzac Day altogether.

Almost invariably described as "radical" in the Western media, Hizb ut-Tahrir, also known as the Liberation Party, was banned in many countries around the world for promoting jihad, including Germany, Russia, China and throughout the Middle East, including Egypt, Jordan and Tunisia, where supporters attempted a *coup d'état* in 1988.

In Central Asia, where repression had intensified since the bombing of Afghanistan, large numbers of its members were in jail. But the Hizb were not banned in the English speaking world. They were particularly active in Britain, Australia and the US; and by 2015 had spread to more than 50 countries, with in excess of a million supporters worldwide. Their flag was the exact same black flag with Arabic calligraphy as the jihadists: God is great, Muhammad is his messenger. Around the world, they continued to make news mostly for encouraging radical dissent or aligning with jihadists.

---

[58] New Zealand Prime Minister joins Australian Defence Minister in failing to name ISIS leader, *The Guardian*, 16 April, 2015.

What made the Hizb so stunning in Australian society was that they were hiding nothing; they invited everyone in to see and listen.

They saw themselves as the proselytizing wing of the jihad movement, and that's exactly what they did, they told everyone what they thought, actively and openly campaigned for membership, and for years their meetings in Australia had been held in packed public town halls. Their members prided themselves on their high levels of educational attainment. They advocated education for both men and women. And they were the subject of controversy virtually everywhere they operated. Barely a chance went by when they did not put out their views. It was their calling, their duty before Allah.

The Hizb produced a steady stream of press releases and reports of far higher quality than most taxpayer funded lobby groups, were openly welcomed into the nation's universities by Muslim Student Associations, and had been operating openly in Australia since the 1990s. They were aligned with mainstream Muslim organisations in their condemnation of Australian terror laws and military involvement in Iraq; and their longing for a transnational Islamic caliphate.

That their views did not accord with those of mainstream Australia, whatever that meant anymore, was entirely the point. They were there to convert the infidels; and, inspired by Allah, that was exactly what they intended to do.

Despite the many contradictions inherent in the celebration of a defeat, Anzac Day was the closest thing Australia had to a holy day. The *communiqués* beginning in 2013 came as a surprise to many pundits and stirred instant controversy; most particularly on talk-back radio. That anyone should dare to question the reverence of Anzac Day, an event which had evolved over the previous century into a sacred day in a not very sacred country, came as a jolt. Those same Australians who promoted multiculturalism howled the instant one of those cultures ran against the country's broader customs.

Although its members refused to vote in democratic elections and openly advocated the overthrow of the UK, Australian and American governments in favor of a caliphate, successive Western administrations had declined to ban them, using as justification the group's own claims that it did not advocate violence.

But the Hizb, and the jihad movement of which they were a part, weren't just espousing Utopian ideals in a free and open marketplace, they were advocating the introduction of the sharia; and the end of the infidel. And ultimately the end of the free speech they had so greatly benefited from.

It was true, in a sense, but disingenuous, to claim they did not advocate violence. To advocate the overthrow of the democratically elected governments, and the mass conversion of the population to Islam, would inevitably involve violence.

But if those goals could be achieved without violence, Insha'Allah, God willing, then all the better.

International analysts regarded Hizb ut-Tahrir as a post-Taliban fifth column and said its sophisticated and well funded propagandizing and appeal across national and ethnic barriers made it a far more potent international force than most other Islamic groups, which had a purely regional focus. The intellectual field work, if you will, and the sophisticated marketing the Islamic State used to such devastating effect had all been pioneered years before by the Hizb.

But despite an intense debate that went back to the Clinton presidency the Hizb had not been designated a terrorist organization by the UN Security Council or the US State Department.

Throughout 2014 and 2015 the government ramped up its rhetoric to get the Hizb proscribed as a terrorist group.

"Hizb ut-Tahrir is an organisation with an ideology which justifies terrorism and that's why I say it's un-Australian," Prime Minister Abbott said. "It's also un-Islamic because no respectable Muslim should have these views. This is an organisation which is very careful to avoid advocating terrorism, but is always making excuses for terrorist organisations, and I regard that as un-Australian frankly. There is no doubt they are an organisation that campaigns against Australian values, that campaigns against Australian interests. They are a thoroughly objectionable organisation." [59]

Lecturing Muslims on what they should or should not believe would get Abbott precisely nowhere; and as the instigator of drone attacks in Iraq which were killing soldiers, civilians and children alike in their eyes he had no moral standing. He could not credibly condemn others for a violence he himself had been party to; and walk away on the high moral ground. While ever Australia was party to war, there would be no winning on the battleground of ideas.

Although its members fervently believed they had been brought to Australia by Allah to help overthrow the government in favor of a worldwide Islamic state, as the group was not illegal membership of Hizb ut-Tahrir did not preclude its members from migrating to Australia.

In other words, Australia's immigration policies encouraged immigrants who made it perfectly clear it was their God given duty to agitate for Sharia law.

---

[59] Tony Abbott renews criticism of Hizb, Jane Norman, ABC, 9 October, 2014.

How was that a recipe for social cohesion?

Former Australian Army officer Bernard Gaynor put it thus: "It is resoundingly clear that the internal danger is growing inside Australia. Although Australians didn't need ASIO to tell them that. The constant barrage of stories about terrorist families, children holding severed heads, and fundraisers that make money for mosques by selling the flag of the Islamic State have driven home the point that we are not the country we were a decade ago.

"To deal with this situation effectively you cannot just tackle the symptoms, but you must also address the causes.

"And the cause of Australia's internal security worries is Islamic immigration. Make no bones about it.

"But no one in power has the guts to say this. This means that we are not doing anything at all effective to protect ourselves internally. The consequence is that we are in no position to effectively deal with the Islamic State, half a world away."

People like Gaynor, and the associated group Reclaim Australia, were almost inevitably decried as right wing and racist; in a media environment which had long abandoned news reporting for advocacy.

The impoverished state of the Australian media of 2015 had much to do with the crossroads the country had reached; it did not report arguments, it took sides, the side they regarded as most progressive or enlightened, and championed that. The bias was as much in the stories they did not run, as those they did; a simple matter of story selection. They chose from a very narrow list.

There had been an in retrospect rapid devolution from debate to propaganda; from reportage to campaigning. The frisson created by dissenting views and the passionate debates they inevitably sparked was entirely lost. The odd climate change skeptic or family law critic or opponent of high immigration rates would have added drama and interest to many a story, and ultimately led to a better informed and less divided public, but they were rarely heard. Instead, people shouted at each other across barely sketched canyons, chasms of misunderstanding.

The taxpayer funded Australian Broadcasting Corporation, which cost the public more than a billion dollars a year and entirely failed in its duty to tell the nation's story, was one of the chief sources of news. In many parts of the country it was the only source of news. Its broadcasts toggled between a narrow band of stories, refugees, racism, multiculturalism, feminism, women in the work place, domestic violence, welfare rights, male abusers, gay marriage aka marriage equality, racism, indigenous rights, indigenous disadvantage, climate change, global warming, environmentalism, emissions trading schemes and a sliding sheaf of social justice related stories. The growing resentment building in the nation's suburbs was ignored. Anyone who disagreed with the corporate ethos was labeled with the cheapest of insults, "racist," "climate denier," "abuser," "sexist," or simply "red neck."

****

Everything was connected: that Alex had been all over every last one of Sydney's inner-city streets, every back alley, all the clubs of the day, as a 24/7 wild child almost half a century before; that he had been busted back to Australia at such a pivotal tipping point in the nation's history; that he had worked at the country's leading newspapers for so many years; that in a clairvoyant mind-map sense he could work out safe passages through unsafe streets; that he now had at his fingertips the means to express that which had been so inexpressible in the days before the internet; all of it felt for magical, or divine, purpose, predestined, if you will. And that he, unlike almost all Australians, understood the Hizb, the intellectual architects of jihad, all because a chief of staff desperate for news one Sunday 13 years before, David King, the best Chief of Staff he had ever worked for, had sent him on a job out to the west of the western suburbs of the city in the wan hope he might be able to get a story out of a town hall meeting being held by a then obscure group, Hizb ut-Tahrir.

Newspapers were perennially short of news on Sundays to fill their Monday editions and on the way to the job David kept ringing, emphasizing just how desperate they were for copy.

Alex had got more than a story.

He had got several stories, a feature and an instant feeling of dislocation; the Australia he thought he knew was not it at all. It was the old reporter's "light bulb moment," the moment Alex realized that all the palaver about community, tolerance and diversity, all the folksy stories he had written over the years about newly arrived Australians, quoting in full the multicultural exponents and refugee advocates, his tacit acceptance of silence and self-censorship and talk of racism as something that had to be expunged from the Australian soul, all of it was leading straight to hell.

In old town halls built at the expense of ordinary ratepayers, the Hizb preached the overthrow of the Australian government, and condemned as un-Islamic, as a betrayal of Allah, the traditionally tolerant Australian way of life, everyone from Christians to Buddhists to gays to Jews to Hindus, from communists to capitalists to those who would dress immodestly on Australian beaches.

That took in most everybody in Australian society bar the Muslims; in a country where it was technically illegal to vilify people on the basis of race or religious creed.

Although they were constantly labeled as radical and decried as active terrorism supporters in many parts of the world, when it came to Australia the Hizb were not in hiding. Details of the meeting had been posted on the AAP news diary; the working list of that day's events which most Chiefs of Staff rely on heavily.

At the meeting an audience of about 400 heard the Government attacked for supporting the US on Iraq and for wasting its resources pursuing Jemaah Islamiah militants after the Bali bombing. The rapturous audience had hung on every word.

In a powerful, hypnotic mix of English and Arabic, speakers warned of the dangers of integration and multiculturalism, Western plots to erode the purity of their belief. They were told to see themselves above all as Muslims and to "dispute the borders we find ourselves living in, and dispute the borders we find ourselves born in." They were taught that capitalist countries gained through the oppression of Muslims.

"Capitalism is a system with no humility, no humanity, no compassion," one speaker said. "Comprehensive peace is mere illusion. Brothers and sisters in Islam, there are two different civilizations, two different ideologies ... which will inevitably clash.

"This is the final type of conflict we have seen over and over again in history, a military struggle with Islam. Crusades continue until today. The truth will prevail over all other ideologies."

Another speaker said: "We are Muslims first and we live in Australia. We must teach our children to live so that when the state is re-established, their loyalty is to the Islamic state."

Overly attentive because there was virtually no media in attendance, after the event wound up the Hizb's press officer was keen to know what he thought, as if there wasn't any way on Earth he could possibly disagree with the strength of their arguments.

Taken aback at the vitriol being directed at virtually everyone in Australia, including the then Prime Minister John Howard, at the time Alex kept his views to himself. In the crush outside the town hall, the press officer looked surprised at his non-committal stance. And soon enough, with a waiting photographer and a driver and a Chief of Staff desperate for copy, they made the journey back from Western Sydney to News Limited's headquarters in Holt Street, Surrey Hills, that place where he spent so many years.

The story ran the next day; and in subsequent days he worked hard to convince the editorial powers-that-be at the paper that the group would make a good subject for a fuller story; and eventually succeeded.

The feature began: "THERE'S a simple reason governments of all stripes are alarmed by Hizb ut-Tahrir. The radical Islamic transnational political party stridently advocates their overthrow. In the place of corrupt Muslim regimes and decadent capitalist governments will rise the caliphate, named for the alliance of states forged after the death of the prophet Mohammad and revered as the purest manifestation of an Islamic state."

It was not as if, with the deteriorating situation in 2015, the Australian security forces had not been fully forewarned. They knew perfectly well what was brewing in the Australian suburbs.

As Alex had observed more than a dozen years before, Hizb ut-Tahrir, was even then making headlines around the world.

In the previous 10 days before the article was published, German police had conducted raids against the group in Frankfurt, Berlin and Hamburg under new anti-terrorist laws, and in Denmark authorities were considering banning the party after the high-profile conviction of its Danish leader for inciting violence against Jews. Just as in Australia, Denmark would later pay a very high price for ignoring the growing jihad movement.

Uzbekistan, one of the Central Asian republics faced with an upsurge of support for extremism among their impoverished populations, called on Britain to label the Hizb a terrorist organization.

The Hizb's rallies and pronouncements had overshadowed activities traditionally associated with the holy month of Ramadan. In Australia, there were calls for the group be placed at the top of the federal Government's list of organizations under surveillance.

In a sense, there didn't have to be much surveillance. The Hizb were out and proud. They made it crystal clear that their aim was to establish Sharia law in Australia and govern according to the rules of Islam. They sought to transform a corrupt society to an Islamic society, and to cleanse it of false creeds.

Anyone who wanted to know more about them simply had to go to their website, Hizb ut-Tahrir Australia, which had a Media Centre and a Multimedia Centre, and was also available in Malay and Arabic. If a journalist wanted to go further they simply had to email or telephone.

It was an easy matter to attend one of their many functions and demonstrations.

As Alex had written so many years before, the Hizb were popular with Muslim youth from the universities of Britain to the slums of Tashkent and the suburbs of Sydney. Their embrace of the internet, promotion of higher learning for both sexes, extensive body of literature, support from women politicized by the imprisonment of their husbands or drawn by its social justice rhetoric, all went to make it a particularly powerful movement.

Hizb ut-Tahrir was founded in 1953, a once obscure splinter group of the Muslim Brotherhood, defining itself as a political party based on Islamic ideology. Founder Sheikh Taqiuddin anNabhani was a Palestinian who believed in establishing a single state across the Muslim world, a political structure in which a caliph — a civil and religious ruler — would be elected by an Islamic council. He believed the Defense Minister in such a structure would then prepare the people for jihad against the non-Muslim world.

Mohammad had predicted the Muslim nation would be divided into 73 sects before the coming of the caliphate, but only one would be the right one. Hizb ut-Tahrir believe itself to be that one.

The group shared many goals with the Taliban, al-Qa'ida, the Islamic Movement of Uzbekistan, Jemaah Islamiah and many other Utopian Islamic groups, including Islamic State.

The Hizb had long been remarkably sophisticated in its propaganda techniques, a sophistication which was a kind of precursor to Islamic State's mastery of the internet, and which surprised the world as horror upon jihad horror mounted internationally.

The Australian's previous coverage of Hizb ut-Tahrir, also written by Alex, had provoked an attack by the Washington-based Muslim Public Affairs Council, which issued an "action alert."

The Council said it was known for combating Hizb ut-Tahrir and no other group had taken on the organization more directly. "Its call that Muslims must not participate in Western politics is a real danger if it gains currency and MPAC has challenged this without compromise," the alert said. "However MPAC is founded on the Islamic principle your brother, for all his failings, is still your brother."

The Council then condemned *The Australian* as Zionist, racist and Islamophobic.

As would become clear in the years to follow, nothing could be more indicative of the tenor of Muslim communities in Australia and where they stood *vis-à-vis* their often uncomfortable relationship with the broader society than the senior Muslim leadership's refusal to condemn the Hizb.

There had been nothing in the stories that wasn't straight reportage. Alex's *Australian* feature was reproduced on a website known as Ummah: The Online Muslim Community, under the headline "More anti-Hizb propaganda from Australia."

The sites editors placed a comment at the bottom of the feature: "We would like to point out that Hizb ut-Tahrir does not have its 'organisational base' in London as the author suggests, nor is the party run or administered from London. The Party's base is in the Islamic World, where it works to re-establish the Khilafah State. It does not regard the Western World as a suitable place to re-establish the Khilafah, rather in the West its members work to carry the Da'wah of the Islamic Ideology - part of which is to present Islam as an alternative to Western Capitalism. This work is solely limited to the intellectual sphere."

"Have it your way," Alex had thought.

The Hizb had never been short of money; but rejected claims they were partly funded by the then world's most famous jihadist, Osama bin Laden.

In the days before the article went to press bin Laden issued direct threats to Australia.

The Hizb ut-Tahrir websites, which had plenty to say on a wide range of topics, were silent on the subject.

The only commentary suggested: "One day soon, this undemocratic war will start. Don't be surprised."

It was on the 12th of November, 2002, that Australian newspapers picked up on the story of the broadcast by Al-Jazeera of an audio-cassette carrying a recorded voice message from the founder of al Qaeda.

At the time Al-Jazeera, in its relative infancy, was only six years old. As the world's first and only international Arabic news network, with substantial resources and considerable clout, Al-Jazeera's sources and journalistic standards were considered impeccable. Its influence, partly founded on its unique access to the Arabic world but also on the fine quality of its journalism worldwide, would build in the years to follow; its footage and news reports widely used by Western media. In 2015 a survey showed that 86 per cent of its Arabic followers supported Islamic State.

The Bali bombings were in direct retaliation for support of the United States' war on terror and Australia's role in the liberation of East Timor, according to the taped message.

During the four-minute broadcast, bin Laden said Australia and other allies would pay dearly for their support of "the criminal gang" in Washington.

"Australia was warned about its participation in Afghanistan, and its ignoble contribution to the separation of East Timor," bin Laden said. "But it ignored this warning until it was awakened by the echoes of explosions in Bali." [60]

In a rallying cry, the taped message carried bin Laden's urged his followers to step up their campaign of violence against the US and its allies, especially those involved in the war in Iraq.

The tape singled out Australia as a close ally of Washington. But it was addressed to "all peoples of the countries allied with the tyrannical US Government" and also nominated Britain, France, Italy, Canada, Germany and Israel.

"You will be killed just as you kill, and will be bombed just as you bomb," bin Laden said. "Expect more that will further distress you."

Responding, then Prime Minister John Howard, the man who took Australia to war in Iraq, said Australians would not be "intimidated by threats from terrorists."

Then Foreign Minister Alexander Downer said the Government would not be blackmailed.

"We will stand by our friends, allies and neighbours in our determination to crush international terrorism," he said.

In February of 2015 the Australian government declared it was seeking advice from security agencies on options for taking action against Hizb ut-Tahrir.

"If cracking down on Hizb ut-Tahrir and others who nurture extremism in our suburbs means further legislation, we will bring it on and I will demand that the Labor party call it for Australia," Mr Abbott said in an address to the National Press Club.

The trouble being that "my brother is my brother," that the Hizb were now closely aligned with many other Islamic groups, their members firmly enmeshed in Australian society. Many of their beliefs were not that far from the Muslim mainstream. Particularly after Abbott himself had taken the country back into the minefields of Iraq and Syria, reaffirming the meta-narrative of Islam under attack from the West.

In 2015, with the country on high terror alert, Tony Abbott's attempts to lay the ground for banning the group were vigorously fought, not just by the Hizb themselves, but by academics who argued listing the Hizb as a terrorist group would only drive its members underground, thereby increasing radicalization in the country's Muslim communities.

In February of 2015, just before his National Security speech, the Prime Minister criticized the Grand Mufti of Australia Dr Ibrahim Abu

---

[60] Bin Laden voices new threat to Australia, Tony Parkinson, *The Age*, November, 2002.

Mohammed for speaking against a possible ban. He said comments by the spiritual leader of Australia's Muslims were "wrong-headed" and "unhelpful."

Mr Abbott said more Muslim leaders must speak out against the rise in Islamic extremism and the growing threat from terrorism. "He himself is not an Islamist," Mr Abbott said of the Grand Mufti. "More and more people are speaking out but certainly those comments attributed to the Mufti don't seem either right or helpful." [61]

Abbott had never criticized any other major spiritual leader in the country.

By the same logic, he should have been criticizing his own security agencies, who in 2005 had found no grounds for banning the Hizb. At the time there was renewed debate over whether they should have been banned after it came under investigation in Britain for links to the London bombings.

Then Attorney General Phillip Ruddock said there was no offence for people holding extremist views. He told parliament: "I asked ASIO for advice on whether there were currently grounds in Australia for listing the organization Hizb ut-Tahrir. ASIO has advised me that at present there is no basis under current legislation for specifying Hizb ut-Tahrir as a terrorist organization under the Criminal Code."

Abbott had been a prominent member of that same government.

At the time Hizb Australia spokesman Wassim Doureihi said it was becoming clear that the issue was not just a question of radicals versus moderates, but of Islam itself. He said the then Prime Minister was suggesting that they should not advocate that Islam was a threat to Western capitalism. A director of the Islamic Council of Victoria, Waleed Aly, said Foreign Minister Alexander Downer's suggestion that moderate Islamic leaders needed to be more vocal in condemning terrorism was "profoundly unfair."

"The suggestion we haven't done enough to condemn terrorism is frankly offensive," Aly said, warning that criticizing radicals could encourage extremist behavior. "If radical groups are truly extreme, they are likely to ignore condemnation and in fact it would embolden and intensify the rhetoric." [62]

But in 2015 there was no logic, no reason, and no easy solution to the increasingly vexed situation the country faced. Whatever analogy you wished to use: the horse had already bolted.

---

[61] Abbott criticises Aust Muslim leader, Sky News, 15 February, 2015.

[62] Pressure makes us stronger: radicals, John Stapleton and Jennifer Sexton, *The Australian*, 25 July, 2005.

Dr Ibrahim Abu Mohammed, an Egyptian-born and educated Australian Muslim scholar and the Grand Mufti of Australia since September 2011, the highest religious post for an Islamic cleric in Australia, said it would be a "political mistake" to ban the group. He said moves against Hizb ut-Tahrir appeared to be motivated by a want for distraction from other political issues. In a video called Muslim Community Confronts Abbott he described the Hizb as a victim of the Prime Minister's paranoia: "Perhaps, you are annoyed because they criticise you. It isn't he who determines the right and the wrong direction. We have sufficient intellect and know well what we are saying."

He said the proposed ban was "an attempt to escape from real dialogue and intellectual engagement" and that this was a way of "keeping people scared and distracted from the real issues and failure of governments and politicians."

"Hizb ut-Tahrir is not against freedom of speech," Dr Abu Mohammed said. "They are actually pro-freedom of speech and they are actually practicing this policy. Those who are against freedom of speech are the ones who are thinking to ban HBT from expressing their thoughts. It's not right on the politicians' side to shift, to create an atmosphere of controversy when they are facing issues within their own party or the government. This is the reason we think is behind it, it's a politician in trouble, wants to switch the light this way."

The same program, Muslim Community Confronts Abbott, also carried an extensive interview with a Hizb spokesman; who declared that while they did not support violence, and wanted to bring about positive change through conviction. "Having said that, we are not passivists, we are Muslims, and as every Muslim knows there is a place for violence in Islam, there is a place for war in Islam; for instance if a land is occupied we will support the right, even the duty, of those people to resist."

The spokesman said Tony Abbott's attempts to ban Hizb ut-Tahrir had to be understood in the broader context of the so-called war on terror. He said anti-Americanism was rife throughout the Muslim world and the war in Iraq was not about combating violence or terrorism, but about targeting fundamental Islamic ideals on the pretext of fighting terrorism.

"Now it is about a war on extremism, but extremism is just about ideas, any idea that is not acceptable to the Western states."

The country's leading Islamic spiritual leader and the Hizb were at one. By calling the Hizb "un-Australian" Abbott was telling all Muslims they were un-Australian; a comment bound to escalate radicalization and resentment.

The Hizb were not some outlying group of radical fundamentalists, they were similar in their beliefs to many other Muslims, they just happened to be more outspoken about it, unafraid of attack, unafraid of criticism, confirmed in their beliefs.

Six months before, a joint statement from all the country's major Islamic groups had condemned the Australian government's involvement in the so-called War On Terror, including Hizb ut-Tahrir.

The Hizb hit straight back at Abbott's speech, issuing a media release titled "Abbott Talks Tough to Mask Weakness."

The release was slugged: "In the Name of Allah, The Gracious, The Merciful."

They made the following points:

1. At a time of immense political pressure and weakness, Tony Abbott is playing tough to score cheap and opportunistic political points. The issue of national security is one conveniently raised only for politically expedient purposes.

2. Mention of banning Hizb ut-Tahrir and further strengthening already overreaching anti-terror laws have little to do with security, and much more to do with silencing dissent. Hizb ut-Tahrir's activities are not illegal and to alter that would demonstrate that the Australian government is willing to change law to suit political agendas and stifle critical voices.

3. Hizb ut-Tahrir is a party of ideas – it is exclusively intellectual and political. To institute measures to ban Hizb ut-Tahrir would be nothing other than an effective banning of certain concepts and discussions that the government is uncomfortable with. This is troubling to say the least.

4. The accusation of Hizb ut-Tahrir being somehow linked to terrorism is a tired and baseless claim that is unworthy of a serious response. The Australian government has no moral standing when talking of terrorism as it supports some of the greatest terrorists of our age, state terrorists such as America and "Israel," as well as dictators in the Muslim world such as El-Sisi of Egypt.

5. Australia's anti-terror laws have already created a two-tiered legal system that treats Muslims not as ordinary people before the law, but as a national security issue to be policed. The cover of legality afforded to the anti-terror laws worryingly justifies state oppression and discrimination.

6. The objective of such talk is to threaten and intimidate Muslims into not accounting the Australian government for its foreign policy crimes and to have them accept a localized, secular version of Islam

that is not the Islam revealed by Allah (swt) to Muhammad (saw). This must be staunchly rejected. Today Abbott is taking aim at Hizb ut-Tahrir, but tomorrow it could be any other Muslim or Islamic group.

Criminologist at the University of Queensland Adrian Cherney said banning Hizb ut-Tahrir would only sharpen the perception amongst Muslims that they couldn't speak their opinions out of fear they would be singled out or labeled as extremists: "The best way to combat a group like that is not to ban them, because banning them will play into their hands, it will embolden them, it will confirm in the minds of people that support them that the government is targeting them and targeting Muslims."

There were multiple contradictions to the debate over banning the Hizb.

There continued to be security incidents worldwide associated with the group.

But at the same time as the Australian Prime Minister Tony Abbott was fulminating over his desire to ban the Hizb, they were, perfectly legally, holding conferences and rallies across North America; including in Washington, Chicago and Michigan.

The Hizb welcomed into the heart of America were exactly same group the Australian Prime Minister Tony Abbott would in 2015 futilely attempt to have proscribed as a terrorist group; who he had repeatedly labeled "un-Australian"; and who far from going into hiding, had continued to brazenly operate, just as if they had Allah on their side.

The mid-June Washington event was called "The Khilafah Conference: Reclaim Your Islam." Its promotional material included images of a satellite circling above the Earth.

Hizb ut-Tahrir openly advocated for a long-term strategy that started with a process of ideological indoctrination and recruitment. The group would then commence a "period of attaining and seizing the reins of power," according to its texts.

Organizers of the Washington conference put out a statement: "When we advertised the conference we did not anticipate the amount of positive response from the people. The response was so tremendous that we will have a larger scale conference after Ramadan to accommodate your response and demand. We promise the conference after Ramadan will be something to remember for years to come both locally and globally by the will of Allah SWT!"

As far as old Alex was concerned, there wasn't much use attacking the Hizb. They had been invited into the country through the front door. They were supported by the Grand Mufti of Australia, the Muslim's spiritual leader. They were invited by Muslim Student Associations to speak at the country's most prestigious universities. They were not saying anything that many Muslims did not already believe; that the prosecution of the war in Iraq by the West was an indefensibly evil crusade against innocent citizens and against the religion, that these were The End of Days, that they were living in a morally degenerate society in desperate need of reform, that the sooner a caliphate was installed the better for everybody, that Allah was the Lord of all the Worlds and Mohammad was his Messenger, and that the sooner the broader population of Australia converted to Islam the better off they would be.

The Grand Mufti's public statements sparked a tirade from conservative columnist Andrew Bolt, who suggested the fact that his making common cause with one of the nation's most extreme groups was frightening: "Most journalists insist there is a difference between moderate Muslims wanting peace and the radical jihadists who are preaching hate. But the Mufti now destroys our work."

Bolt said the Grand Mufti was legitimizing the rage and demands of Islamist terrorists and his comments made the Muslim community a legitimate target of suspicion.

He called for the Grand Mufti to be sacked.

Bolt summed the arguments up thus: "Why is the Government worried about Hizb ut-Tahrir?

"It's because, yes, although it says it opposes terrorism, Hizb ut-Tahrir tells followers Australia is 'at war with Muslims.'

"It's because Hizb ut-Tahrir claims 'Abbott has been leading the way in demonising Islam and Muslims,' and that by fighting the Islamic State, his Government 'will be responsible for the repercussions that ensue.'

"It's because it warns: 'Even if a thousand bombs went off in this country, all that it will prove is that the Muslims are angry, and they have every reason to be angry."

"It's because it refuses to criticise IS, saying 'ISIS or al-Qaeda ... exist as a reaction to Western interference in the Islamic lands.'

"It's because it defends Australians who fight for IS, and says Muslims are 'forced to react' against our 'Western violence.'

"It's because it claims 'wherever the Jews thrive, corruption abounds, and asks: 'Who will set the world free from the Israelites, so that the world will be able to say that it has rid itself of that hidden evil?'" [63]

The Grand Mufti hit back: "This journalist does not dictate what we should do and what we shouldn't do. He also does not decide whether what we have done is enough or not and we do not work for anyone for

---

[63] Grand Mufti in shocking defence of evil fanatics, Andrew Bolt, Herald Sun, 23 February, 2015.

whom we must file a report. What does he have to do with the Muslim community and what right does he have to meddle in its internal affairs? He has no right to involve himself in this way. It is perhaps reflective of the spirit of supremacy and marginalisation that this journalist is accustomed to." [64]

Successive governments had known perfectly well that they were bringing into Australia people whose religious beliefs dictated that they dedicate their lives to campaigning for the overthrow of democracy and the institution of an Islamic government. And if not, intelligence officers had known exactly what the Hizb believed in for more than 20 years. Their cautionary notes, if there were any, were ignored, or pounced upon by bureaucrats higher up the food chain; the devotees of the state creed of multiculturalism who refused to accept that jihadists were in their midst and posed a genuine danger to the security of the nation; that their bureaucratic vision of nirvana, a Godless paradise that bore no resemblance to the conformist, socially conservative world of Australia's of the past was a concocted chimera. That Australia had been a far freer and more egalitarian country before they laid their fingers all over it.

"Believe in everything and you believe in nothing," as the Hizb said.

It had all come home to roost.

****

In a famous interview with ABC presenter Emma Alberici, spokesman for the Hizb Wassim Doureihi repeatedly refused to condemn the tactics of Islamic State in Iraq and Syria.

The Hizb had made headlines before; but in some strange soporific way, with the waves crashing against the shores and summers stretching into infinity, Australians weren't listening.

This time around the interview brought some genuine public awareness.

Doureihi deflected questions back onto the violence perpetrated by governments of America and Australia.

"No-one legitimately or sincerely is discussing what Western governments are doing in the Muslim world," he said. "Groups like ISIS or Al Qaeda don't exist in a vacuum. They exist as a reaction to Western interference in the Islamic lands and they view themselves, rightfully or wrongfully, irrespective of my opinion or otherwise, as a resistance effort to what they regard as an unjust occupation.

---

[64] Muslim Community Confronts Abbott, OnePath Network, 19 February, 2015.

"I come from a very clear point of view that, as Muslims, we have a fixed moral compass that says it's unequivocally, under any conditions, an aberration to kill innocent civilians.

"Tony Abbott cannot say that. John Howard dismissed the slaughter of half-a-million civilians as an embarrassment. Let's talk about morality here. Let's talk about who is the greatest threat to civilian life."

At one point, the Lateline host asked: "Are you outraged by the image of an Australian-born child of seven-years-old holding up severed heads like trophies in Iraq or Syria?"

Doureihi replied: "Let me tell you what I am outraged by..." before an angry Alberici admonished him for avoiding the question.

Towards the end of the interview, an exasperated Alberici said: "Can you do me a favour? But will you do me a favour and answer one question?"

Instead of answering further questions about Islamic State's conduct, Mr Doureihi repeatedly railed against Western governments and the media.

Alberici persisted with her line of questioning, and eventually Doureihi terminated the interview.

The Prime Minister weighed straight in, congratulating Alberici on being a feisty interviewer and reiterating his frustration at his inability to ban the group due to legislative complications: "Hizb ut-Tahrir is an organisation with an ideology which justifies terrorism and that's why I say it's un-Australian. It's also un-Islamic because no respectable Muslim should have these views." [65]

****

By mid-2015, relations between the government and the Muslim community had for all intents and purposes broken down

If nowhere else, the television station Al-Jazeera carried images of civilians and children killed by allied bombs.

Tony Abbott's rhetoric of "Team Australia," his dismissal of Islamic State as a "death cult" and fundamentalist Muslims as un-Australian, along with his participation in the bombing of Muslims in Iraq continued to sour relations.

As one journalist asked: "Would it not be a bitter irony, too, that in our desperate attempts to stop homegrown violent extremists and to deter Australians leaving to fight overseas, we were actually fanning the radicalisation we seek to counter?

---

[65] Tony Abbott backs Emma Alberici, Latika Bourke, *The Sydney Morning Herald*, 9 October, 2014.

"Abbott has presided over a breakdown in the relationship between many Muslims and their government. As the government reminds us daily, it has a duty to protect Australians. That is a complicated duty requiring a balance between powers and resources for intelligence agencies and police and maintaining the civil freedoms that supposedly define us.

"The Australian Prime Minister can be a rhetorical wrecking ball, but in no case has his lack of subtlety been more damaging than his remarks about Muslims. The media does not deserve to be let off the hook, either. Journalists have to cover this story, but at times parts of the media have inflamed fear and mistrust. In turn, many Muslims have come to mistrust and fear the media. But it is the Prime Minister who is critical in setting the tone for national conversation on these issues and Abbott has presided over a breakdown in the relationship between many Muslims and their government." [66]

****

There was no major terrorist attack on Anzac Day.

But in a sense Islamic State had won anyway.

The name of Islamic State, the fear of Allah the All Merciful, was everywhere; and the kafir had been forced to spend millions of millions of dollars in extra security costs.

Fear of consequence would undoubtedly diminish Anzac Day crowds in years to come, just as it had limited other major events in other countries. Anzac Day of 2015 would, Alex believed, come to be a defining moment in Australian history, as the country adjusted to a New World Order.

The aim was to instill fear into the population in an attempt to trigger a mass conversion of the population to Islam.

They wouldn't know where, they wouldn't know when, but the day of reckoning for the unbeliever was coming as assuredly as night followed day.

Australia wasn't the only country waking up in shock to a new world order; written by Islam at the End of Days.

In Britain, prior to the May 2015 elections, there were a number of demonstrations by Muslim groups against democracy.

In Regent's Park, that finest example of the skills of British horticulturalists and landscape artists through which Alex had occasionally wandered, Islamist Anjem Choudary, along with a number

---

[66] Tony Abbott's rhetoric on Muslims is damaging and dangerous, Gay Alcorn, *The Guardian*, 17 June 2015.

of other speakers, addressed a rally. One of the placards read: "ALLAH IS THE ONLY LEGISLATOR."

Choudary had previously served as Chairman of the British Society of Muslim Lawyers.

Until it was banned he was also the spokesman for Islam4UK, an Islamist group proscribed under the UK's counter terrorism laws in 2010 after it announced plans to protest the public morning of UK armed forces personnel killed on active service.

"No to democracy, No to freedom," Anjem Choudary shouted through a microphone. "No to liberalism, no to secularism. No to Christianity. No to Judaism. No to Sikhsm. No to Buddhism. No to Socialism. No to Communism. No to Liberalism. No to Democracy. Democracy, go to Hell! Democracy, go to Hell!"

The crowd repeated the phrase "Democracy, go to Hell!"

Then Choudary continued: "Democracy, hypocrisy! Democracy, hypocrisy!"

Each phrase was repeated by the crowd.

There had been similar sentiments expressed at rallies, meetings, mosques and Islamic Centres in Australia for years.

Nobody, outside the believers themselves, had paid much attention.

Back in 2002, after the success of the Hizb stories, Alex was encouraged by the Editor in Chief to write more about terrorism.

Alex could see how dangerous the situation was. He had young children to protect. He promptly pretended to lose interest.

He did not wish to carry any swords for anybody, not for any ideology, not through the crazed and vexed circumstances that were modern Australia. Certainly not so Rupert Murdoch could make yet more money with sensational headlines.

Thirteen years later Islamic State was raging across the world; Islam was constantly in the news.

And Man Haron Monis, said to have been radicalized by Hizb ut-Tahrir, rose from where he had been sitting in the Lindt Cafe, drew a gun and told customers to stand with their hands up.

And Australia finally became the frightened country it should have been all along.

SECTION THREE: WITHOUT HISTORICAL PRECEDENT

THE BUILDUP HAD been long and hard.

Throughout 2014 and 2015 there were a series of disturbing incidents; with politicians warning the terror threat in Australia was at its highest level in history, with relations between the government and the Muslim minority entering a new low, and with the nation having once again become involved in military action in Iraq and Syria.

In June of 2014 ginger-haired Sydney teenager Abdullah Elmir told his mother he was going fishing when he disappeared from his Bankstown home in Western Sydney. In Iraq, he adopted the name of Abu Khaled. He appeared in several propaganda videos for Islamic State surrounded by black flags and a crowd of mujahedeen. It was the first time Islamic State had used an Australian jihadist in one of its major propaganda videos and mentioned the Australian Prime Minister specifically. His family claimed he had been brainwashed and described him as academically bright and caring.

Elmir declared: "This message I deliver to you, the people of America, I deliver this message to you the people of Britain, and especially, I deliver this message to you the people of Australia. And I say this about your coalition. Bring every nation that you wish to come and fight us, it means nothing to us, whether it is 50 nations or 50,000 nations it means nothing to us. Bring your planes, bring everything that you want to us because you will not harm us. Why, because we have Allah's blessing, which is something you do not have. Is it not apparent to you, how are these victories possible?

"To the leaders, to Obama, to Tony Abbott, I say this, these weapons that we have, we will not stop fighting, we will not put down our weapons until we reach your lands, until we take the land of every tyrant, till the black flag is flying in every single land, until we put the black flag on top of Buckingham Palace, until we put the black flag on top of the White House, we will not stop and we will keep on fighting, we will defeat you." [67]

In mid-2015 came the news that Elmir had married a jihadi bride, a schoolgirl from the UK. He told the *UK Daily Mail* ISIS members were itching to do an attack in Britain, where the threat level was severe, meaning an attack was highly likely.

---

[67] Australian teenager Abdullah Elmir appears in Islamic State video threatening PM Tony Abbott, ABC, 21 October, 2014.

Elmir also praised the work of the Tunisian massacre of 38 tourists: "May Allah bless the man who slaughtered those filthy infidels and May Allah grant him the highest level in Jannah (Paradise). May the kuffar that this man killed taste the heat of Jahannam (hell) and their families be reunited with them in there.'

Elmir's comments came after the Foreign Office warned the remaining 3,000 Britons to leave Tunisia amid increasing fears of repeat attacks on Western tourists.

There were also concerns about the galvanizing impact Elmir's worldwide fame, or infamy, was having on those he had previously tried to convert in Western Sydney.

A manager at the Bankstown Multicultural Youth Centre, Sarkis Achmar, said there had been groups of men in traditional Islamic clothes mixing with boys between the age of 13 and 16 at an outreach event, and encouraging people including Emir to start preaching to them. Elmir warned that if they did not convert to Islam they would go to hell.

Achmar said he was concerned other young people in the Bankstown area were still being radicalized. "It's definitely still brewing in Bankstown and brewing in other places as well," he said. "You will see that they will try to do an act on Australian soil because, if you look at history and what's happened overseas in every other country, it's what they do. It's all about instilling fear and having ownership." [68]

In July came the news of the first Australian suicide bomber in Iraq, who went by the nom de guerre of Abu Bakr al Australi. Adam Dahman had just turned 18 when he strapped a belt bomb to himself and detonated it in a busy marketplace near a Shi'ite mosque in Baghdad, killing five people and injuring 90. He was understood to have links to a group who had previously planned to bomb the Melbourne Cricket Ground.

The Islamic State group claimed responsibility for the attack, hailing him a knight and a martyr.

Islamic State posted on Twitter: "Abu Bakr Al Australi may Allah accept him targets a Shi'ite temple the Militias use as HQ & Kills and injures 90 militiamen." [69]

---

[68] Islamic State: Australian teen Abdullah Elmir tried to infiltrate Sydney youth welfare groups to recruit people, Bankstown worker says, Brendan King, ABC, 16 June, 2015.

[69] Sydney teen kills five in suicide bombing on crowded Iraqi market, Simon Benson & Ashlee Mulany, The Daily Telegraph, 19 July, 2014.

Friends said two years before he had been a fun loving teenager who played football and was interested in fast cars and girls. Then he became devout.

"It is just appalling that a kid of this age would want to do something like this, waste his life," an Australian security officer said. [70]

Picturesque rhetoric from the Australian government said fundamentalists were cruising the internet like predators seeking out the young and the vulnerable. Prophet Muhammad himself reportedly said that men under the age of 25 were best suited to martyrdom. Many young Australian jihadists simply felt they were following a religious edict.

There was concern that the suicide attack could spark unrest between Sunni and Shia communities. The government urged calm, claiming radicals represented a tiny minority in the Australian-Muslim community.

At the time Islamic State had overrun much of northern and western Iraq and was fighting on battlefronts across the country. It had already seized Mosul and was vowing to push south to the capital. [71]

ASIO estimated at the time there 150 Australians were involved in Syria and Iraq with about 60 fighting in the region. Four major attacks on Australian soil had been thwarted in the previous decade. There were also serious concerns over the terrorism threat within Australia posed by returning fighters.

In August the Prime Minister Tony Abbott and Attorney General George Brandis announced a range of new counter terrorism measures, including an additional $600 million in funding to security agencies and new laws lowering the threshold for arrest without warrant for terrorism offences.

The official press release read: "The threat to Australia and Australians from extremists is real and growing. Australian citizens and dual nationals are currently fighting overseas in Iraq, Syria and other conflicts, committing unspeakable atrocities and honing terrorist skills. Many violent jihadists will attempt to return home."

The Government's public information ended with a tilt at ideology: "Terrorists and violent extremists represent a fringe minority and an affront to the values of all Australians. The Government will continue to work closely with communities, including the Muslim community, to address radicalisation and the threat that it poses."

---

[70] Sydney teen kills five in suicide bombing on crowded Iraqi market, Simon Benson and Ashlee Mullany, *The Daily Telegraph*, 19 July, 2014.

[71] Iraq suicide bomber was Australian, News, July 18, 2014.

Daniel Baldino, editor of *Spooked: The Truth About Intelligence in Australia*, criticized the legislative free-for-all gifting power to the executive branch and security sector which had occurred since the Twin Towers attacks: "It is a shame that the Coalition has decided to paint their security framework by staring into a broken and outdated rear mirror.

"It is wrong to presume that increased budgets will automatically lead to better security. Such an approach can wrongly presume an intelligence system is hopelessly broken in the endless pursuit of absolute security or even act to encourage the scapegoating of the intelligence sector.

"Improvements in performance might be better achieved by addressing items such as improved coordination between agencies, building corporate knowledge and memory or improving analytical capacity. We have seen plenty of warning signs from the US that its own cash frenzy has created bigger but more unwieldy bureaucracies, reinforced outdated work habits and spurred the wasteful duplication of security efforts." [72]

Unlike the broader Australian community, the Muslim community were united in their condemnation of the new terror laws.

From groups like Hizb ut-Tahrir, which the government wanted to ban, to mainstream organizations, including academics and numerous Islamic centers, 80 Muslim groups signed a joint statement which read in part:

"In the name of Allah, most Gracious, most Merciful.

"These laws clearly target Muslims and they do so unjustly. Whilst the language of the law is neutral, it is no secret that in practice these laws specifically target Muslims. Prime Minister Tony Abbott's commentary in selling these laws also makes this clear.

"The primary basis of these laws is a trumped up 'threat' from 'radicalised' Muslims returning from Iraq or Syria. There is no solid evidence to substantiate this threat. Rather, racist caricatures of Muslims as backwards, prone to violence and inherently problematic are being exploited. It is instructive that similar issues about Australian troops travelling abroad to fight or Jews travelling to train or fight with the Israeli Defence Force are simply never raised.

"The Muslim community is being asked to sign off on laws and policies that have already been decided. Prime Minister Tony Abbott is merely seeking approval under the cover of consultation. He seeks that the Muslim community be on board because the policy entails the

---

[72] Not so smart: the Coalition intelligence review repeats old mistakes, Daniel Baldino, *The Conversation*, 25 June, 2013.

community policing itself. We refuse to provide such a rubber stamp on what is an unjust and hypocritical policy. We also reject government attempts to divide the Muslim community into 'radicals' and 'moderates' and to use the community for its agenda.

"It is evident that the 'war on terror' has been a failure.

"After thirteen long years, everyone can see that the world is not a safer place. Rather, violence and instability is noticeably more prevalent. The approach of continuously ramping up laws, lowering legal standards, spending more on defence and intelligence agencies is not working. Over $30 billion has been spent in Australia on this war yet the threat is 'as high as it has ever been' according to the Prime Minister."

When he declared military involvement in Iraq the following month Prime Minister Tony Abbott knew perfectly well he did not have Australian Muslims onside.

Fast forward six months and the rhetoric from both sides had simply grown more inflamed.

Delivering his national security statement in February of 2015, Abbott said: "I've often heard Western leaders describe Islam as a 'religion of peace.' I wish more Muslim leaders would say that more often, and mean it."

If the country wasn't at war with Islam, the Prime Minister certainly was.

Questions pertaining to the Muslim minority; and to terror in Australia, played in vivid imagery across the media, settling misapprehension into the public imagination. With great assistance from the government.

****

On the streets of Sydney the scenes simply grew more degraded by the day.

Having not so cleverly locked himself out of his 24-hour shared office one early morning in May, Alex went for a longer than usual wee hours walk, through the Dead Zone, past the bug-eyed ice addicts of Australia's largest city, Sydney, searching for a cafe where he could sit and have a "large, strong flat white."

In the entire district of central Sydney there was no such place.

He went into a Kings Cross convenience store for cigarettes, having relapsed on the nicotine. Cigarettes are the first defense, an old mentor once taught him. The radio in the store was streaming Arabic; and while he had struggled at odd times to learn various phrases, the only word he recognized was *jihad*.

To the best of his knowledge, all the convenience stores in Sydney that were open 24-hours had begun life as immigration scams. There wasn't any way they made enough money selling the odd packet of cigarettes or sweets to an increasingly impoverished population to justify staying open.

He ended up at the only fast food outlet he knew of that sold decent coffee.

"No chairs, nowhere to sit," he complained to the Asian woman behind the counter.

"It's changed a lot," she said.

"Where were you born?" he asked.

"Vietnam," she replied.

"Öh, I've just been there," Alex said. "Lovely country. District One. Ho Chi Minh City. Not like here, dead," he said, gesturing at the abandoned scene outside. "I don't want to be here anymore."

She smiled at him as he left.

Australians didn't smile at each other anymore.

He took his coffee and slice of carrot cake and, in the absence of anywhere else, went to sit at the local bus stop.

It was covered in vomit.

So instead, he found himself sitting beside the Alamein Fountain, that place where he had spent so much time as a teenager in the late 1960s; watching the crowded, thronging, bohemian streets, a place he had loved so much.

Now he looked down almost empty streets; and if he hadn't felt so fired up, would have felt exactly what the rest of the country felt: despair.

For weeks, testing the temperature, in response to his casual, seemingly innocuous queries, everybody he met said much the same thing. The NRMA man, "you used to be able to get ahead," the woman at the pharmacy, "nothing works," the woman at the Telstra shop, "things are getting harder." "Sydney's not a friendly city," he had said to the woman at the pool. "It's worse than ever," she replied.

"I think we're in the middle of a really bad depression," a cutter, as the old Australian expression for character went, in a pub in the tiny foothill town of Drake. "There was a market here on the weekend, plenty of people. Nobody spending money, all the stall holders said."

"Australia is a police state," a man by the pool commented.

"I'm a teacher and it's shit," said another.

"You hardly want to turn the radio on anymore," he overheard a lawn mower man say.

A truck driver relayed stories of predatory police booking his colleagues for ludicrously minor or imagined offenses.

There was no arguing. One thing was for sure: the country was depressed.

Not even the Alemain Fountain was working anymore. Once, revelers had delightedly filled it with bubble bath at every opportunity. Now it was stained and silent.

Alex sat under the surveillance cameras up on the light poles. These days the police didn't even have to get out of their chairs to check what he was up to.

Even the seagulls looked bored. The carrot cake was stale, and he threw half of it to the birds, swilled his coffee and walked down to Elizabeth Bay, that place where, in some way, his adult journey had begun.

Past where the Sebel Townhouse once was; that rock and roll hotel where all the visiting stars had stayed; much to the fascination of the rest of Sydney.

Past the Monks and the neighboring complexes of upmarket flats which populated the elite sweep down to the water; the rich, as always, protected from the streets.

And he walked past that most pivotal of buildings in his life, a tall block of flats from the 1930s and looked through the now locked front doors. He'd swear the carpet was the same as it had been almost half a century before; but he couldn't be sure. In his day it had been known as Withering Heights; after the number of gay lads that occupied it. In a land of Sharia, they would have all been stoned to death.

A later generation would call the building Gotham City.

In those days Alex had been welcome anywhere.

He had worked out, during those long adventurous parties that went on for days, how to get up on to the top of the building, through a broken lock, although of course you weren't meant to be there. He would sit up there on the roof scattered to the four winds while his friends partied in the apartments below, and watch the sun come up over the harbor, the delicate shades of pastel and the darkness of the water emerging into light, and think, it's so beautiful, why aren't there people on top of all the rooftops, watching the sun come up.

But there never were.

It was here, in those shattered moments in the gathering dawn that he had come to the conclusion, after so many efforts to be so many things, a musician, a painter, a prostitute, that he would adopt the honored role of observer. And thus it was, almost half a century later, that he continued the decision he had made all those years ago on that rooftop; splintered in the dawn, with no idea who he was or why the agonies of childhood would not go away, to be a watcher on the watch, to be invisible in the fabric, to write.

Almost all those gay lads he used to party with were long dead. And he was now a man in his sixties.

There had been no contingency plans. They had never intended to grow old.

In contrast to days of yore, when Kings Cross had a reputation for being a dangerous place but was in fact safe partly because of the number of people on the streets, now they genuinely were dangerous.

The ice addicts, particularly because of the material with which it was cut, were unpredictable and desperate. The personality decay associated with its use made them more amoral than any other drug user. And the fractured, depressed, uncaring nature of the society made them indifferent to consequence. They couldn't have cared less about the people they robbed; the punters or each other. The old camaraderie of thieves had disappeared from the Australian consciousness.

On his way back to the office he walked over the street embedded line from that most tenderly lyrical of Sydney poets, Kenneth Slessor: "You find this ugly, I find it lovely."

The line was from a Kenneth Slessor poem called William Street, the closest thing to a boulevard the city had. The street was significant to many Sydneysiders because it lead directly to what was then one of the largest billboards in the country, the famous red Coca Cola sign, and was the gateway to the Cross, to a nightlife and a bohemian culture largely nonexistent in the rest of the country.

Now William Street was just another dreary transport route. For much of the previous century it had seemed like an avenue leading to multiple excitements, nights that turned into days, a place that ran 24 hours.

Slessor would never have believed the decrepit state the area had sunk into under the scarifying tutelage of Clover Moore and the NSW State Government.

All Alex could do was look on in in some kind of funk; the poem of lost times a signally romantic hymn to a no longer romantic place:

The red globe of light, the liquor green,
The pulsing arrows and the running fire
spilt on the streams, go deeper than a stream;
You find this ugly, I find it lovely

Smells rich and rasping, smoke and fat and fish
and puffs of paraffin that crimp the nose
of grease that blesses onions with a hiss;
You find it ugly, I find it lovely

The dips and molls, with flip and shiny gaze
(death at their elbows, hunger at their heels)
Ranging the pavements of their pasturage;
You find this ugly, I find it lovely.

Slessor couldn't have realized he was writing an epitaph.

He had been talking about the crowded, haphazard, atmospheric streets of Kings Cross and its surrounds, the colorful personalities, the dense street scenes of Australia's own demimonde.

Old Kenneth wouldn't have found much to write about in 2015. Apart from a few jerking ice addicts, jumped up on the jump with which the rotten stuff was cut, the occasional prostitute so old she looked like she should have been in a nursing home or the occasional toothless wonder hoping for a sight impaired client, the streets were empty.

Corruption, malfeasance and abuse of office came in many forms; and like many of her generation Sydney Lord Mayor Clover Moore had proven utterly incapable of separating the personal from the political. She constantly and repeatedly, in Alex's humble view, and the view of many of the city's business people, misused her position to perpetuate her own agenda.

Her deeply undemocratic policies of blocking off roads into the entertainment district over the weekend and of making it almost impossible to find a parking spot had already aggravated the social divides of the inner-city into haves and have nots; into those who had inner-city property; and those who did not.

Jihad within and jihad without.

Screwed by the left and screwed by the right.

Lloyd Rees, that most accomplished and most loved of Sydney artists, once declared: "A city is the greatest work of art possible."

And such art should be available to all its residents; not just those who lived in fashionable inner-city houses and had parking stickers; or didn't need a car because they were so close to the city's amenities.

Including those plebeians who could be so shocking as to want to visit a red light and entertainment district on the weekend; instead of facing closed off signs forbidding their entry.

Rees was best known for his love of Sydney and his sublime drawings of its sandstone cliffs. He had died much revered in his 90s. He would, one could safely assume, have been deeply horrified by the visual assaults and the commercial connivances that the Sydney City Council had inflicted on the city.

In 2015, down William Street flags advertising everything from ANZ bank to alcohol to fast cars to coming corporate sponsored events fluttered from twee aluminum alloy ribbed anti-graffiti anti-poster light poles promoting whatever corporate sponsor the Sydney City Council was in bed with this week.

And the city was a damn sight uglier for it. The Council was selling space which should belong to everyone, not just to corporate interests; public space, visual space, stolen through a contrivance of public and private interests.

It was safe to assume Lloyd Rees would have been scandalized.

The two meter-high flags were an eyesore across the entire center of Sydney, a misappropriation of public space from which the Council made millions; money which it in turn misused for its own ideological purposes or to channel money to its favorite causes and a whole network of suppliers and consultants being grossly overpaid to provide next to nothing.

The sanitization of Sydney was almost complete, the streets were frighteningly quiet.

****

One of the drivers of the violent race demonstrations of 2015 was the suppression of dissent and unfashionable views; and not just by the cliques which controlled much of the media agenda. Attempts to restrict the freedom of the press came from both the left and the right of politics. The previous Labor government had attempted to pass ridiculous laws requiring news stories to pass a "public interest" test, that is, whether or not they were in the interests of the elected government.

The Abbott government reduced free speech by introducing legislation that included provisions for jailing journalists for up to 10 years if they disclosed information that related to a "special intelligence operation." The government left ambiguous what a "special intelligence operation" was, leaving it up to agencies to decide. In other words a journalist who accurately and fairly reported a botched government operation or the malfeasance or incompetence of an agency could be jailed.

In a speech marking the 100th anniversary of the allied assault on Gallipoli and his grandfather Keith Murdoch's famous assistance as a newspaper man in the exposure of the military fiasco that had gone on there, Lachlan Murdoch lamented that Australia had fallen to its lowest level in ten years on Freedom House's annual index of media freedom. Australia now ranked 33rd, behind Belize. Twenty years before, Australia had ranked ninth.

"We have literally hundreds of separate laws and regulations that currently govern the working press," he said. "Trust us, we're from the government' seems to be a common theme when attempting to censor the media. Our freedom of speech and freedom of the press are not things we should trust blindly to anyone. We should be vigilant of the gradual erosion of our freedom to know, to be informed, and make reasoned decisions in our society." [73]

While Australians lamented the *Charlie Hebdo* killings, the magazine could never have been published under Australian law.

Boring as it may sound, the saga over the attempted repeal of Section 18C of the Racial Discrimination Act exemplified much about the difficulties of Australian governance; the abandonment of freedoms in favor of attempts at perceived legislated ideals, at social outcomes which defied legislation; a kind of passive aggression worse than any original crime.

Section 18C of the Racial Discrimination Act 1975 read: "(1) It is unlawful for a person to do an act, otherwise than in private, if: (a) the act is reasonably likely, in all the circumstances, to offend, insult, humiliate or intimidate another person or a group of people; and (b) the act is done because of the race, colour or national or ethnic origin of the other person or of some or all of the people in the group."

Repeal of the 18C, which stifled debate on issues of concern to many Australians, was an Abbott election promise. Essentially the laws made it illegal to hurt the feelings of others; not a prescription for a vigorous democracy.

The lightning rod for the debate was columnist Andrew Bolt, labeled by his numerous critics as conservative, right wing, rabid and a few less polite appellations. Bolt's power came from his columns, printed in several different Murdoch tabloids; and in more recent times by a television program The Bolt Report.

Sometimes secret networks or little understand societal pressure points only became visible once illuminated, synapses activated. In a sense this is what Bolt did when he was closely identified with fight over 18C, which became known simply as the "Bolt laws."

Prior to that few Australians had ever heard of 18C, and as for the Racial Discrimination Act, the only thing which most people knew about it was the name, which seemed fair enough. That the Act could be misused as a suppressor of free speech had not been a question in the public conscience.

---

[73] Keith Murdoch's deeds still relevant in digital world, says his grandson Lachlan Murdoch, *Herald Sun*, 23 October, 2014.

In 2009 Bolt wrote three articles: "It's so hip to be black," "White is the New Black" and "White Fellas in the Black." The articles suggested it was fashionable for "fair-skinned people" of diverse ancestry to choose Aboriginal racial identity for the purposes of political and career clout.

Whether you agreed with the sentiments or not, they were widely held views. Nine fair-skinned people identifying as Aboriginal sued Bolt and his employers.

The courts, predictably, fell against Andrew Bolt.

The debate ran throughout the first year of Abbott's Prime Ministership. There were rallies and public meetings across the country, along with thousands of submissions to government.

The Muslim community was vociferous in their opposition to reform.

The Prime Minister took proposed changes to the laws off the table in August of 2014, saying they had become a complication in the government's relationship with the Muslim community. He betrayed his supporters and broke yet another election promise.

"When it comes to counter-terrorism, everyone needs to be part of Team Australia," Mr Abbott said. "The Government's proposals to change 18C of the Racial Discrimination Act have become a complication in that respect.

"I don't want to do anything that puts our national unity at risk at this time and so those proposals are now off the table. It is, if you like, a leadership call that I have made after discussion with the Cabinet today. In the end, leadership is about preserving national unity on the essentials and that is why I have taken this decision." [74]

Bolt said it was "desperately sad that freedom of speech had so few defenders."

Human Rights Commissioner Tim Wilson said: "This government has squibbed at this important opportunity to allow for the human right to free speech in Australia."

That the debate was deeply hypocritical was evidenced six months later when the spiritual leader of Hizb ut-Tahrir Australia, Ismail al-Wahwah, described Jews in an online video as the "most evil creatures of Allah." There were no court cases, no public ballyhoo, no taxpayer funded litigation.

"Moral corruption is linked to the Jews," al-Wahwah said. "Prostitution in the world began with the Israelites. Usury and gambling began with the Israelites. Killing began with the Israelites.

---

[74] Government backtracks on Racial Discrimination Act, Emma Griffiths, ABC, 6 August, 2015.

"If the Jews were given the whole world, they would want the heavens. That is the nature of the Jews. It is a delusion to think that there can be peace and coexistence with the Israelites, with the Jews.

"There is only one solution for this cancerous tumour: It must be uprooted and thrown back to where it came from. They have corrupted the world with their corrupt media. The Israelites have corrupted the world with so-called art, cinema and corrupt films, and with sex trade, drug trade and moral depravity. They have corrupted the world in every respect.

"They will pay with blood for blood, with tears for tears, and with destruction for destruction."

Abbott had abandoned modest democratic reforms to promote freedom of expression while Muslim groups peddled anti-Semitic diatribes online with impunity.

****

In August of 2014 the use of violent propaganda videos by Islamic State was only just beginning to shock the West.

Particularly striking to Western sensibilities was the use of children in execution videos; with a number of scenes of children executing infidels.

Outrage was sparked by pictures of a seven-year-old Australian boy holding up the head severed head of a Syrian soldier.

The boy was dressed in a blue Polo top as he used both hands to hoist the decapitated head.

His father, Khaled Sharrouf, posted the image on Twitter with the words: "That's my boy!"

Sharrouf also posed in battle fatigues with his three children, aged four, six and seven, each of them armed with machine guns.

The photographs were intended to provoke; and indeed did evoke a kind of shock of distance from normality, dysfunction, terror, a world far from safe suburban homes and quietly reconciled lives.

Abbott said the picture was evidence of the hideous atrocities Islamic State were capable of: "We see more and more evidence of just how barbaric this particular entity is." [75]

Other pictures posted on social media showed Sharrouf crouching over dismembered corpses and preaching in front of an Islamic State flag.

---

[75] The photo that will shock the world: jihadist Khaled Sharrouf's son, 7, holds severed head, Kelmeny Fraser, *The Daily Telegraph*, 11 August, 2014.

In tweets taunting the Australian Federal Police Sharrouf wrote: "U can't stop me and trust me if I wanted to attack aus I could have easily" and "I love to slaughter use (sic) and ALLAH LOVES when u dogs r slaughtered."

In June, the first disquieting winter month of 2015, came the news that Sharrouf, along with fellow Australian Islamic State fighter Mohamed Elomar had been killed in a drone strike in Mosul.

Whether the drone strike was Australian was not clear from the news reports.

His mother-in-law, in a statement provided to the media through her lawyer, pleaded with the Prime Minister to help with the return of her daughter Tara and Sharrouf's five children, her grandchildren: "They want to come. Our country is a country of many faiths and backgrounds. It is my belief that Australia is an open hearted country. The time is ripe for compassion and empathy.

"I accept that some will be critical of my daughter, who followed her heart and has paid an enormous price.

"I implore these people, including the Prime Minister Mr Abbott, who is a man of faith, to remember John 8:7 — 'He that is without sin among you, let him first cast a stone at her.'

"Mr Abbott, I beg you, please help bring my child and grandchildren home."

When asked how authorities would care for Sharrouf's children, Abbott replied: "The children of these particular criminals will be dealt with in the same way the children of criminals are normally dealt with."[76]

Well, go Tony, Alex thought.

That'll show 'em.

The sins of the father. As written in the Book of Exodus: "I am a jealous God, punishing the children for the sin of the parents to the third and fourth generation."

While unconfirmed, Mohamed 'Moey' Elomar was believed to have been killed in the same drone attack as his friend Sharrouf.

He was once one of Australia's rising boxing stars, boasting a near unbeaten record in the ring. In 2008 he was Australia's super featherweight titleholder.

By July of 2014, he had managed to shock Australians by posting pictures on social media of himself holding up the severed heads of two Syrian soldiers. He sported a beard, sunglasses tucked into the top of his shirt and a big, broad grin.

---

[76] Khaled Sharrouf's mother-in-law begs Tony Abbott, Andrew Greene and Ashleigh Raper, ABC, 24 June, 2015.

Elomar had been particularly active on Twitter spreading jihadist propaganda. Australian authorities issued an arrest warrant. He was alleged to have been radicalized at the Global Islamic Youth Centre in Liverpool, run by the "hate preacher" Sheik Feiz Mohammed, an Australian of Lebanese descent born in 1970, an al-Qaeda supporter known as Australia's most dangerous preacher. Elomar's brother Ahmed was serving four years jail for bashing a policeman during Hyde Park riots in 2012. [77]

At the same time, demonstrating why the Sharia appeared to be taking such easy hold in Australia, all the economic grace notes were bad. As one letter writer summed it up: "Unemployment is rising, industries are shutting down, business and consumer confidence is at an all-time low, closures and downsizing in the retail market are common, interest rate cuts are not kick-starting the economy and employers don't seem to be creating new jobs..." [78]

In March of 2015 two teenage Australian boys were stopped at Sydney Airport on suspicion of heading to the Middle East to join foreign fighters.

They were star pupils at one of Sydney's most elite selective schools, Sydney Boys High. In years gone past the school had been the subject of scandal in that there were almost no Anglo Saxon students who attended; a story immediately buried under a torrent of accusations over racism.

The two boys, 16 and 17-years-old, were attempting to travel to Turkey, a major transit point for Islamic State fighters.

The pair had also been watching videos by Sheik Feiz.

Apart from some levels of surveillance, the authorities took no action against him. The Muslim community did not speak out to condemn him. He garnered thousands of followers in Australia and around the world. The schoolboys of Sydney were just the latest in a string of people who had been inspired by him.

Sheik Feiz was one of the inspirations behind the Boston marathon bombings, in which three people were killed and 264 injured. Chechen bomber Tamerlan Tsarnaev posted a link on his YouTube page to Sheik Feiz's sermon on the Dangers of Harry Potter: "This film whatever you think about it glorifies, magnifies, promotes paganism, promotes idolatry, promotes evil. Harmless!? Teaching your children idolatry, magic, the drinking of unicorn blood?! This is the monoculture of

---

[77] Mohamed "Moey" Elomar goes from celebrated boxing champion to wanted terrorist, *The Daily Telegraph*, 31 July, 2014.

[78] Garry Dunne, *The Daily Telegraph*, 6 March, 2015.

Western culture, Western lifestyle. Look at the way they are dressed. Even in cartoons, they glorify nudity." [79]

A generation of Australian children learnt to love reading thanks to J.K. Rowling's immensely popular Harry Potter series.

There would be no reading of popular novels if the jihadists had their way.

His many controversial actions included encouraging the beheading of Dutch politician Geert Wilders: "Anyone who mocks our learning, laughs at the Islam and degrades it must enter death—decapitate him, cut his head off."

Sheik Fiez also claimed that "Jews are pigs who will be killed at the end of the world."

He preached that children should be encouraged to be jihadists: "We want to have children and offer them as soldiers defending Islam... Teach them this: there is nothing more beloved to me than wanting to die as a mujahid. Put in their soft, tender hearts the zeal of jihad and a love of martyrdom." [80] Intelligence Risks CEO Neil Fergus said: "It's not the schools. The schools in the main have been incredibly responsible. The issue we've had locally is a couple of these hate preachers, self-styled preachers. We have a lot of material on the internet that is very confronting, very violent and that is attracting a certain style of person. But there is other much more subtle propaganda going out there which is showing footage of the refugee camps ... and appealing to ... the wider Islamic population to come and do their duty." [81]

Sheik Feiz Mohammed headed up the Global Islamic Youth Centre in the western Sydney suburb of Liverpool, reaching a community of more than 4,000 Muslims and providing spiritual sanction for Islamic violence. His website Faith over Fear, linked to the Centre, called on Muslims to sacrifice their lives to the West. He studied under Sheik Mohammed Omran, one of the founders of the jihadist movement in Australia. Sheik Feiz fled to Lebanon in 2005 to escape constant surveillance by the Australian Security Intelligence Organisation; relocated to Malaysia to complete his studies and returned to Australia in 2011, when he opened up a prayer hall in Auburn in western Sydney.

[79] Were Boston Marathon bombers followers of Harry Potter-hating Australian sheik and pro-al-Qaeda preacher, Daily Mail UK, 20 April, 2013.
[80] Muslim cleric urges children to be martyrs, NBC News, 19 January, 2007.
[81] Teen terror suspects attended exclusive Sydney School, James Thomas, 7 News, 18 March, 2015.

One of his last publicly known addresses was a luxury retreat in the Southern Highlands.

Australia had knowingly played host to one of the world's preachers of violent jihad and done nothing about it.

Tolerance of intolerance is cowardice.

****

In the same month that Sharrouf's 7-year-old son was posing with the head of a severed Syrian soldier, retiring Director-General of ASIO David Irvine addressed the National Press Club in Canberra. His speech was a rare window into the thinking of Australia's lead security organization. He made the claim that the terrorist threat within Australia was real but manageable: "The great evil of terrorism, from whatever source, is that it is designed to strike fear and cause mass casualties among innocent civilians. Such threats can come from a variety of religious and ideologically focused groups, from the right or the left.

"But our principal concern has for more than a decade been the threat from terrorism by extremists adhering to a particularly violent interpretation of Islam. In the case of al-Qa'ida and its various offshoots in the Middle East, Africa and South East Asia, not to mention the West, the intent is to punish, to foment social upheaval, destroy the public's confidence in their governments. It is a doctrine of hate, brutality and inhumanity.

"Australians have not been immune from such violence. Over one hundred Australians have died in terrorist incidents in the past twelve years. True, we have not had a terrorist attack on Australian soil in that period, but planning for a number of mass casualty attacks on our soil was detected and the attacks were thwarted by ASIO and its state and federal law enforcement partners.

"We have long been monitoring a small number of Muslim Australians who support violent extremism and who frequently express the aspiration of conducting terrorist attacks in Australia. We have needed to be in a position to move quickly, to nip things in the bud, as soon as such people moved from talk to active planning to final preparations. It was not only groups who were of concern; a recurring nightmare has been the so-called lone-wolf, radicalised over the Internet, who had managed to avoid coming across our radar.

"In the past two years, however, the situation in Syria and now Iraq has radically complicated the threat, adding energy and allure to the extremist Islamic narrative. The draw of foreign fighters to Syria and Iraq is significant and includes more Australians than all other previous extremist conflicts put together. The number of Australians of potential security concern to ASIO has increased substantially."

Irvine said ASIO estimated there were some 100 people in Australia actively supporting extremist groups, recruiting new fighters and grooming new suicide bombing candidates, as well as providing funding and equipment.

"Not all of those Australians will return, but some tens of Australians have already returned and a good number of these remain of concern to the security authorities – people with potentially enhanced religious commitment to violence in the name of a distorted brand of Islam – and training in the use of weapons or bomb-making."

The retiring Director-General then went on to push the official line: "ASIO recognises that the tiny number of violent extremists does not represent the Islamic communities of Australia – we are talking about a few hundred aberrant souls in a community of nearly half a million – and it is grossly unfair to blame Muslims, who see themselves as a committed component of Australia's multicultural society, for the sins of a tiny minority."

Deleted from some transcripts of the speech was the perhaps inelegant phrase "who nevertheless can make a rather big bang." [82]

Muslims themselves had never said they were proponents of multiculturalism. They may have been in the country in such sizable numbers as a result of multicultural policies, but that was an entirely different matter.

The website for Hizb ut-Tahrir Australia declared: "There remains a dangerous plot of the West which remains hidden from the non-alert Muslim. You will hear some Muslims defending integration. This is to say that Jews, Christians, Hindus, homosexuals, capitalists, communists and Muslims should be in a free and equal association and each of them constitutes part of the whole. Muslims living in the West must realise that we are not a minority which can easily melt into the Anglo-capitalist way of life, abandoning the perfection and mercy of Islam."

Irvine ended his spiel on terrorism with the claim that the country should recognize that the strongest defence against violent extremism lay within the Australian Muslim community itself. By year's end the Prime Minister himself had escalated his criticism of the leadership of Australia's Muslim community. By year's end, following renewed military intervention in Iraq, relations with the Islamic community would be at new lows. And by year's end Australia would have seen two

---

[82] Director-General of ASIO David Irvine addresses the National Press Club, ABC, 27 August, 2014.

terrorist attacks on home soil; and the capabilities and competencies of Australia's security agencies called into question.

****

Much happened in September of 2014 and the Prime Minister had much to say as he committed the nation to a Holy War. Within the half year, much of it would come to seem very hollow indeed.

In a journalistic career spanning decades, Alex had never been successfully sued. One of his favorite journalistic mottoes was: "Let them hang themselves."

To begin, Abbott warned Australian Muslims they would be acting "against God" if they joined Islamic State.

Lecturing the good Muslims of Australia on what they should or should not believe was never going to get the government very far.

In a round of media interviews on that first day of Spring prominent television personality Lisa Wilkinson asked: "Critics say that this latest situation in Iraq is proof that the 2003 war on terror was a mistake and only gave rise to a much more dangerous jihadist movement. Why have you decided to involve our military in yet another conflict in Iraq?"

The Prime Minister replied: "Lisa, they are two very different situations. In 2003, there was a campaign in Iraq against the will of the Iraqi government. What's happening now is an involvement, essentially a humanitarian involvement, and it is at the request of the Americans with the support of the Iraqi government."

Good question.

Feeble answer.

Amidst the round of media interviews the Prime Minister repeated the mantra: "We have seen the beheadings, the crucifixions, the mass executions, the driving of innocent people from their homes, the destruction of ancient communities. It is important not to stand aside in the face of what is pure evil."[83]

In a radio interview the next day with another dominant media personality, talk-back host Alan Jones, the Prime Minister declared: "These are dire and dreadful things that we are discussing, but sadly, sometimes dire and dreadful measures are necessary in response to the pure evil that we are now seeing across a large swathe of the Middle East thanks to this hideous movement. The difficulty here is that these people do exalt in death; they absolutely revel in killing.

---

[83] Prime Minister's website, Transcripts, 1 September, 2014.

"We've seen in the century just gone, the most unspeakable things happen, but the atrocities that were committed by the Nazis, by the communists and others, they were ashamed of them, they tried to cover them up. This mob, by contrast, as soon as they've done something gruesome and ghastly and unspeakable, they're advertising it on the internet for all to see which makes them, in my mind, nothing but a death cult and that's why I think it's quite proper to respond with extreme force against people like this."

Within months the situation in the Middle East had seriously deteriorated, the threat to the West had escalated and Obama's strategies were being seriously questioned, if not ridiculed. It became rapidly clear that what was being described as a humanitarian mission was nothing of the kind; that there was nothing humanitarian about dropping drones on mujahedeen and their families, talk of disrupting and degrading Islamic State was fanciful nonsense, and that far from acting as the "the strong arm of Australia," the country's military operations had increased the domestic terror threat.

Military operations would be strictly limited to airstrikes, Abbott declared in taking the country to war that Spring, as if high-tech killings would somehow keep Australian personnel safe and absolve the country of any true crime against humanity. While numerous military experts decried the use of drones and airstrikes as inhumane and counterproductive, no such doubts lay with Australian Prime Minister Tony Abbott: "Air strikes may not roll back their existing conquests, but air strikes can certainly prevent or hinder – very substantially hinder – new conquests."

A kill was a kill; whether it was high-tech or low-tech, whether it was a laser-guided bomb or a slit throat.

The type of warfare which the Anzacs had known, courage and personal sacrifice, was a thing of the past.

There were no official estimates on how many people Australia's bombs had killed: mujahedeen, old men, old women, mothers, fathers, children by the score. Innocents who died for being who they were; for being of the Muslim faith.

Australian taxpayers would never know the numbers; what their religious and political affiliations had been, what their lives and dreams once were.

There were differing reports on the numbers of civilian casualties from coalition airstrikes. One group, Airwars, a project aimed at tracking international airstrikes, claimed that it could demonstrate that at least 57 missions had killed civilians, with 459 verifiable civilian deaths between mid-2014 and mid-201; an5. More than 5,800 coalition strikes had killed some 15,000 militants and led to 48 suspected friendly fire deaths.

A report from the group stated: "Almost all claims of noncombatant deaths from alleged coalition strikes emerge within 24 hours — with graphic images of reported victims often widely disseminated. In this context, the present coalition policy of downplaying or denying all claims of noncombatant fatalities makes little sense, and risks handing Islamic State and other forces a powerful propaganda tool." [84]

The linking of engagement in the Middle East to images provided to the media of men flying FA-18 Super Hornets at high altitude, to a heightened terror alert within the country, to terror raids in major cities, the shooting and killing of a young Muslim man outside a suburban police station in Melbourne, to debates over the wearing of the burqa in Parliament House in the nation's capital Canberra, all of it clashed or converged with sentiment on the ground, with increasing reports of racist insults or attacks, a rise in anti-Muslim sentiment and a renewed virulence of debate within the nation's chattering classes, both left and right.

The Americans released so called "bomb-camera" footage, showing the destruction of targets, but Australia did not.

Defence head Air Chief Marshal Mark Binskin defended Australia's refusal to release the footage. "I don't want to get into glorifying what's happening out there," he said. "This isn't a video game. This is the real world. That camera footage shows people dying and I don't think we should glorify that." [85]

David Kilcullen was among a number of counter insurgency experts highly critical of drone warfare: "These strikes are totally counter-productive. It is a strategic error to personalise the conflict in this way, it'll strengthen the enemy and weaken our friends. How can one expect the civilian population to support us if we kill their families and destroy their homes?" [86]

Drone warfare raised profound moral, ethical and legal questions, none of which were being canvassed with the public by the Australian Prime Minister. There was no national conversation.

---

[84] Report: US-led strikes in Iraq, Syria kill 459 civilians, Associated Press, 3 August, 2015.

[85] 'This isn't a video game' - footage of Australian bombs hitting IS targets won't be released, Max Blenkin, *The Sydney Morning Herald*, 13 October, 2014.

[86] David Kilcullen: The Australian helping to shape a new Afghanistan strategy, *The Independent*, 9 July, 2009.

The Prime Minister of Australia knew perfectly well when he committed the country to the most inhumane form of warfare ever devised that many senior military strategists, theoreticians and authors believed that drones were counterproductive, and would make a bad situation in the Middle East a damn sight worse.

As military insiders warned, tactics swallowed strategy.

The Australian people heard nothing about these complexities, and saw not a shred of doubt from their Prime Minister.

Yet internationally there was spirited debate, including a spate of books, *Predator: The Secret Origins of the Drone Revolution*, *Kill Chain: High-tech Assassins* and *A Theory of the Drone*.

In *Kill Chain* author Andrew Cockburn wrote that for years critics had railed against the injustice and capriciousness of killer drones, citing the lack of due process in selecting targets, the collateral civilian casualties invariably accompany the strikes, and the backlash from the growing numbers of families and communities radicalized by experiencing the strikes. But beyond these tangible consequences, the combination of technology and the policy of targeted killing had challenged some of the more basic ways in which human beings and political powers existed in relationship to one another.

He called for a moratorium on their use, saying they placed entire target populations under a siege mentality; as the drones could hover for hours or days over their targets before unleashing their weaponry.

Critics argued that the dramatic escalation of their use during the Obama administration from a few hundred to many thousands was more of a legacy of his Presidency than Obamacare.

"My powers of empathy, my ability to reach into another's heart, cannot penetrate the blank stares of those who would murder innocents with abstract, serene satisfaction," Obama had written in a Preface to *Dreams From My Father*.

Obama was responsible for killing thousands; mechanically, at a distance. No blood splashed on his hands, no mud on his boots.

Philosopher Gregoire Chamayou observed in his book *A Theory of the Drone* that not since the debates over nuclear warfare had an American military strategy been the subject of such worldwide concern over the development of increasingly inhumane forms of warfare.

He described the killer drone as "a dream of a weapon" resulting in confrontation without combat, no prisoners and no sure expectation of victory.

For the first time in history, Chamayou argued, a state had claimed the right to make war across a mobile battlefield that potentially spanned the globe, respecting no borders. In drone warfare, the whole world was a "hunting ground," the target was unable to retaliate, no quarter could be given in case of last-minute surrender, and only one side risked being killed. Drones represented a fundamental transformation of the laws of war that had historically defined military conflict as between combatants.

As more and more drones were launched into battle, war transformed into a realm of secretive, targeted assassinations beyond the view and control not only of potential enemies, but also of citizens of the perpetrating democracies.

Drone warfare took away the traditions of battle, which by nature was limited and allowed for reciprocity.

A review of *A Theory of the Drone* in *The Washington Post* observed: "Ultimately, drones are the opposite of warfare as we have long understood it: a warrior culture in which readiness to kill has been inseparable from willingness to die. With drones, the ethics of warrior cultures have been superseded, and the warriors have turned into invulnerable, cold-hearted executioners. In addition, the rules and values of counter terrorism have replaced those of counterinsurgency, blithely exchanging the so-called battle for hearts and minds with a staccato delivery of death from above. With drone warfare, there is no victory, just perpetual elimination, a 'periodic reaping' that Special Forces operatives ... cynically call 'mowing the grass.'

"The use of drones to conduct warfare has destabilised the rules of war and weakened the moral fibre of warriors."

Chamayou reasoned that ultimately the assumed right to assassinate from the air was a forceful distortion of the law of warfare. By eroding the all-important principle of distinction, mixing up combatants and noncombatants and defanging accountability for assassination, drone warfare had caused a profound crisis in the legal theory of war. The revolution was astonishing to behold, "for we are now living in an unprecedented age of one-way-only armed violence, war without combat."

****

In a country where many of its inhabitants had little fondness for Americans, including the tens of thousands of Vietnamese who had settled there after the Vietnam War, Abbott's ceaselessly praised the America's military misadventures and pushed his view that America as a force of good in the world.

Abbott claimed US President Barack Obama had acted with "reason and appropriate anger" to a situation that was "abominable, unspeakable, repellent, abhorrent..." [87]

The obsequiousness reached absurd levels. Abbott declared in one interview: "I think that the world should be grateful to President Obama for taking the action that he has. He hasn't been trigger happy, he hasn't rushed in, he has been very careful about this and I think that's to his credit because the last thing any of us should want to do is rush into a difficult conflict in the Middle East. By the same token, none of us should want to stand by while an avoidable, preventable genocide takes place, and that's why I think President Obama's actions have been wise and just." [88]

The rhetoric was reminiscent of a bygone era.

In October 1966, Lyndon Baines Johnson became the first incumbent US president to visit Australia, conducting a five city three day thank you tour for Australia's emphatic support for the war in Vietnam.

Nearly a million people lined Sydney streets to catch a glimpse of the presidential motorcade on its way to a state reception at the Art Gallery of NSW, where a bush park had been assembled with koalas, kangaroos, wallabies and an echidna.

Many in the crowd waved placards: "All the Way With LBJ."

A glimpse is all that most of them got because anti-war protesters disrupted the route, forcing the motorcade to finish the journey at high speed. On Oxford Street, protesters lay before the motorcade; on Liverpool Street, women banged fists on the car carrying the First Lady. [89]

Famously at the time, Premier at the time Robert Askin was reported to have declared: "Run the bastards over."

Just as it had been in the 1960s and 1970s with Australia's support of America in its conduct of the Vietnam War seriously backfiring, so it would equally prove in 2015 with its support of America in the Middle East.

The views Abbott was expressing were the discredited views of someone who had supported the Vietnam War.

Abbott was meant to represent all Australians. He was representing himself; there were very dark forces abroad.

---

[87] Official transcripts, Prime Minister's website.

[88] Transcripts, Prime Minister of Australia, 1 September, 2014.

[89] LBJ came all the way - but few followed, *The Sydney Morning Herald*, 12 November, 2011.

****

On the 12th of September the government announced that based on advice from security and intelligence agencies the National Terrorism Public Alert level would be raised from Medium to High. The threat level was determined by the Australian Security Intelligence Organisation (ASIO).

The government claimed the advice was not based on knowledge of a specific attack plan but rather a body of evidence that pointed to the increased likelihood of a terrorist attack in Australia.

An official statement declared: "Security and intelligence agencies are concerned about the increasing number of Australians working with, connected to, or inspired by terrorist groups such as ISIL, Jabhat al-Nusrah, and al-Qaeda. The threat they pose has been increasing for more than a year. Raising the alert level to High is designed to increase vigilance and raise awareness in the community. While it is important the public are aware of the increased threat, Australians should continue to go about their lives.

"Owners and operators of critical infrastructure and places of mass gathering are encouraged to review their security plans and update their contact details with their state or territory police counter-terrorism unit."

Three days later, with no prior attempt to convince the public of the need to go to war and with little apparent consultation with the nation's military, Prime Minister Tony Abbott once again declared the country was at war, this time with Islamic State.

"The death cult," as Abbott continued to repeatedly label them.

Whether or not participation in the Iraq conflict would make Australia safer, as the Prime Minister claimed, Australia was at it again.

The greatest betrayal is by those put into positions of power, those one should be able to trust.

Abbott announced that 200 elite special-forces soldiers could be on the ground in Iraq within days after his government had agreed to an American request to provide planes and 600 personnel to the Middle East as part of a multinational strike force against Islamic terrorists in Iraq and Syria.

There was an initial estimated cost of half a billion dollars; no exit strategy, no end date, no realistically achievable outcome. And the intervention was highly likely to backfire.

"Go forth and set the world on fire," St Ignatius of Loyola, the founder of the Jesuits said.

Sometimes to Alex, in those early morning hours when his own mind was on fire, the Jesuit trained Australian Prime Minister was taking the words literally.

In previous weeks US President Barack Obama, or Barack Hussein Obama as so many of his critics kept insisting, had admitted that America had no strategy to deal with Islamic State while blaming his intelligence officials for the country's lack of preparedness, and for the deteriorating situation in the Middle East.

The rapid recovery from no strategy to a policy of "degrading and destroying" Islamic State and the many deaths which would inevitably result was at odds with Obama's relaxed demeanor, and images of him, immaculately tailored, swinging golf clubs during his holidays at Martha's Vineyard.

The soaring rhetoric for which Obama had been famous, making him one of his country's greatest teleprompt readers if not presidents, appeared ill-fitting for declarations of war, even in the manufactured solemnity of presidential media conferences; for sending American soldiers to their deaths; or for killing religious warriors on Arabic soil.

His golfing holiday coincided with the beheading of an American journalist. A video was released of American Steven Sotloff, in which he declared that he was paying the price for American intervention. A masked ISIS figure spoke directly to Obama: "Just as your missiles continue to strike our people, our knife will continue to strike the necks of your people. We take this opportunity to warn those governments who've entered this evil alliance of America against the Islamic State to back off and leave our people alone." [90]

Abbott's mid-September announcement that Australia would be joining America in yet another coalition also came within hours of another televised beheading, this time of British aid worker David Haines, father of two. Abbott declared: "This death cult is uniquely evil in that it does not simply do evil, it exults in evil. This death cult has ambitions way beyond those of any previous terrorist group."

He was also quick to link the Middle Eastern conflict to the terrorist threat within the country: "This is not just an international security situation, but it is a domestic security situation." [91]

The bizarre nature of Australia's involvement in Iraq, the fact that Tony Abbott appeared to take no military advice and sought no broader

---

[90] ISIS video shows beheading of American journalist Steven Sotloff, CNN, 9 September, 2014.

[91] Abbott declares war on Islamic State 'death cult,' Mark Kenny, *Sydney Morning Herald*, 15 September, 2014.

consultation before taking the nation to war, was evidenced in part by a piece in *The Australian* written by John Lyons.

Some of the criticism of the story focused, as armchair critics were wont to do, on the reporter. Alex had known John Lyons since the 1980s when they were on *The Sydney Morning Herald* together.

Lyons had a somewhat imperious air at odds with the average reporter; and had the managerial caste of 1980s totally boxed. With a pompous mien which confounded the hierarchy, he quickly rose from the news floor to the lofty heights of editor; and remained there in the decades to follow.

Alex remembered John Lyons for drunken parties at his house long ago, before the Sydney property wagon steamroller had barely begun to roll, making many an undeserving character rich. And before alcohol became unfashionable.

As well, of course, for his seriously well polished articles, all of which took weeks to write and which the editorial hierarchies would gift him all the time he required; much to Alex's envy. Humble hacks on the highways of print like himself were expected to turn around a feature in a single day.

But whatever Alex's occasional stabs of passing resentment over the years, one thing was for sure: Lyons was not the type of journalist to get a single detail in a story wrong.

The piece began: "Tony Abbott suggested a unilateral invasion of Iraq, with 3500 Australian ground troops to confront the Islamic State terrorist group.

"Flanked by his chief of staff, Peta Credlin, in a meeting in Canberra on November 25, the Prime Minister said the move would help halt the surge of Islamic State in northern Iraq.

"After receiving no resistance from Ms Credlin or his other staff in the room, Mr Abbott then raised the idea with Australia's leading military planners. The military officials were stunned, telling Mr Abbott that sending 3500 Australian soldiers without any US or NATO cover would be disastrous for the Australians." [92]

That the Prime Minister, after the long and troubled history of American and Australian involvement in Iraq and the hostility of the general population to foreign military adventures, was making such proposals without prior consultation was nothing short of bizarre.

Peculiarly, as a matter of such import, the decision to assist in the bombing of Iraq, would not have passed what in Australia is often called "the pub test."

---

[92] Tony Abbott sought military advice on go-it-alone invasion of Iraq, John Lyons, The Australian, 21 February, 2015.

Any normal person sitting on any normal bar stool would have told him: "What the... Remember the Weapons of Mass Destruction that never existed?

"Remember that you've got half a million Muslims in the country now, whether we like it or not, who will be inflamed by the decision. Remember that Iraq and Afghanistan have been the main drivers of domestic terror threats for the past 20 years.

"Remember you've got more than a quarter of a billion Muslims directly to your North in Indonesia who regard America's bombing of Iraq and the hundreds of thousands of deaths which have resulted as the greatest act of terror in history.

"Remember that the majority of the population is against Australia being involved in foreign wars.

"Remember that most Australians don't like Americans in any case, and thought John Howard was a joke for toadying up to George Bush.

"And wake up to the reality of what you are doing. You are raking billions of dollars off the backs of hard working Australians to enter a morally indefensible war you cannot win."

But common sense and good governance were entirely absent in the Abbott government's drift towards electoral oblivion.

****

The mistakes of the Abbott government began early and lasted long.

The fear and antipathy that was seeping through the country ran in parallel with a cascade of falling grace notes on economic news, "Economy Darkens"; and as spirits dived at the impossibility of confronting the terror from within and the terror from without, so too did the nation's once natural optimism and overblown confidence of its place in the world.

On election night, in his victory speech, Tony Abbott declared: "Australia is open for business."

Many Australians thought that at last the legislative shackles, onerous taxation and multiple compliance burdens, the apparent antipathy of government to individual enterprise, was over. That they finally had a Prime Minister who understood the problems of small business; that the good times were back.

But nothing happened. There was no reduction in taxes. The cost of electricity remained at ludicrous levels, despite the well documented impacts it had on the cost of living and the cost of doing business. Money did not start flowing through the economy again. Petrol taxes went up, a broken election promise. Many people now kept their car travel to a minimum because of the cost of travel. No more visits to grandma each weekend. No more Sunday drives, once a feature of Australian suburban life. More and more activity ceased. Taxes on pensions went up. Another broken promise.

Telecommunications remained extremely poor and outlandishly expensive. Even the smallest cafes and restaurants across Asia had perfectly decent Wi-Fi. There was barely a coffee shop in the whole of Sydney that offered internet access for its customers. Many people could not get ordinary mobile phone coverage, and the internet remained hapless in much of the country. An additional levy on foreign property buyers was so paltry as to prove nothing but an insult to a population incensed by the fact that the wealthy from Communist China were buying much of the country's choicest real estate, from swank Sydney pads to some of the world's best farmland. The national debt continued to rise.

"It was not true," said Michael Blaimey, proprietor of The Little Ox, a cafe towards the bottom of Oxford Street. Following a habit of a lifetime, Alex would go there many a morning as the earliest opening cafe he could find.

"When it comes to business, Australia is chronically ill. When will politicians ever make decisions for the people rather than for their members to stay in parliament?

"The low interest rate environment has created a commercial real estate bubble in which rents have outpaced the growth of businesses in the last decade. Rents are so high that most businesses are unprofitable.

"The tax structure is outdated.

"The GST is a debacle, small business compliance is unbearably complex, it is a paperwork nightmare."

Nationally the deficit had blown out to more than $50 billion, and gross debt was skyrocketing towards $667 billion. The country was borrowing $1 billion a month just to pay the interest on debt.

The shopping malls and High Streets remained as grim a reminder of past economic policies, with shuttered shops and struggling businesses now a feature of most suburbs. It was as if the place had suffered a massive heart attack so fierce that nobody understood what had happened; slabs of memory, historical memory, had gone missing. Australians didn't know who they were anymore.

****

Tony Abbott's first major gaffe was on the always vexed playing field of gender.

There was one woman appointed to his first cabinet, Foreign Minister Julie Bishop, front woman for the bloated Department of Foreign Affairs and Trade.

Predictably Abbott's decision to appoint a cadre of suits to his Cabinet provoked howls from women's lobby groups. Alex was as sick to death any man of the Marxist feminist ideology which had pervaded and distorted most Australian social policy, and which derided the traditional roles of men as protectors and providers, instead painting them as oppressors and abusers.

Men in Australia were routinely ridiculed as bashers, the indoctrination beginning in the schoolyard.

"Why would any man want to live in Australia?" the good Muslim who fixed his computer demanded to know when the conversation drifted to the state of the nation. He then proceeded to tell his own tales of injustice at the hands of the country's despised family law system.

Many men, Muslim or not, could tell similar stories. Ankle bracelets with GPS locators for male perpetrators of domestic violence, ran the headlines in the adjoining days.

But you could never win an argument on gender in modern Australia in 2015.

And in the case of Tony Abbott's Cabinet the feminist lobby groups were entirely correct.

It was a simple matter of social equity.

Of all the charismatic black holes who had graced ministerial offices over the preceding conservative governments, it was impossible to believe that Abbott could not find plenty of women to fill Cabinet postings.

Apart from that, it was just stupid politics.

And for a professional politician, a gaffe which those around him should never have allowed to occur.

Nineteen men in dark suits and dark ties. You could smell their stale breaths and stale ideas from a hundred years away.

The next clutch of Abbott gaffes, don't talk about the war, involved the waste of hundreds of millions of dollars of public funds on Royal Commissions which produced little the public did not already know and provided no political dividend. Royal Commissions were often criticized as lawyer festivals; in effect gifting money away from the working class to the professional class.

Lawyers competed with each other to run up as many billable hours as possible.

The inquiries were into the conduct of trade unions, decades old allegations of sexual misconduct in institutions and pink bats, the ridiculous home insulation scheme which cost the taxpayer $2.2 billion, again gifted money away from workers towards people who already owned their own homes, and led directly to the deaths of four young tradesmen. Another stupid and expensive idea courtesy of Kevin Rudd.

The public already knew that some senior union officials had used union funded credit cards to get up to a bit of hanky panky in brothels, and Australians, above all, hated class war.

The extended inquiry into sexual misconduct in institutions may have produced some moving and genuine stories of abuse, but it also produced a considerable number of implausible stories. Many of the allegations, including those aired in the media, were against people who were no longer around to defend themselves.

The government would have been better off conducting inquiries into the present day conduct of the nation's scandal ridden family courts, children's courts and child protection services; all of which had serious systemic problems which would have benefited from public exposure.

Instead the only real outcome was, surprise surprise, lawyers calling for more money to conduct ever broader inquiries. There was, again, no political dividend.

The catalogue of gaffes culminated with the bestowing of an Australia Day knighthood on the Duke of Edinburgh; a decision made solely by Tony Abbott, a so-called captain's pick.

"Abbott's Australia Day Knightmare," trumpeted the tabloids.

The positive symbolism of the day was instantly destroyed.

England's royal family had little or no relevancy to most Australians; apart from the soap opera of their privileged lives. Australia was founded by convicts, victims of the brutality of the English upper classes. And by 2015 many Australians came from cultures with no connection whatsoever to the Royal Household of England.

News Limited commentator Andrew Bolt got it exactly right when he declared that the knighthood would be the death knell of Abbott, from that minute on he would be a dead man walking.

The decision, which played to Abbott's own peculiar instincts, exemplified what he had most lost in office: an understanding of the people for whom he served.

Australia Day, or Invasion Day as the indigenous called it, and the days that followed were cold, overcast and wet in Sydney and surrounding regions.

On Oxford Street the Islamic ban on entertainment was increasingly in place.

The Phoenix Club, virtually the only late night early morning club left in the entire city, was closed down and its invariably colorful cast of customers, a feature of early morning scenes on the strip, disappeared.

Australia Day was an occasion to think about where the nation was heading; and Alex grabbed a reporters pad and jotted down notes on what he saw; shop after shuttered shop.

Just over the rise from Taylor Square, what was once a busy and successful restaurant precinct, was full of abandoned enterprises. Next to Tool Shed Adult Concepts there was a For Lease sign on an empty bar; some fittings remaining. Next was H & R Block, with its largely empty foyer. Next to that an abandoned cafe, old mail was scattered on the damp floor.

The Bookstore Darlinghurst had few customers, and the books in its window display referred to the past: Retro London, Retro TV, Old Sydney. Adjacent, a graffiti paneled hoarding bore an about-to-lapse notice of consent; while nearby another abandoned shop, plaster hanging from the ceiling.

Australia Day.

****

Australia's disastrous military involvement in Iraq stretched back a quarter of a century; and in a two party system, just as in 2015, both sides of politics were complicit, and guilty.

In August, 1990, Iraq's leader Saddam Hussein ordered his army to invade oil-rich Kuwait. The United Nations Security Council authorized a US led military coalition which included Australia.

The operation became known as Desert Storm.

In 1991, following more than a month of aerial bombardment, the Americans mounted a swift ground assault. More than 100,000 Iraqis were killed; while only 200 coalition combatants died. Australia's involvement was limited to providing naval support in the northern Persian Gulf, deploying three guided missile frigates, a destroyer and two support ships.

That first time around, Australia might have been able to avoid loss of life and appear to be a player in the wider world of war, but the country's ethically dubious involvement came at a cost not just in coin but in identity. And laid the path for greater disasters to come.

Prime Minister at the time of Desert Storm Bob Hawke committed troops to the first Iraq War, a controversial move in a country which had seen too many of its young men die in distant wars. He slickly purloined what was an electoral risk into an issue of national pride. To question the country's commitment to Iraq was to denigrate, as the spin went, some of the world's finest soldiers.

As a news reporter with pad in hand, back in 1991 Alex had been on board the destroyer for the first farewell of Australian troops to Iraq, watching proud sailors and soldiers pose with their families and with the then Prime Minister.

Having neatly survived the country's natural anti-war sentiment post-Vietnam, and as common Australian decency would dictate, Bob Hawke was determined to farewell the troops personally.

As history would have it, the anti war protestors marooned at the naval gates were probably right. Australia should have stayed well out of it.

Hawke was a masterful old-style grin and grip politician who could work any crowd.

As a general news reporter based in Sydney Alex had been obliged to follow him around on numerous occasions. Hawke was not a humble man, but he had the gift of convincing the voters that he was one of them, in a bygone era of Australia which lived by the motto, "never trust a man who doesn't drink."

You would never have known Bob had any more brain cells than your Average Joe Blow.

Hawkie, as he was almost universally known, wasn't about to let on to the great unwashed know that he had ever read a book or could see straight through them in a micro-flash.

Australians loved him. That he was clever was forgiven or forgotten.

In that Arcadian world prior to the Twin Towers turning security worldwide on its head Hawke wasn't the type of Prime Minister to hide behind a screen of police and national security. He lingered on the ship for hours, shook the hands of every soldier and sailor he laid eyes on and wished them all good luck.

After the official proceedings were over, Hawke wandered the battleship decks, cheerfully posing with the proud families of the soldiers.

Alex followed the Prime Minister, his circling minders and his ever despairing security detail.

Follow in Hawke's wake as a reporter and virtually all one ever found were fans. And so it proved on the day the country sent the first contingent of soldiers off to Iraq.

"Hawkie shook my hand, he touched me here, he kissed me on the cheek, I'm not going to shower for a week," one of the mothers clutching children gushed.

"He asked after my grandmother, he remembered her from the teachers union, and said he was sorry to hear she had passed away," another threw in. "He wanted to know the names of my children. He posed for a picture with them. When I told him one of the kids was sick, he said he knew an asthma expert, and would get one of his staff to send me the details."

All of this and more from the devoted constituents left in his wake. Hawke didn't win four elections in a row without a gift.

During his entire time on board the naval ship, Alex heard not one whisper of doubt about the nature of Australia's involvement in Iraq.

Outside the heavily fortified Australian Navy docks at Woolloomooloo protestors waved placards and chanted anti-war slogans with little effect.

Journalism dignifies the extremities of any debate.

However few journalists bothered with the anti-war protestors on that day. Hawke had starved them of media oxygen and once again stolen the show.

The fact that he was sending soldiers to a dangerous and far off place where Australia had little business being purely to support the American Alliance was lost.

With no loss of life, and with Operation Desert Storm deemed a success and anti-war protestors marginalized, Hawke emerged from the conflict without apparent guilt or consequence.

No such easy absolution would exist for subsequent politicians leading Australia into Iraq.

****

One night at work late Alex lost his lighter; and so, craving nicotine, he wandered outside the 24-hour office where he worked and went looking for a light.

He ducked up to the corner of William and Bourke and bummed a light off a "tranny," this one young, would have made a pretty boy; but as a woman trapped inside a man's body, would forever be at the edge of societal reaches. Would never be accepted. She had the sad brazenness of many of her ilk. He liked them, these empathetic window panes between genders and social norms; had written about them at various times.

The thing that struck him the most from his research was that transgenders, far from being marginalized, were often valued and loved in cultures other than Christian, Muslim or Jewish, in countries where a vengeful Abrahamic God did not hold sway.

Alex exchanged a light for a cigarette; and then stood outside the Egyptian's 24-hour convenience store and watched as she bent down to negotiate a price with a passing silver-colored car, just as transsexuals had done for decades in that exact part of the city.

It had always been dangerous work; but now, with religious zealots roaming the streets, many of whom believed that transsexuals should be killed, beheaded, burnt alive or shoved off buildings, considerably more dangerous than ever before.

Alex could only hope that the young man/boy/woman/girl would not meet a violent end.

It was probably a wan hope. Most of them did not live long.

As he smoked outside the Egyptian's shop, listening to the sound of Arabic radio, he looked out across an almost deserted William Street; an occasional police car, an empty taxi, many of them, he suspected, working for someone else, the all-seeing eyes of any large city.

Tony Abbott had told the long-suffering people of Australia to go about their daily lives, not to let the terrorists win.

But that was not what was happening on the streets.

****

By late May of 2015 inner-city Sydney had been swept almost entirely clean; as if preparation for a terrorist attack.

On the streets of the Cross there was not even the usual assortment of vagrants, much less punters spilling from the clubs. There weren't even any drunks slumped in corners. At the main intersection in the Cross Alex passed a pile of abandoned clothes lying on the pavement, the last belongings of some fallen angel, the typical collection; as if, broken winged and flapping on the ground, they needed to cling to something from normalcy, a bag of dirty laundry.

But the fallen angel herself had already been swept away.

Just like the streets, swept, swept entirely clean.

Welcome to the Sharia.

It was as if the Muslim ban on entertainment was already in place.

The Islamists had won with barely a shot, barely an execution.

The police may have swept every vagrant and every prostitute from the streets; the bars might be empty, the roads deserted and the shops shuttered, but to get Biblical about it, no one knew the time and the place.

As any journalist knew, fear of a story was a far greater weapon than the story itself, fear of attack was a far greater weapon than the attack itself.

That was the power of fear.

Drunken kafir at play in the city's few fleshpots were not the only targets. The authorities could attempt to minimise the potential loss of life as much as they liked, there were always buses, ferries, trains, official functions, orchestrated community events.

As Alex walked the inner streets of Sydney, he often passed the old Darlinghurst Mental Hospital where the inspired Australian writer Henry Lawson had been repeatedly confined for alcoholism.

On the walls of the renovated building were engraved words from one of his poems, After All:

The light of passion in dreamy eyes, and a page of truth well read,
The glorious thrill in a heart grown cold of the spirit I thought was dead,
A song that goes to a comrade's heart, and a tear of pride let fall
And my soul is strong! and the world to me is a grand world after all!

Let our enemies go by their old dull tracks,
and theirs be the fault or shame
(The man is bitter against the world who has only himself to blame);
Let the darkest side of the past be dark, and only the good recall;
For I must believe that the world, my dear, is a kind world after all.

The poem was written in 1896.

They were optimistic lines from a not always optimistic man.

As he scanned the streets for danger, Alex wondered what Henry Lawson would have made of the coming Sharia, of the multiple failures of Australian democracy, of the vanquished fields of play in now darkened streets; whether he would have seen any grounds for optimism at all.

****

While Australia had been shocked and transfixed by the demolition of the World Trade Centre, it was the Bali bombings of 2002 which first genuinely brought the the new age of terror into Australian homes.

Eighty eight Australians were amongst the 202 people killed in the attack; with the dead including 38 Indonesians and 20 other nationalities. A suicide bomber detonated a bomb in his backpack, causing patrons to flee into the street. Twenty seconds later, a second bomb hidden inside a white van outside the Sari Bar opposite went off.

Horrific images of dismembered bodies, corpses lined up in makeshift morgues, the injured overwhelming local hospitals, distressed tourists fleeing the island; all of it flooded through the media and through all their lives; and on that news floor where he spent so much time.

It was a loss of innocence.

In *Australian Jihad* Chulov recorded the scene through the eyes of two federal police officers who happened to be in Bali at the time: "As they neared Jalan Legian, the main thoroughfare through Bali's party central, they saw people staggering towards them. Some appeared unhurt but shaken; others were wounded, their blackened, torn beach gear covered in blood; and yet more were cradling the scorched, lifeless bodies of friends and strangers... All around them was bedlam. Jagged glass, twisted pieces of metal and chunks of masonry littered the road. So too did something less familiar, pieces of human bodies. There were people dead in the ruins, and dying in the streets."

Dispatched by the newspaper to cover the aftermath, Chulov recorded the chaos of the morgues and hospitals, the bodies lined up in lines under the tin roof of an outdoor corridor, covered in white plastic.

As so often, it was the detail which told the story: "Body parts of those people who hadn't endured the blast intact were assembled in a pile under the thatched awning of an outdoor pagoda not far away. A charred arm seemed to be reaching desperately from the middle of the heap . . . It was the small things that really hammered the catastrophe home, such as the shoes piled a metre high on the footpath . . . Some still contained the remains of their owner's feet."

Mastermind of the Bali bombings, Indonesian cleric Abu Bakr Bashir, later to pledge allegiance to Islamic State, had been to Australia on at least 11 occasions prior to the Bali bombings, beginning in 1988, drumming up support for his terrorist group Jemaah Islamiah. He was treated with reverence as a senior cleric, provided accommodation, a driver and funds.

In reported comments he told one group of willing listeners it was a rejection of the faith to live quietly in a non-Muslim country: "The Islamic faithful in Australia must endeavour to bring about an Islamic state in Australia, even if it is 100 years from now." [93]

In an address at the Tempe mosque, a southern suburb snuggled in next to Sydney Airport, Bashir told a gathering: "An opportunity exists for us in Australia, and the conclusion of my preaching today is to invite all of you to strive to uphold the Islamic faith in this country, and to work towards the creation of an Islamic state in Indonesia. Do not

---

[93] Australian Jihad, Martin Chulov, Pan MacMillan, 2006.

let there be someone here who in their heart is not comfortable with the challenge. If you are not comfortable with the challenge you are not comfortable with your faith.

"If we are going to defend anybody we should defend Muslims. Outside of this people are our enemies and we have no sympathy for them. Even if we appear congenial on the outside, in our hearts we have no sympathy. May God bless the struggle of our brethren in Australia, who have demonstrated such loyalty, despite being surrounded by non-believers."

In a sermon given two weeks after the bombing, Chulov recorded that Bashir was resolute in his condemnation of the lifestyles of non-Muslims: "There was no show of sympathy for the victims from the Indonesian cleric, no softening of his rhetoric at a time when mercy could have been reasonably expected. Instead, Bashir seemed to use the moment as an opportunity to ram home the message that the holidaymakers on Bali who drank, danced and dallianced had through their behaviour invited this evil."

Alex had been working as a general news reporter on *The Australian's* news floor when the Bali bombings occurred that October of 2002.

It was his job, as befell lowly general news reporters after any disaster, to ring the relatives of the deceased, to knock on their doors, to extract whatever photographs and information was possible, to turn grief into print; to make private pain a consumable product.

Alex had been the first journalist on the phone to a father who had just been told by the Federal Police his son had been killed in the Bali Bombings. The man had literally just put down the phone when Alex rang. Too shocked to have put up any defenses, too soon for government media officers to move in to protect him, the man poured out his stunned disbelief, the only interview he was to give in those early days.

Pictures showed his son to be a well-educated, well-groomed young man in his early 20s, good looking, successful, happy, his whole life in front of him, clearly loved by his parents and his three brothers; a son that any father would have been proud of.

The family were clean cut, healthy, successful, decent, the sort of family Alex could only dream of creating.

Of all the death knocks he had done; as these terrible cold-calls were known, this was one that would stay in his memory forever.

But there had been other slabs of refracted horror in those days following those bombings in Kuta on the 12th October, 2002.

At Sydney Airport he had been part of the newspaper's determination to pursue every last single survivor as they flew in from Bali; the melee of the city's media determined to get whatever they could, to feed the maul of their ever demanding editors and chiefs of staff.

While the public liked to dismiss them as "vultures," as he had been called on more than one occasion, most journalists and photographers on these jobs are perfectly decent people; just doing their work, mostly boring, sometimes inspiring, often enough ethically compromising.

Already Alex was one of the oldest and most experienced general news reporters in the country; and it often fell to him to do the dirty jobs.

On that particular night, with people putting in long extra hours in the wake of the bombing, he was sent out to the airport with a photographer with one specific instruction: to get shots of a family with two young girls who were returning to Australia.

The children had not yet been told they had lost their mother in the bombings.

Renee Nowytager, a multi-award winner, a magnificent photographer to work with, was on duty that particular night. Neither of them liked the job; and both had concerns about the ethics involved. But concerns over what was right or what was wrong on any particular news job didn't always get you very far.

You either did the job, or found yourself another line of work.

The pair were old hands and knew all the secret security exits the airport guards used to hustle out high profile visitors; or in this case grieving families, giving them an advantage over many of the less experienced personnel from other news outlets.

As the airport security yelled abuse at them and the family pleaded to be left alone, they got the shot the paper wanted; the grieving family fleeing across the airport car park carrying the two young girls; causing great distress to them in the process.

They felt lousy about it; a job's a job but pursuing children who had just lost their mother across a car park was about as low as journalism went.

Later in the night, after having rushed back to the office to file for the first edition, the paper decided the pictures were too confronting and would cause distress to the family.

They could have told them that before being ordered to harass a family enduring some of the worst moments of their lives.

With the fear of terror having well and truly filtered into the Australian consciousness, on New Year's Eve of that same year, 2002,

Alex was dispatched to Bondi Beach for what some might unkindly call a "beat-up."

"Bondi had all the ingredients for another Bali disaster," he wrote. "Just as for the Sari Club, young people from all over the world have heard of the Bondi Hotel and the other bars and backpacker joints that occupy the checkered streets back from Australia's most famous beach.

"Just as Bali was the play place for the Australia's young and young at heart, so Bondi has become for the British.

"While their fellow countrymen freeze in the European winter, they come in their tens of thousands every summer for what has become an essential rite of passage.

"For these legions of the young, Bondi means only one thing – a good time before getting back on to the treadmill of work or university – sun, sex, and surf all rolled in to a whopping good time in a friendly place where the locals speak English and the exchange rate makes a cheap destination.

"That's exactly why Australians liked Bali. It's exactly why there were so many in the Sari Bar back on October 12."

The story ended with a quote from Ben Pavilion, a 21-year-old computer operator from Sussex, who said Bali was in the back of everybody's mind, but you couldn't stop living your life.

"Everyone comes here," he said. "It's the best place to be. We're all just having a good time, man."

Imram Samudra, one of the Bali bombers later executed for his role in the terror plot, described Bali as the immoral place in Indonesia and said the dignity of Islam and Muslims would be restored by removing Western influences.

In 2005 four Australians died in another series of attacks in popular tourist locations Bali.

But for the decade following, remarkable as it seemed, there were no further attacks.

Nor were there any attacks on Bondi Beach, no matter how obvious a target.

In 2015 the Australian government officially warned there was a high threat of a terrorist attack in Indonesia. A Department of Foreign Affairs statement read: "We continue to receive information that terrorists may be planning attacks in Indonesia, which could take place at any time."

****

Despite a largely pacifist anti-war population, in March of 2003, with Prime Minister John Howard in power, Australia participated in the US led coalition that invaded Iraq searching for weapons of mass destruction. This time around, the United Nations refused to authorize further military intervention.

John Howard was almost single-handedly responsible for taking Australia into Iraq, a decision made against the wishes of a significant proportion of the population; while his fiscal and social policies, including high immigration intakes and increased levels of business and personal taxation, significantly contributed to the hapless, ethnically, religiously and economically divided state of Australia in 2015.

Having learnt from Hawke's performance, Howard, just as had his political predecessors, won the day with shameless appeals to Australian nationalism.

History would not look kindly on what came to be known as the "mother mistake," the first and biggest of them all.

By one of those uncanny accidents of history, Howard had been in Washington at the time of the September 11 attacks in 2001.

For the first and only time in Australian history, on 17 September, 2001, he invoked the security provisions of the ANZUS Treaty between America and Australia, which required the two countries to come to each other's aid in the circumstances of an attack on home soil.

In what came to be regarded as one of his finest speeches, Howard told the Australian parliament: "The world has changed. We are all diminished, we are all changed, and we are all rather struggling with the concept that it will never be quite the same again. There is united, righteous, deep, seething anger around the world at present. But, as the months go by and as perhaps the early dividends of retaliatory action are not ready and not apparent, some of that anger may subside; and some may argue that the extra miles that are required to be travelled are not really worth it. But, if those who died last Tuesday are not, in the judgment of history, to have died in vain, there is an obligation on all of us to persevere, to travel the distance, to persist and to root out the evil that brought about those terrible deeds. But, in the process of responding, we must do so with care as well as with lethal force. We should understand that barbarism has no ethnicity and evil has no religion."

The course Howard, set with his speech and parliamentary resolution, took Australia to Afghanistan and Iraq. The commitment Howard made was not just to the alliance but to George W Bush. The "Push With Bush" was to impose great political costs on Howard and Tony Blair, and significant alliance burdens on their nations. Iraq divided Australian politics while, by contrast, the major parties maintained their consensus on the commitment to Afghanistan over the 13 years of what became Australia's longest war; and cost the lives of 41 Australian Defence Force personnel. [94]

Once again the anti-war movement was largely starved of oxygen.

Come 2015, there were few in Australia who did not see the country's involvement in the Iraq War of 2003 as a tragic blunder; a political and humanitarian disaster. Some estimates placed the number of civilian and military deaths at more than 600,000.

As counter terrorism expert David Kilcullen put it, the invasion of Iraq in 2003 was the greatest strategic mistake made by a major power since Hitler's invasion of Russia, a "collective madness." Since the war had gone so badly, Australians had a tendency to blame the Americans; but "it is as much our fault as anybody else's."

Referring to the increasingly dangerous situation in which Australian troops had been placed in 2015, he said: "Whatever we have been doing to date for the past ten months, it ain't working. ISIS would not exist except for the 2003 invasion. It is a creature of the invasion. It is a bit of a fantasy to think that we can keep our boys safe by keeping them behind the wire. The wire is not going to be much of a protection if this thing continues to escalate." [95]

Sheik Hilali, imam of the country's largest mosque at Lakemba and the most prominent Muslim spokesman of the time, told Alex in an interview on the occasion of his resignation: "Australia was seen as a potpourri of the world, as a bunch of roses, now it has a bad smell because of the foreign politics of the Howard government. The policy that aligned Australia to the US has brought us discredit and disgrace. I want to fight to have Australia stand on its own two feet."

But in Howard's time the conflict in Iraq was so distant, the deaths of the nation's soldiers so few, the rightness of the cause so confounding, most Australians had little sense of their country being involved in a war or in military operations far afield at all. And little understanding as to why.

The Army sent a 500 strong Special Forces team supported by three Chinook helicopters and a number of other military aircraft, including 14 FA/18 Hornets, while the Navy deployed three ships and a clearance diving team.

The cost to Australia of involvement in a war its people largely did not support was an estimated $5 billion.

---

[94] Great Australian foreign policy speeches: Howard on 9/11 and the US alliance, *The Interpreter*, 14 August, 2014.

[95] The Rise of ISIS and Its Threat: David Kilcullen in conversation with Robert Manne, La Trobe University Ideas and Society session at the Wheeler Centre, May, 2015.

The combat troops were withdrawn in 2003, but Australian troops were redeployed in 2005.

Also in 2005, Howard made front page news for all the wrong reasons. "Police taped terror plot to kill Howard," ran one headline.

Action and reaction.

The story concerned two Melbourne terror suspects who discussed killing John Howard and his family, launching a large-scale attack at a football game and causing carnage at a train station as part of a religious war in Australia.

Surveillance transcripts between Muslim cleric Abdul Nacer Benbrika, 46, and Abdulla Merhi, 20, were tendered to court.

"If they kill our kids, we kill little kids," Benbrika said. "We send a message back to them. That's it, an eye for an eye. You shouldn't just kill one or two or three. Do a big thing, like Spain." A reference to the 191 people who were killed when ten bombs exploded on four Madrid trains.

That the country had no allegiance to a shambolic Iraqi government, that Australia's security interests were, if anything, compromised rather than buttressed by military involvement, that previous operations had been largely against the will of the people, and had on a number of counts been ineffective and counterproductive, none of it seemed to matter.

John Howard, who lost power in 2007, had been unable to fix many of the country's bureaucratically enhanced social problems and questions of governance, held more than 100 parliamentary inquiries without instituting a single one of their recommendations, segued and double-danced his way through controversial issues from global warming to family law without providing leadership, destroyed much of the nation's raffish character with obeisance to bureaucratic creeds and chained the nation's businesses with ridiculously complex legislation including the Goods and Services Tax.

But he could take the country to war in an instant.

The diminutive Australian had been famously welcomed at George Bush's ranch, and media and government flunkies touted the friendship between the two leaders. More than a decade later, Howard finally admitted embarrassment at the lack of Weapons of Mass Destruction, but disingenuously denied the deteriorating circumstances in Iraq and the rise of the Islamic State had anything to do with actions of the past. And refused to actually apologize to the Australian people for taking them to war on a lie, the non-existent WMD.

Alex had always been privately opposed to Australia's involvement in Iraq, partly just a reflexive anti-war sentiment from his student days during the Vietnam War. Partly because he just could not see how the invasion of a sovereign country was justifiable, or in any case what a conflict on the other side of the globe had anything to do with a remote country like Australia. Occam's Razor, the simplest truth is the best truth: "What's it got to do with us?"

****

Action and reaction.

Also in 2005 came news of what was then the largest counter terrorism operation in Australian history, named Operation Pendennis.

The leading figure in the planned terrorist attacks was radical Melbourne Muslim cleric Abdul Nacir Benbrika, who had been caught on surveillance tapes saying they were planning "something big"; saying he wanted to kill thousands of Australians: "We'll damage buildings. Blast things. Thinking big not small." [96]

Targets were alleged to include the Melbourne Cricket Ground on Grand Final Day and the city's leading Crown Casino, along with Sydney's Holsworthy Army Barracks and the Lucas Heights nuclear reactor.

Benbrika was due for release in November, 2017, and faces deportation under new citizenship laws introduced by the Abbott government. Counter terrorism officers said he had continued to radicalise supporters while in jail, some of whom were now fighting for Islamic State in the Middle East.

Much of the detail of the case would not be revealed to the general public for many years, following the issuing of 21 suppression orders by the Victorian Supreme Court. The orders were not to be lifted until 2011.

Suppression orders were meant to ensure a fair trial, but as far as Alex was concerned often gifted additional powers they did not deserve to the legal profession and limited the flow of vital information to the public.

The operation came after a tip-off from a member of Melbourne's Muslim community and another tip-off from a Sydney chemist concerned about the quantity of chemicals being purchased which could be used for making explosives.

ASIO and the Australian Federal Police, as well as Victorian and NSW police, were involved in uncovering the plots.

---

[96] MCG bomb plot terror chief faces deportation, Keith Moor, *Herald Sun*, 17 February, 2015.

The foiling of the potentially largest terror attacks in Australian history was seen as perhaps the greatest triumphs of Australia's security forces.

Eight men were arrested in Melbourne and another seven in Sydney.

Greg Barton of the Global Terrorism Research Centre at Monash University said: "The broad overall effect of both of the Pendennis cells, the Melbourne and Sydney cells, was that this was the most comprehensive and serious terrorist plot so far. It appears that some of the men knew much more about what was going on than others, and in particular, four men in Melbourne were in regular contact with their colleagues in Sydney and appeared to be very knowingly well down the path towards preparation for terror." [97]

After a lengthy trial process, in 2009 Benbrika and seven of his Melbourne followers were found guilty of planning a terrorist attack on Australian soil. Later the same year five Sydney men were found guilty of planning the same attack, and four men pleaded guilty to lesser charges.

Just prior to his arrest Benbrika told the Australian Broadcasting Corporation: "I am not involved in anything here. I am teaching my brothers here the Koran and the Sunnah and I'm trying my best to keep myself, my family, my kids and the Muslims close to this religion." [98]

One member of the Sydney cell, Khaled Sharrouf, after his release in 2009, became notorious for joining Islamic State in the Middle East and having his 7-year-old son pose with the decapitated heads of Syrian soldiers. He used his brother's passport to slip the country.

In 2005, hours after the Pendennis raids, then NSW Police Commissioner Ken Moroney said authorities had "disrupted a large-scale operation which, had it been allowed to go through to fruition, we certainly believe would have been catastrophic."

Prime Minister John Howard told Sydney radio: "The idea that terrorists are people that are flown in from another country to do their wicked deeds and then flown out is completely altered."

On the same day one of those arrested, known as Yusef C, told police the Prime Minister had struck no fear in their hearts, and they would destroy the wrongdoers: "The annihilator of the tyrants and of the infidels, this is who we worship, who do you worship, Howard and the legislations? Your democracy, full of hypocrisy, is that it?

---

[97] Two terrorist cells worked together to plot attacks, ABC, 19 September, 2011.

[98] Two terrorist cells worked together to plot attacks, Alison Caldwell, ABC, 20 September, 2011.

"We worship Allah ... Sharia law is gonna prevail throughout this land, it's gonna be ruled by it, you tell Howard this, tell him Islam is gonna rule this land. Sharia law, Sharia law, you poofter, Sharia law, go and learn about it because you are us. The land, all the lands, all the lands is Allah's lands, Allah created it and he's given it to the Muslims. The one and only law that's worthy, worthy of ruling mankind, no democracy rubbish. It's full of shit. So you tell Howard this and pass it on to Bush the motherfucker."

In 2014, just prior to the country going on to high terror alert, came reports that members and relatives of the cells were a continuing threat.

Journalist Rachel Olding wrote: "A new generation of radical young Sydney Muslims is carrying forward the extreme beliefs of its elders, with frightening vigour. Almost a decade after their arrest, much of the most comprehensive terrorism cell in Australian history continues to menace the country with the same messages of violence and anti-Western hate, which are being spread either by cell members or some of their close relatives. Close relatives of the Sydney cell's ringleader Khaled Cheikho and his nephew Moustafa Cheikho, who are both in a high-risk prison unit, continue to pose a security threat to Australia, authorities believe."

In his sentencing remarks in 2009, Judge Anthony Whealy said the cell members showed little remorse and few signs of deradicalization. Many "wear their imprisonment like some kind of badge of honour," he said.

A court found all nine Sydney cell members had vast quantities of extremist material, including thousands of images and videos of executions, and they shared the same violent hatred of non-believers and intolerance of Australia. [99]

As Martin Chulov wrote in *Australian Jihad*, in 2004, when the tip-off for Pendennis first came in the Australian security agencies were still in the fledgling phases of understanding how best to conduct counter terrorism operations. They were short on Arabic speakers; and found it difficult to calibrate the difference between incitement to terror and the freedom of speech they tolerated.

The impact of the home-grown jihadi phenomenon had well and truly rattled Australia's security apparatus and the impact of the operation would resonate for years to come.

"As had happened in the United States, Britain, Europe and Asia," Chulov wrote, "Australia's police and intelligence agencies had been

[99] Terrifying legacy emerges from success of Operation Pendennis, Rachel Olding, The Sydney Morning Herald, 24 August, 2015.

slow to catch on to the global jihad evolution. And when they finally did sense the danger, they struggled to match it with the jihadis who threatened Australians' very way of life. It wasn't a failure rooted in a lack of interest or a disregard for an escalating situation. The inability of the West generally to get on top of the emerging threat can be attributed to a failure to apply one of the basic tenets of warfare – to know one's enemy." [100]

****

Everything was connected, or God spoke through coincidence, as the saying went.

In 2015 Alex became involved in the publication of a book *America's Destruction of Iraq* by a West Point graduate Michael O'Brien.

If his private views that Australia had no business being in Iraq needed any further confirmation, that book proved it.

America's Destruction of Iraq was particularly interesting for being written by a staunch conservative rather than a liberal academic; and could not have been more critical of America's adventurism in Iraq.

O'Brien was a former political appointee in the administration of George W. Bush, and had an abiding contempt for the political and military mismanagement of the Iraq War, officially referred to as Operation Iraqi Freedom. A graduate of West Point and former Infantry officer, O'Brien saw the Iraq War from the inside out—not as a soldier but as a contractor advising the new Iraqi Army and Ministry of Defence on base and facility reconstruction, and acquisition of land and Forward Operating Bases originally built for Coalition forces.

One of the farces of the war was that those bases were built without any proper land title. It seemingly never occurred to anyone in the administration that the land on which military facilities were being built might already be owned by an Iraqi, who soon enough would want their land back.

"Compounding in outrage, compelling in detail," as Alex had written for the book's press release.

O'Brien condemned the waste of tens of billions of U.S. taxpayer dollars and the needless loss of American and Iraqi lives.

He argued: "The Bush administration's desire for war was built on fabrication and the political agendas of its senior advisors. But it is the generals for which O'Brien saves his greatest disdain because they should have known how to properly execute the war, and the courage to tell their political superiors the truth.

---

[100] Australian Jihad, Martin Chulov, Pan MacMillan, 2006.

"*America's Destruction of Iraq* is a detailed example of the 'military-industrial complex' President Eisenhower warned America of in 1961. In a way only a contractor with a military and political background who was at the heart of America's reconstruction of Iraq could do, O'Brien exposes military intervention in Iraq for what it is: a disaster equal to or worse than the quagmire of the Vietnam War. Americas Destruction of Iraq details the deception and mismanagement of America's involvement in Iraq since 1991, and continuing through to the present day."

And Australia had gone right along for the ride.

****

In the increasingly racially and religiously charged world post September 11 and the invasions of Iraq and Afghanistan, the atmosphere of the city darkened.

Many people believed that Sydney would see a terrorist attack – and probably sooner rather than later.

Distrust of Muslim minorities intensified; and was promptly returned in full.

The city's talk back radio shows went feral.

The "if you're not happy here go back where you came from" sentiment was a feature of talk back radio. "They're like black flies buzzing in the ceiling, threatening to take over," one caller declared.

Then Prime Minister John Howard bought into the heightened tensions over Australia's immigration rates by announcing that prospective immigrants would have to pass a basic knowledge or "citizenship" test. Alex had been sent out to vox pop anybody he could corner at Central Station, five minutes from the office. No need to go too far.

The story observed that: "Most Australians approached by this newspaper yesterday would have failed a basic citizenship test. They could not cite the citizenship pledge, did not know the five fundamental freedoms of Australians, did not know any of their basic responsibilities as citizens and could not guess the year of Federation."

All those we questioned knew that John Howard was the Prime Minister, could describe the Australian flag and understood it was compulsory for Australian citizens to vote.

Many could not name the Australian floral emblem, the wattle, and had little idea of the country's population size, 20 plus million.

Many also did not know the year in which Captain Cook claimed Australia for Great Britain (1770), or the year in which British settlers first arrived (1788).

But not one of them could repeat the pledge expected of new citizens: "From this time forward, under God, I pledge my loyalty to Australia and its people whose democratic beliefs I share."

Nor did they know that the five basic freedoms of Australians were: freedom of speech, association, assembly, religion and movement.

****

Sydney's first race riots in December of 2005 led the evening news bulletins, were plastered over the nation's front pages and made international news. The riots erupted on one of Sydney's most southern beaches, Cronulla. Volunteer surf lifesavers had been assaulted by a group of young men of "Middle Eastern appearance." There were violent incidents on buses, trains and in surrounding suburbs during the following weeks.

It was not an easy job to cover, and multiple reporters were assigned to the task, Alex being one of them.

On the Sunday following the first outbreak of violence, as reporters struggled to work out the best vantage points to cover the unfolding drama, the crowd, fueled by alcohol and years of simmering, unfocused, unformulated resentments, turned violent.

Messages circulated among Cronulla residents called on them to "reclaim the beaches," while countering texts urged the "Lions of Lebanon" to fight.

The tribal groups of white Anglo-Saxon surfers born and bred on the beaches were angry over the behavior of some of the Lebanese men coming in from the Western suburbs. From a culture where modesty was emphasized, the gauche reactions of Lebanese men to the scantily clad women sunning themselves and flirting blatantly with their boyfriends, or let's face it, sometimes with each other, were a scene of adolescent, testosterone fueled fantasy almost beyond imagining.

The beach tribes and the Lebanese lads came from different worlds.

In Australia, the second, third, fourth generation whatever Anglo Saxons accustomed to the blazing white heat and the vivid coloring of the beaches in summer were immured to the sight of exposed flesh; accustomed to the brief-flash flesh dreams of suntanned, exposed curves of both men and women; thought nothing of it.

But in a place like Sydney, where the communities of the city were divided by ethnicity and religion, a journey from the Western suburbs to those in the East could cover just as big a cultural crossing as the Bosporus.

The youth of Western Sydney, coming from strict Islamic cultures, were entirely unused to seeing exposed flesh. To them, making that often rare trip to a place they felt they did not belong, to the Australian beaches, was an entry into Sodom and Gomorrah, to a place of licentiousness and decadence they had only heard the preachers at their local mosques tell of in scandalized and cautionary tones.

It would never cross their minds to marry a woman who would do such a thing; bare their flesh to strangers.

The Sunday following the first outbreaks of tension, when, as usual, Alex was working, a crowd of more than 5,000 Cronulla residents and their supporters had gathered by midday. It was the largest and most violent backlash against Muslim minorities the country had ever seen.

In an attempt to quell tensions hundreds of police lined all the roads on the way in to the beach, searched the cars for weapons, and turned back anyone they thought posed even the slightest threat.

That was one occasion when Alex and the photographer, Renee again, prominently posted the sign "Media" on the front windscreen of their news car. Access and position was, as always, everything.

A 33-year-old man became the first person to be charged for inciting racial violence by forwarding text messages.

A man "of Middle Eastern appearance" was surrounded by a crowd outside a Cronulla hotel and attacked.

Local, state and federal government apparatus went into propaganda overdrive to try and quell a situation deteriorating by the day.

Ultimately some 300 people were arrested. The flow of suspects through Sydney's old sandstone building the Central Local Court kept reporters and photographers busy for weeks.

There was a strong police presence on Sydney's sun drenched beaches throughout the normally peaceful Christmas and New Year periods.

Alex was repeatedly sent out to Cronulla to monitor the situation.

The removal of an Australian flag from the roof of a Returned Services League clubhouse and its burning in front of a crowd of 150 men was incendiary.

New anti-terror laws granting police additional powers were rushed through parliament.

Men gathered outside the Lakemba mosque, inflamed by rumours there was going to be an attack on the mosque itself.

"I haven't seen so many weapons since Beirut," one man said.

Muslim spokesman Keysar Trad said: "What we have seen over the past few days has no place in Australia. It is something you would expect in a barbaric, savage country. We can all celebrate our differences and love of this country."

For months politicians struggled to deal with or accept the origins of Sydney's racial tensions, papering over the social and ethnic divides.

A year on from the riots, in December 2006, Alex was once again sent out at Cronulla; to report what was basically a non-story: "Beyond the extra police, including riot squad and mounted police, and a few members of the Australia First party, there were few signs that the area was once a focus of conflict between local Anglo-Saxons and Muslims from other parts of the city.

"Most locals just want to put the whole sad episode behind them.

"The occasional Australian flag, perhaps controversial in the circumstances, fluttered from the front of flats and units. One dog wore sunglasses and an Australian flag tucked into its collar.

"Beyond that, it was another quiet day at the beach."

****

Ethnic tensions and misunderstandings increased throughout the early years of the new millenium, and with the clashing state creeds of multiculturalism and feminism, much of it had to do with gender.

The Australian newspaper where Alex had worked for so many years was front and centre of one of the major contretemps.

Sheik Taj All-din Hilali gave a weekly address to Muslim women at the Lakemba mosque in Sydney'as west.

The sermons were broadcast on Muslim radio.

Hilali's sin had been to suggest that the scantily clad women on the country's beaches were akin to leaving uncovered meat out for a dog. In other words, or at least in the way the mufti's critics interpreted the matter, these women were asking to be raped.

Arabic was a language of strong imagery; and could easily be misinterpreted in translation.

Barely concealed nudity had been part of Australia's beach culture since the 1960s; and the Sheik's comments were seen as a full frontal assault on Australia's way of life and as offensive to women, at a time of increasing ethnic tensions.

The story was "broken" by journalist Richard Kerbaj, an Arabic speaker of Lebanese Christian background. He won the most prestigious prize in Australian journalism for his efforts, a Walkley Award; although in reality he had to do little research but listen to the radio.

As far as Alex was concerned, the story was a nonsense. Many Christian denominations also encouraged modesty of dress and did not support the liberal dress codes of Australian beaches. It wasn't all that long past in Australian history when women were forbidden in front bars of hotels; contained to the Lady's Lounges at the back. But in the trample to secular enlightenment, the country's own modest past was forgotten.

Another Sunday for Monday, another news organization desperate for news. *The Australian* ran the story on the front page that Monday in 2006. And the country promptly went mad; a media driven picnic of racial and ethnic hysteria.

As always, talk back radio lit up.

Gatherings of journalists parked outside the Lakemba Mosque were demanding an interview with the bewildered Sheik, who had not had any intention of provoking a controversy.

Hilali was a polite man with a devoted family who had founded the Australian Muslim Women's Association. The attacks were perceived by his many followers as entirely unfair.

For day after day in the baking sun, Alex had been a part of the horde of reporters and photographers gathered outside Australia's largest mosque.

Police were in prominent attendance. Journalists were warned they were not safe. The taxpayer funded Australian Broadcasting Corporation hired security for their reporter, much to the amusement of everybody else.

On that Monday morning Sheik Hilali had appeared much more subdued than Alex had ever seen him. He had read the headlines describing him as a "heartless ignorant man" who should be sacked and deported.

"My comments are misunderstood," he told the attacking media throng in the following days. "I respect the lady in Australian society. Australia is a free country."

Sheik Hilali apologized for the misunderstanding and said his speech had been intended for Muslim women in Australia.

At the height of the furore, having spent days waiting for the Sheik to do something, anything, Alex described the scene at Friday prayers for the Saturday edition of the paper: "While the rest of the country expressed outrage at his comments, Taj Din al-Hilali enjoyed rock star status when he arrived at Lakemba Mosque.

"He was smiling when he exited Sydney's now infamous mosque, clearly buoyed by the backing he had received inside, where 5000 worshippers shouted their support during the midday service.

"He was surrounded by more than 200 fervent supporters as he made his way to a waiting car."

Asked if he would resign, Hilali said: "After we clean the world of the White House."

The crowd erupted in applause.

Minutes before Hilali had implored thousands of worshippers not to attack the waiting media pack, but to be polite, smile and walk away.

His followers did exactly as they were told.

Many of those dispersing from the mosque carried a flyer from Hizb ut-Tahrir that described the controversy surrounding the Sheik's comments as the latest chapter in Australia's demonization of Islam and the Muslim community.

The flyer read: "In an age of heightened hysteria generated as part of the 'war on terror,' the media and politicians of all persuasions have wasted no time inflaming popular sentiment concerning the question of Islam and its role in Australian society."

****

As a young man Alex had taken every opportunity to travel.

He stayed several times at a beach on Penang island known as Batu Ferringhi.

In the 1970s it was little more than a haphazard shanty town strung along a beach; but by 2015 was a major resort lined with high rise hotels.

Back then he had always liked the feel of disembarking from the rattly bus that travelled from the town, when he had invariably sat squashed in with the local villagers and their chickens and their cheerful chatter.

He would often visit a Muslim village a little way inland, set on the floor of a valley surrounded by steep flanked hills, sit and have tea, watching the goings on of village life. One day, there were always children squalling everywhere, the boys, well young teenagers they were, approached him at the tea shop with enormous excitement.

They had a plan that would make Alex's day, make every body's day. They could barely contain themselves with the delight they felt as they whispered their daring scheme in schoolboy English.

They had spotted one of their school friends secretively borrowing a blanket from the back of his mother's house.

They all knew he was sweet on a neighborhood girl.

They surmised, particularly after they had spied on the movements of the girl, that the pair were going to sneak off into the steep forests that surrounded the village: and kiss!!!!

In a society like that, fornication was something beyond comprehension; but to see a girl and a boy kissing; Allah could not be more kind.

And thus it was, that Alex found himself climbing up slippery, narrow paths through a rain forest in a queue of 10 or so adolescents; it was a steep climb, and took almost an hour, but the group knew the spot the couple were likely to be heading for.

And then, they rounded the corner of the steep path, and there they were, the young couple, in a clearing, fully clothed, sitting on the blanket borrowed from a washing line, staring doe like into each others eyes on the opposite side of a ravine, caught in a patch of sunlight breaking through the trees.

They were so entranced with each other that they never noticed the gang of excited boys.

The queue all made shushing gestures, absolute silence had to be maintained.

And then the most extraordinary thing happened: the young couple kissed.

The boys were agog with excitement.

As an honored guest, Alex was shuffled to the top of the queue, so that he, too, could get a good view.

And sure enough, there they were, the young couple, doing that most daring of things: kissing.

After ten minutes or so, worried that they would be spotted by their friend, the group turned around and inched back down the steep slope.

As soon as they were out of hearing range, they burst into wild whoops of laughter; and all the way down the steep slopes, kept breaking into laughter.

They wanted to know if people who were not married did this in Alex's country.

Kissed before marriage?

He replied yes; and their eyes grew rounder still.

And then, when they finally all got down to the flat valley where the village lay, they went back to the tea-shop. Laughing and laughing with delight; they had never seen anything so extraordinary; done anything quite so naughty.

Alex was under strict instructions not to tell any of their parents, with whom he was friendly, what they had done.

He promised; and as the afternoon wore on, they would disappear back into their own houses, only to appear a few minutes later and come over to where he sat at the tea shop, and secretively, so no adults in the village would find out, reprise the whole event, and giggle and giggle and giggle.

Life could not have been better, God more kind, it could not have been a more wonderful day.

****

In September of 2014 fears of attacks by fundamentalist Islamists had yet to be realized. One of the only elements of surprise within Australia was that security and intelligence forces had unto that point successfully thwarted plans for terrorist attacks on Australian soil.

On the 18th of September more than 800 officers from the AFP and NSW Police Force conducted 25 search warrants across Sydney in the suburbs of Beecroft, Bellavista, Guildford, Merrylands, Northmead, Wentworthville, Marsfield, Westmead, Castle Hill, Revesby, Bass Hill and Regents Park. It was the largest counter terrorism operation in Australian history.

The raids reportedly brought to a halt plans to carry out random beheadings in Sydney and Brisbane, drape the victims in the Islamic State flag, film the executions and have the videos distribution by the Islamic State's media arm.

Sixteen people were detained. [101]

Members of the Sydney Muslim community attended a rally in Lakemba organized by Hizb ut-Tahir on the same day waving placards "Raids terrorise women and children" and "We won't stand by as Muslims are vilified." One organiser said: "Let me say clearly even if a single bomb went off even if a thousand bombs went off in this country all it will prove is that Muslims are angry."

In response to the news founder of Murdoch University's Security, Terrorism and Counter terrorism studies program Sam Makinda said "having supported the invasion of Afghanistan in 2001, Iraq in 2003 and so on, Australia had long ago painted itself as a target." [102]

Senior Gold Coast imam Imraan Husain said the decision to send Australian soldiers to the Middle East was marginalizing Muslim youth. "It takes them towards radicalisation," he said.

The raids were as a result of contacts with the group from from Mohammad Ali Baryalei, 33, Australia's most senior Islamic State member, who was in the Middle East. He had allegedly called contacts in Australia and asked them to carry out the a campaign.

---

[101] AFP Media Release 18 September, 2014.

[102] Australian Police Foil Islamist Terror Plot, TIME, Ian Lloyd Neubaeur, 18 September, 2014.

The Prime Minister declared the exhortations to commit violent acts against members of the public were "quite direct exhortations, were coming from an Australian who is apparently quite senior in ISIL to networks of support back in Australia to conduct demonstration killings here in this country." [103]

Baryalei had a long and colorful history in the part of Sydney that Alex knew well, Kings Cross. He had been a former bouncer come spruiker at The Love Machine strip club and had a reputation as a drug user.

In April of 2013 he travelled to Syria; where authorities claimed he began fighting for the notoriously violent jihadist group Jabhat Al Nusra, later switching to Islamic State. Authorities suggested that he had recruited half of the 60 Australians who at that point had travelled to the Middle East to fight with Islamic State.

Baryalei began life as a member an aristocratic Afghani family with historic connections to the last King of Afghanistan. His family fled the country after the Russian invasion and he arrived in Australia at the age of seven.

A video produced before the raids shows him exhorting his followers: "Islam means submission to the one true God and the Muslim is the slave of God."

A subsequent investigation by the ABC labeled Baryalei as a "drug-abusing brothel tout with underworld connections who found radical Islam after years of physical abuse and mental illness." [104]

"He was a big party animal," a former friend told the ABC. ""He drank a lot, was a big smoker, he liked drugs, loved women and could be violent. He was protective of his friends and that could make him very violent. He gambled a lot ... He once won $8,000 or $9,000 on the pokies, then played it back down ... and he loved cocaine."

Severely depressed in 2009, Baryalei began attending the mosque and following Islamic preachers on YouTube. He grew a beard, studied the Koran and developed a disdain for Western culture. He became the front-man for a global preaching movement called Street Dawah, devoted to converting people to Islam. It is believed to have operated as a major recruiter for those wanting to travel to the Middle East for jihad.

---

[103] Australia's most senior Islamic State member 'arranged for random beheadings in Sydney, Brisbane, Karl Hoerr, Lucy Carter and Staff, ABC, 18 September, 2014.

[104] Mohammed Ali Baryalei: Australia's most senior Islamic State member loved cocaine, Sean Rubinsztein-Dunlop, ABC, 25 September, 2014.

In a video recorded a day after anger against an anti-Islam film led to riots in Sydney's Hyde Park, he begged Allah to make him and his followers "shaheed," or martyrs, and declared his mission to expose the failings of the Western world.

"Our purpose is to better the community because where we are living, the community is not good. There's landmines all around us and what are the landmines? Pornography, alcohol, drugs, prostitution, brothels, girls ... violence, crime."

Of Baryalei terror expert Greg Barton said: "The fact that he's got at least 30 young Australians to join him is, for a guy who seems in many ways quite unremarkable is a remarkable achievement. And he's certainly not senior, but he's rising through the ranks, as indeed are a number of foreign fighters." [105]

Baryalei would get his wish to become a martyr, with reports he was killed by allied airstrikes in October of 2014. Whether they were Australian bombs that killed him would probably never be revealed.

Omarjan Azari, 22, was accused of conspiring with Mr Baryalei and others to act in preparation or plan a terrorist act or acts.

During the raids in Brisbane police arrested suspects who had machetes, swords, balaclavas and military fatigues, allegedly in preparation for carrying out simultaneous attacks.

The ABC reported that police made their move to disrupt the group of mostly Afghan Australians 48 hours after a phone call which the Prime Minister described as a direct exhortation to conduct demonstration killings.

Commonwealth prosecutor Michael Allnutt told Sydney's Central Local Court the alleged offense was "clearly designed to shock, horrify and terrify the community."

Allnutt said there was a plan to commit extremely serious offences that involved an unusual level of fanaticism. He told the court the arrests were "an immediate reaction to a clear, imperative danger."

The front and back gardens of a number of at least some of the 24 properties were excavated; and at least one property was examined with metal detectors.

The swoop took place on the same day that 10 Australian military aircraft, 400 support personnel and 200 special-forces troops were dispatched to the United Arab Emirates as part of the US-led coalition against IS militants in Syria and Iraq.

As the raids were being conducted Abbott told members of the Australian Defence Force heading to the Middle East: "You are

---

[105] Islamic State release 'a game changer' warns terrorism expert, Leigh Sales, ABC, 22 September, 2014.

deploying in preparation for combat operations, but it is an essentially humanitarian mission to disrupt and degrade the operations of ISIL, and in so doing, to protect the people of Iraq, but more than that, in so doing, to protect the people of the wider world, including Australia.

"Regrettably, around the world and in this country itself, there are people who would do us harm. There are people who hate who we are and how we live. They hate our freedom, our tolerance, our democracy. You are there to protect us. You are the long, strong arm of Australia."

****

The day after the largest ever counter terrorism operations in the Australia's history, Abbott informed the public: "Earlier this month, I was advised of chatter amongst these terrorist networks of a potential attack on Government, government people, Parliament House. In response, I spoke with the presiding officers. I commissioned an urgent review of security at Parliament House. On receipt of that review, I wrote immediately to the presiding officers asking them to implement this review. That implementation is now taking place and as a result of that review the Australian Federal Police will be in charge of not just the external security of Parliament House but the internal security as well. There will be armed Australian Federal Police present in and around our national parliament at all times." [106]

As Australia was marching off to war in the Middle East, so Islamic State were taking it to the West, with renewed calls for attacks on Australia.

A statement from the official spokesman Abu Muhammad Al-Adnani stated: "O Americans, and O Europeans, the Islamic State did not initiate a war against you, as your governments and media try to make you believe. It is you who started the transgression against us, and thus you deserve blame and you will pay a great price. You will pay the price when your economies collapse. You will pay the price when your sons are sent to wage war against us, and they return to you as disabled amputees, or inside coffins, or mentally ill. You will pay the price as you are afraid of travelling to any land. Rather you will pay the price as you walk on your streets, turning right and left, fearing the Muslims. You will not feel secure even in your bedrooms. You will pay the price when this crusade of yours collapses, and thereafter we will strike you in your homeland, and you will never be able to harm anyone afterwards. You will pay the price, and we have prepared for you what will pain you.

---

[106] Official Transcript, Prime Minister's Web Site, Joint Press Conference, Sydney, 19 September, 2014.

"So O muwahhid, do not let this battle pass you by wherever you may be. You must strike the soldiers, patrons, and troops of the tawaghit. Strike their police, security, and intelligence members, as well as their treacherous agents. Disrupt their sleep. Embitter their lives for them and busy them with themselves. If you can kill a disbelieving American or European – especially the spiteful and filthy French – or an Australian, or a Canadian, or any other disbeliever from the disbelievers waging war, including the citizens of the countries that entered into a coalition against the Islamic State, then rely upon Allah, and kill him in any manner or way however it may be. Do not ask for anyone's advice and do not seek anyone's verdict. Kill the disbeliever whether he is civilian or military, for they have the same ruling. Both of them are disbelievers. Both of them are fighters, so it is permitted to shed their blood and take their money."

Australian terrorism expert Greg Barton told the ABC: "I was chilled because, surprisingly, it's beautiful. It's lyrical like an Old Testament prophet. And I'm very, very worried about the persuasive power it's going to have on young people, including young Australians. I think this is quite a game-changer. It means that IS is now turning its energy outwards and is going to usurp the role of al-Qaeda and I think we're seeing a lot of challenges coming from this. Adnani speaks sparingly. It's only every couple of months we hear from him … but his messages are devastatingly effective." [107]

In the October issue of *Dabiq*, under the title Indeed Your Lord is Ever Watchful, Islamic State declared: "At this point of the crusade against the Islamic State, it is very important that attacks take place in every country that has entered into the alliance against the Islamic State, especially the US, UK, France, Australia, and Germany. Rather, the citizens of crusader nations should be targeted wherever they can be found. Let the muwahhid not be affected by "analysis paralysis" and thus abandon every operation only because his waswās (whispers from Satan) and "perfectionism" pushes him towards an operation that supposedly can never fail – one that only exists theoretically on paper. He should be pleased to meet his Lord even if with just one dead kafir's name written in his scroll of deeds, as the Prophet (sallallahu 'alayhi wa sallam) said, "A kafir and his killer will never gather in Hellfire" [Sahih Muslim].

"Every Muslim should get out of his house, find a crusader, and kill him. It is important that the killing becomes attributed to patrons of the Islamic State who have obeyed its leadership. Otherwise, crusader media makes such attacks appear to be random killings.

---

[107] Islamic State release 'a game changer' warns terrorism expert, Leigh Sales, ABC, 22 September, 2014.

"Secrecy should be followed when planning and executing any attack. The smaller the numbers of those involved and the less the discussion beforehand, the more likely it will be carried out without problems. One should not complicate the attacks by involving other parties, purchasing complex materials, or communicating with weak-hearted individuals. "Rely upon Allah and stab the crusader" should be the battle cry for all Islamic State patrons." [108]

The lone wolf call.

****

By mid-2015, along with other commentators, counter terrorism expert David Kilcullen was arguing Islamic State was increasingly looking like a government which utilized terror rather than a terrorist organization per se: "Islamic State controls territory and population, governs cities, levies taxes, disposes of substantial economic and military resources, and is in the process of redrawing the map of the entire Middle East through aggressive (largely conventional) military conquest.

"It does have an international terrorist network as well, and its reach on social media — along with its ability to radicalise people in the West and draw recruits from across the world — is dangerous.

"But its most threatening aspect of its state-like nature, which has turned a longstanding Sunni-Shia cold war into a hot conflict that is dragging in regional and global powers such as Iran, Turkey, Israel, the Gulf states, Saudi Arabia, Russia and, of course, the US and allies including Australia, New Zealand, Canada and Britain, along with several European countries. At least five of these states are present or threshold nuclear powers, so that — in a worst-case scenario — the escalating regional conflagration centred on Iraq and Syria even carries the ultimate risk of a nuclear exchange.

"What is clear is that we need to start treating Islamic State as what it is — more than just a terrorist group or an extremist death cult but, rather, something that looks increasingly like what it claims to be: a state." [109]

As extremely clever as Kilcullen was, there were points with which Alex could not agree.

A military man, Kilcullen came up with military solutions.

The problem was, as Alex saw it, and as the Muslims themselves said, was that you could not bomb an idea; and the further escalation of the conflict could only make a diabolical situation worse.

---

[108] Dabiq Issue 4, 1435.

[109] How to Defeat Islamic State, David Kilcullen, *The Australian*, May, 2015.

The more you attempted to destroy it, the further the idea of jihad would spread, a perhaps vile, certainly brutal plasma of spiritual insanity and dark worship of even darker lords and jealous gods splashing out across national borders, a spiritual malady originating with Abraham, curdling through the excesses of the Christian church, including the Inquisition, and now inflaming Muslims across the world, transforming and changing as it spread.

In those feverishly calm hours of the early morning there came the voice: "The only solution is a magical one."

In other words, in a theological debate, in a world under threat from fanaticism and religious zeal, with notions of God and the purity of belief, of the power of the infinite, of the Lord of the Worlds driving blind obedience and horrific massacre, inflamed by the West's own Christian zealotry, military missteps and self-righteous but nonetheless barbaric murder by high-tech drone, only the divine, or divine argument would implement the necessary change; a different world, a world before the Abrahamic God gripped the imagination, stole the souls of millions.

As Wood had written, Islamic State contained within itself the seeds of its own destruction.

Inflexible in its interpretations, promoting an arid world of blind obedience, without literature, art, film, music, without respect for civilizations been and gone, without respect of so many people, from the Buddhists to the indigenous, there was only so far it could go; before, like other totalitarian movements, it would burn out or collapse in upon itself, under the weight of that very human longing, to be free.

Ordinary people, family men and family women, took up arms and massacred, whether they were Sunnis beheading apostates or Western operatives guiding drone strikes and planning military operations.

Was this really a world they wanted for their children to grow up in? A world where children held up the heads of executed soldiers for the camera, or participated in ritualistic slayings, or, in the West, soldiers dropped drones on foreign lands to achieve precisely nothing but the loss of life, treasure, self-respect? Or spent their days at computer screens monitoring the lives of citizens, waiting for the order to determine who would live and who would die? Where Western leaders could determine, without any recourse to due process required in their own countries, who to execute?

Though rarely painted in such terms, in a sense, it was possible to see a gathering counter reaction, the battle between those who were attempting to trigger mass conversions to Islam and the unquestioning worship of Allah, and those who were trying to trigger an enlightenment.

The Rising of Islam was countermanded by The Rising of the Network.

The same internet technology that Islamic State had used to such devastating effect, to spread terror, shock, to inflame sensibilities, to coalesce fighting forces and spread their ideology, allowed for the aggregation of some of the world's cleverest minds and enabled the creation of new social networks, new ways of thinking, new societies unconfined by locality, national borders or philosophical and theological creeds.

None of the millions engaged in the stunning creativity of this new world wanted to be stoned to death for daring to think outside defined theologies or belief systems.

2015 began with the news that 13 teenage boys had been publicly executed by Islamic State in the city of Mosul for watching on television an Asian Cup soccer match between Jordan and Iraq. The match had been played in Brisbane, Australia.

Before they were killed, their "crime" was announced over a loudspeaker. The group Raqqa is Being Slaughtered Silently, one of the only dissident journalist groups briefly operating inside ISIS controlled territory, reported: "The bodies remained lying in the open and their parents were unable to withdraw them for fear of murder by the terrorist organization."

Every one of those kids had parents, siblings and relatives who loved them, who had cared for them since they were babies, who invested in them all the hope of the future, of a better life.

Was this really the future ordinary people wanted to create for themselves and their children?

Iraq won the match 1:0. [110]

For every action there is an equal and opposite reaction.

All the millions of sympathizers of Islamic State worldwide, all the proponents of its bleakly proscribed view of spirituality, of subservience to a single deity, could, in the 21st Century, access millions of books and movies, listen to popular music, peruse images of the greatest works of art and literature, pursue the lives, work and biographies of thousands of history's most gifted creators, easily, rapidly, cheaply.

The social media technology being used as such a devastatingly effective indoctrination tool on the battlefield of ideas could equally become a tool of personal liberation, and turn against its jihad masters. The population need only grow tired of subservience, of living in fear, of having others tell them how to live. Thanks to the startling

---

[110] ISIS executes 13 teenagers for watching soccer match, New York Post, 19 January, 2015.

technological developments of recent years, each of those dead teenagers could access everything from the worthy to the risqué on their smart phones within seconds. Yet they died for watching a soccer match.

In a time when conspiracy theories were running rampant, and fantasists would have their way, there was nonetheless no doubt the Rise of Islamic State was paralleled by the Rise of the Network Society.

Just as jihadists could share their advice on the best encryption programs and Australian teenagers could download execution videos at the click of a smart phone app, so too could anyone access an enormous range of views on God, religion and the spirit world, from the remarkably obscure to some of the world's most powerful and transcendental spiritual texts.

The internet was not a technology which could be contained for one theological, personal or political cause.

It could equally well be used for enlightenment as for fanaticism.

The world's hyper-clever, once isolated in their own communities and dysfunctional in their own lives, considered geniuses, drunks or eccentrics, could now communicate online at any time of the day or night; and multiple interest groups spawned across the globe.

Like the stars, a hundred million lights could never be extinguished.

****

Things made so little sense in 2015, including the conduct of political leaders, from the streets to the corridors of power, that sometimes Alex thought the deconstructionists of the 20th Century, the Frankfurt School and all the theorists who had plotted and polemicized over the overthrow of Western civilization in all those towers of academe must have won the day. They just hadn't bothered to tell the people, who kept thinking that somewhere, somehow, common decency and due process would triumph.

On either side of the 24 hour communal office where he was working the empty shop fronts were badged "Sydney City Council Making Space for Creativity."

Building for the Future declared further signage; and an early-Kandinsky style set of geometric blocks had the words: "Built." and "those" set into it; whatever that meant.

As in so many other parts of the inner-city, all these so-called Creative Spaces were vacant. Perhaps it was cleverer than it initially appeared. Perhaps they were part of some city-wide art installation, a postmodernist post structuralist post whatever art project; empty art, empty of heart. Oh if only he could decode the signifiers.

These disciplines, the academic deconstruction of everything the culture had been, and what ordinary people thought it was, were entirely revolutionary in content and intent; and remarkably obscure. That had never stopped the halls of academe being jammed with students doing media and communications degrees; the same generation of lieutenants and useful fools who, as they took up their posts inside the media, would so ably destroy the integrity of the journalistic profession.

There were only a few hundred people on Earth who could fully, genuinely understand the esoteric texts of the postmodern narrative, the works of the communist and Frankfurt School inspired French philosophers who had been its founding fathers.

His friend Wanda Jamrozik, one of the brightest people he had ever met, had been one of those few.

Wanda had become another disturbed, dark pit stop memory. Another death. Another funeral. Alex had become immured to the deaths of friends, but not that one, in January of 1996.

He had known she was using heroin again, although she would deny it to his face in the cafes surrounding News Limited's Australian headquarters in Surrey Hills.

She had come over to the dark side, the Evil Empire of Rupert Murdoch as they had both always thought of it as, and its signature masthead *The Australian*, not that long after him; another refugee from the pogroms of Fairfax, the terrible management styles of the 1980s and 1990s.

Wanda had been at the height of her powers and the height of her fashionability. And she had died in the most pointless, loneliest of ways; just as so many far less famous people had before her.

"Wanda was someone who was educated despite her teachers," Dr Braham Dabscheck, then of the University of NSW, wrote in an obituary. "A number of things dominate my memory of Wanda. Firstly, her love of life and sense of fun. She had a wicked sense of humour. Secondly, the range of her interests from films and books, through politics, world affairs, sport and to the history of ideas and philosophy. Thirdly, her intelligence and lack of respect for cant and hypocrisy. To my mind Wanda is best remembered as an intellectual larrikin. Fourthly, and mostly importantly, her sense of humanity and friendly disposition.

"If an anthology of Wanda's writings were to be published readers would be struck by two things. She wrote about anything and everything. The second would be the quality and breadth of her analysis. She was an intellectual in residence at a newspaper."

As a woman with substance abuse issues living in a defacto relationship, Wanda too, no matter how gifted, would have been stoned to death come the Sharia. There would be no room for intellectual larrikins. And not much room for newspapers either.

****

The streets of Sydney were quiet in the days and nights following the Martin Place siege. People chose to stay home rather than risk being out and about where they could be subject to lone wolf attacks or public massacres.

Perhaps the truth of the disaster enfolding the country came not with government announcements but with the death of a single teenager.

Jake Bilardi was a thin, pale faced teenager from a non-Muslim family in the Western suburbs of Melbourne.

Long-haired and awkward, he looked exactly like every other gawky, uncomfortable suburban kid, those who, rather than experiencing the flowering of youth, did not settle into their own physical frames until later in life.

He looked like he should have been hiding from his parents in the garage, working out how to make bucket bongs, conspiratorially smoking marijuana with his neighborhood mates; a cohort of misfits just as uncomfortable in their own skins as himself.

Instead, already under observation for his online behavior, he evaded security forces and left Australia for the conflict in the Middle East, where he willingly gave up his life as a martyr for Islamic State. He was 18 years old. Bilardi had been five years old at the time of the September 11 attacks.

Before his Twitter account was suspended the teenager posted: "Martin place was just the beginning for you dogs." And: "What we have in store for you dogs will make 9/11 look like child's play."

On Thursday March the 12th of 2015 came the news that Jake Bilardi had died in a series of coordinated Islamic State suicide bombings in the Iraq city of Ramadi in which at least 17 people were killed and dozens injured.

Police confirmed that they found material including chemicals to make Improvised Explosive Devices, IEDs, at the boy's home; and that he had been planning terrorist attacks in Australia, on shopping malls and cafes, before realizing he had attracted too much attention from the authorities. [111]

Jake Bilardi's last will and testament, so to speak, was in the form of a blog.

While, cruelly perhaps, the authorities took the blog down, ensuring his death was even more pointless than before, thanks to Google's cache system in the days following his death it was easy enough to find.

Why should a testament which might help the broader population to truly understand what was incubating in their suburbs be concealed from public view?

At one time Jake Bilardi dreamed of being a political journalist; and he clearly had the talent.

His final post was remarkably well written and well argued for someone his age. Many of those commenting on the blog remarked that he would have made a great journalist.

The post was called "From Melbourne to Ramadi: My Journey."

It began: "With my martyrdom operation drawing closer, I want to tell you my story, how I came from being an Atheist school student in affluent Melbourne to a soldier of the Khilafah preparing to sacrifice my life for Islam in Ramadi, Iraq. Many people in Australia probably think they know the story, but the truth is, this is something that has remained between myself and Allah (azza wa'jal) until now.

"My life in Melbourne's working-class suburbs was, despite having its ups and downs just like everyone else, very comfortable. I found myself excelling in my studies, just as my siblings had done, and had dreamed of becoming a political journalist. I always dreamed that one day I would travel to countries such as Iraq, Libya and Afghanistan to cover the situations in these lands. I was intrigued by the conflicts in these countries and I was bent on understanding the motivations behind violent political and social movements. While the rise of the Taliban in Afghanistan, Jabhat al-Nusra and the Islamic State in Syria and Ansar Dine/MUJAO in Mali occupied my mind day-in-day-out, I also took interest in the rise of violent street gangs in Mexico, El Salvador and Brazil. Through my research I found a common link between all these organisations, they are made-up of oppressed and neglected people seeking their own form of perceived justice.

"But let's go back a little further..."

In the preceding years, Bilardi's entire generation had jumped online.

While other teenagers were sneaking looks at naughty pictures, endlessly interacting with their friends on Facebook or playing complex

[111] Blog shows Australian teen reported dead in Iraq suicide attack had planned bombings in Melbourne, Michael Safi, *The Guardian*, 11 March, 2015.

computer games, Bilardi researched the Taliban and al-Qaeda, and was fascinated by Osama bin Laden: "May Allah have mercy upon him."

Jake was decidedly pleased with the laptop-in-schools program, which allowed him to surf jihadist sites while bored in class. The provision of laptops to Australian school children was yet another expensive, failed, flash-in-the-pan government program dreamed up by the then Prime Minister Kevin Rudd, who had made a campaign promise that every Australian child would be given a computer and Australia would become the clever country. The scheme was launched in 2008 and given the tag Digital Education Revolution.

In 2015 Australia had the 44th slowest internet in the world. As some theorists suggested, in the population cohorts in countries with good high quality and an education system which showed people how to use it, the populace was becoming smarter. In countries with poor quality internet and an education system which did not support it, it was creating a drive towards superficiality and group think, a narrowing of ideas, the ponding of ignorance.

Not only were the computers easily misused, the rapidly evolving technology and the advent of smart phones meant that virtually every child who wanted one already had a computer at their fingertips, of the style and model they wanted, not some clunker a government boffin dictated.

As usual, the taxpayers of Australia would have been better off if the government had kept its ideas to itself.

Like many others, Bilardi became radicalized by the West's involvement in Afghanistan and Iraq: "I saw the Taliban as simply a group of proud men seeking to protect their land and their people from an invading force, while I did not necessarily agree with their ideology, their actions were in my opinion completely justified. I saw the foreign troops burning villages, raping local women and girls, rounding up innocent young men as suspected terrorists and sending them overseas for torture, gunning down women, children and the elderly in the streets and indiscriminately firing missiles from their jets. Who was I to believe was the terrorist? I saw similar events unfolding in Iraq where the mujahedeen were valiantly fighting the occupation.

"I read and viewed images of the inhumane torture in Abu Ghraib prison as well as many other atrocities committed, primarily by the Americans, with also cases of torture, summary executions and massacres of civilians being carried out by military personnel from other nations of the coalition. I was beginning to learn that what the media was feeding us was nothing but a government-sponsored distortion of the reality. The image of the American hero waving the US flag on top of a Hummer rolling through Baghdad was nothing but the soft cover to a brutal untold story."

Bilardi explored in considerable depth the failings and hypocrisies of Western democratic systems, "every day the Americans are firing missiles at innocent Muslims," and said he woke up to the reality of the ideology of democratic systems, that they were nothing but systems of lies and deception. He quoted former Russian dictator Joseph Stalin: "The people who cast their votes decide nothing, the people who count the votes decide everything." People are convinced they are free at the same time as they are oppressed.

The manufacture of consent.

Celebrities and false realities were thrown into the spotlight to distract people from what was going on: "This was the turning point in my ideological development as it signaled the beginning of my complete hatred and opposition to the entire system Australia and the majority of the world was based upon. It was also the moment I realised that violent global revolution was necessary to eliminate this system of governance and that I would likely be killed in this struggle."

Bilardi documented his path to jihad, reading the Koran, the deceptiveness of the unbelievers. He wrote that he began to truly understand, after years of study, the motivation of the mujahedeen, the doctrine of jihad and its superiority in Islam. "As the Messenger of Allah, Muhammad ibn Abdullah (peace and blessings be upon him) said: 'The head of the matter is Islam, its pillar is the prayer and its peak is jihad.' I now for the first time truly understood why there were Islamic armies from Mali to China, from Chechnya to Indonesia, it was an obligation upon every able Muslim to fight, an obligation that a person who dies without having fulfilled, he dies upon a branch of hypocrisy as stated by Prophet Muhammad (peace and blessings be upon him)."

Jihadi Jake, as he was nicknamed by Islamic State, posed with mujahedeen fighters before his martyrdom operation. He was reportedly full of happiness in the weeks before he got in a bomb-packed SUV and attacked an Iraqi army outpost in Ramadi. The Iraqi army said the attack was unsuccessful, causing only his own death. Islamic State media said Abu Abdullah Al-Australi, Bilardi's nom de guerre, was part of a coordinated suicide attack in Ramadi with 13 car bombs claiming 10 lives and injuring 30.

Posts on Islamic State linked social media accounts commented on Bilardi's "weak body," that he was from an atheist family and that he had sold his soul to Allah cheaply. [112]

---

[112] Jihadi Jake Bilardi was 'weak' and 'sold his soul cheaply,' says Islamic State online propaganda, James Dowling, Herald Sun, 17 March, 2015.

****

In the same month that Tony Abbott was making his national security announcement, February of 2015; came Sydney's Gay, Lesbian, Bisexual, Transsexual and Intersexual Mardi Gras, previously known simply as the Gay Mardi Gras.

The event had gone from being a protest movement against police harassment in the 1970s to the country's largest street parade; but by 2015, with the threat of terror attack, a shuttered economy and rabid licensing laws, was in serious decline.

Alex was waiting for an attack.

As a general news reporter considered something of an inner-city expert, Alex was often dispatched during the 1980s and 1990s to cover the Mardi Gras. Alex remembered the wild, vivid days of the early Mardi Gras, the cheering crowds, the sense of being part of a bold new enterprise, a more compassionate, enlightened, future.

Now the Australian Federal Police, the Australian Defence Force and the Royal Society for the Prevention of Cruelty to Animals all marched in the parade; a once revolutionary movement integrated into the mainstream.

As the years had rolled by, AIDS victims had become an increasing part of the parade, ending some years with a hundred or more desperately ill gay men being pushed in wheelchairs up Oxford Street by volunteers, a terribly sad end to the sequins and chaps, the out loud and the out proud.

Alex had interviewed many of those desperately sick men, leaning down to hear their hoarsely whispered voices.

For most of them, being wheeled up that strip would be their last Mardi Gras.

There was a room in one of the hotels at the bottom of the strip where, with medical staff in attendance, those too sick even to be wheeled up the strip would be gathered so that they could look down at the parade; their parade, their moment when history finally recognised them. Finally recognised what they had been through, who they had been.

In 2015 Alex kept playing that song by the apostate transsexual Antony Hegarty, You are My Sister:

We felt so differently then
So similar over the years
The way we laugh the way we experience pain
So many memories
But there's nothing left to gain from remembering

Faces and worlds that no one else will ever know
You are my sister
And I love you

By 2015 Sydney's extremely colorful history of giant dance parties, wild bars and wild orgies had faded into history, the victim of zealous council officials, police sniffer dogs, insurance companies, over-regulation, the ever increasing loss of personal freedoms, the bankruptcy of a culture.

The scene had devolved, the party scene vanquished. The common lament now was how bad things were; how dreary the scene, how dead the bars, how dangerous the streets.

On Oxford Street middle-aged gay men past their prime times of outrage lamented the passing of the 1980s and 90s, when the place really did rock. And when, of course, everybody had wanted them in some universal congress of the flesh. "When did the wowsers win?" Alex asked airily to the passing parade one evening.

But won the wowsers had.

Streaked through the whole of Sydney gay life of the era had been an ultimate sadness as death followed death, and AIDS decimated the scene.

"I've been to so many funerals I've lost count," became almost a greeting. Alex had seen enough of Islamic State propaganda on the subject; the gay men hugging their captors before being stoned by the mob, shoved off buildings and if still alive, killed, or hung up and crucified in the town square; the Birth of Fanaticism, the monotheistic faiths. Quite why a God could care who slept with whom Alex would never understand.

This was the pluralistic world for which they had fought? Open minded, tolerant, diverse? Accepting?

Alex had seen enough of the howling of the mob in his own life to truly hate thugs.

Back then, in the early days of the AIDS epidemic, Alex had been there on Mardi Gras night, in that room full of dying gay men, a working journalist, leaning down with note pad in hand, trying to hear what they had to say.

Most of what came out of their mouths was just desperately sad wry camp, ultra-black-death humour, giving one last Julie Garland impression, happy to have been noticed by someone, a reporter from *The Sydney Morning Herald* no less.

Some of them just wanted to make sure he got their quote right, because it would be their last testament on Earth.

They had come out in the days when none of what they got up to was legal or socially acceptable, and now they were dying for their courage.

There would be no compassion under the Sharia; they would have been stoned to death, shoved off buildings, crucified, burnt alive; sick or not.

Reach back through time.

Reach back in time. Stone them to death for being born different. Go on. Stone them, stone them all to death.

Tolerance of intolerance was cowardice.

Too right.

Ironically, the Muslim look was in on Oxford Street; unshaven, masculine, chunky, dark, Middle Eastern. "You're looking butch dear," they would have cooed in the old days as they air-kissed each other in dimly lit bars.

****

One evening Alex ran into an old friend he had long assumed was dead.

"Justin!" Alex said as his brain and odd circumstance continued to enforce a tracking back through a difficult past. He embraced someone he barely recognised, an older man with an eccentric mustache. Justin had been very handsome in his day, clean shaven, a deft hand with a joint, often enough his apartment a regular stopover on a night out.

And soon enough, being in a particular mood, Alex said exactly what was on his mind: "I've thought of you a few times lately, wondered what had happened to you. I assumed you were dead, along with everybody else."

"I've thought of you, too," he said. "Whenever I think of journalism, what a terrible state it is in these days, I think of you."

Justin had been one of the first of the crowd to come out as HIV positive, back in the 1980s when the gay disease was barely understood.

"It's the drugs," he said, referring to the combination retro-viral treatments which had prolonged the lives of so many HIV positive people, turning the grim reaper into a chronic but manageable disease. "I saw some statistics the other day. Something like 24% of those who contracted it in the 1980s are still alive. But I never thought of myself as lucky, as one of those who would be fortunate enough to be in a minority, to still be here."

Several times through the evening Alex said more or less exactly the same thing: "I had assumed you were long dead. It's very nice to see you alive."

Later they did what they had always done, and went back to Justin's. And Alex remembered all too clearly a different Justin, when they had all gathered in the darkened, candle lit reaches of his apartment, through long evenings of fun and intrigue and outrage; in the days, when everything they had done had been on a different ledge.

In the early hours Alex walked back home through empty streets.

"TERROR WATCH: 400 Stopped At Airport Every Day" the banner outside the news agency on Oxford Street declared.

The Sydney Morning Herald reported that counter-terrorism officials were stopping more than 405 people a day at Australian airports as they ramped up efforts to detect potential jihadists slipping out of the country: "The alarming figures from the recently established Border Force Counter-Terrorism Unit have added further fuel to the debate over the merits of cancelling passports, preventing travel and keeping jihadists in Australia, where they are 'ticking time-bombs.' The assessments are not random and involve specialist officers pulling suspicious travellers aside and asking them a series of questions to determine their risk to national security."

Unit teams at eight airports conducted 75,906 real-time assessments between August and February. [113]

Initial results suggest a sizable number of travellers were being caught with extremist material on their phones. Many more had been pulled off planes, had luggage searched and been forced to re-book flights.

Muslim community leaders said most were legitimate travellers who were being unfairly profiled and targeted.

The Grand Mufti of Australia, Dr Ibrahim Abu Mohammad, condemned the "extremely unprofessional" and "seemingly random yet profiled manner" of the assessments following the detention of a senior imam.

Sheikh Shady Alsuleiman, who was travelling with a group of pilgrims to perform the Hajj in September of 2014 when he was detained for more than two hours in Sydney and missed his flight.

In its first three weeks of operation Border Force Counter-Terrorism Unit teams in Sydney and Melbourne reportedly intercepted 11 terror suspects, seized three devices containing extremist material, denied one Malaysian man entry to Australia and pulled dozens of people off flights and placed them under surveillance. The Border Force Counter-Terrorism Unit was rolled out to eight airports, costing $50 million over four years and employing 80 specialist officers with

---

[113] Border Force Counter Terrorism Units ramps up efforts, Rachel Olding, The Sydney Morning Herald, 16 March, 2015.

enhanced powers to intercept inbound and outbound passengers of national security interest.

Two men were stopped in August with tens of thousands of dollars in undeclared currency and extremist propaganda material.

Controversial preacher Mohammed Junaid Thorne, a Saudi Australian of aboriginal heritage, said he was the only traveller pulled aside at the boarding gate for a flight from Sydney to Perth on March 9. He missed his flight but was later released.

Thorne was on the Australian Federal Government's terrorism watchlist for his inflammatory social media posts and for lectures indicating support for Islamic State.

Thorne had been a contentious figure in Australia for some time, giving a series of lectures nation wide at Islamic centres known for their hardline views, including the iQraa Islamic centre in Brisbane, the subsequently closed Al Risalah Islamic centre in Bankstown in Western Sydney and the also subsequently closed Al Furqan Islamic centre in Melbourne.

After the Charlie Hebdo killings Thorne tweeted: "If you want to enjoy freedom of speech with no limits expect others to exercise freedom of action." [114]

By midyear, after once again having his Twitter account blocked, Thorne was declaring on his Facebook page: "Pondering over the few incidents that took place in the recent months, any person that desires to be fair and just can only reach one conclusion: Being a Muslim is a crime in itself in this country, and you have to be prepared to face the full force of law, even if you haven't done anything wrong... may Allah keep all Muslims safe from the oppressors. Ameen."

Also critical of upgraded control procedures at Australia's airports was Joseph Wakim, founder of the Australian Arabic Council. He said innocent Muslims were purposely not speaking Arabic at airports to avoid being embarrassed by the crackdown.

****

There was no terrorist attack on the Mardi Gras in 2015; although Alex had perched on the steps at the back of the Stonewall Bar as if he had had the prescience to stake out the Sari nightclub in Bali on the night when 88 Australians had been killed in a terrorist attack in 2002.

He had no premonition that there would be an attack. It just seemed logical that if you were going to make a statement, that would

---

[114] If you want to enjoy freedom of speech with no limits expect others to exercise freedom of action, Daniel Pietrowski, *UK Daily Mail*, 8 January, 2015.

be the spot. Alex might not show up for work as a journalist anymore, but he had once had a knack of being in the right place at the right time, when it suited him, and while he was not convinced there would be an incident, it was worth being there in case.

Fortunately, for the thought of blood and dismembered bodies, howling sirens overwhelming screams and people fleeing in panic made him sick, he waited for a disaster that never came; the shock of invisible assault.

This was the 37th Mardi Gras, and considering that it celebrated lifestyles which were anathema to members of the Muslim minority, with the rise of Islamic State and in the wake of the Martin Place attack, the Stonewall was an obvious target; a valuable, high profile recruiting tool.

And an easy one. There was no way a parade involving so many people, attracting such large crowds and traversing such a long central city route, could be easily policed. The news would have spread around the world in a few short minutes. Spectacular. There would be no safe gay pride march on Earth after that.

Instead of joining the crowds lining Oxford Street to watch the floats, he watched them on two separate screens from within the Stonewall bar. A loud drag queen urged the crowd to celebrate the Mardi Gras moment. "Ladies and gentlemen," she would drawled repeatedly in her loudest, most cutting tones; following up with a string of double entendres. The show was not very entertaining, but from the massive eyelashes to the troweled on makeup to the long, brightly flowing dress, the entertainer had achieved his goal: he looked fabulous.

The crowds were down from their peak; in previous years Alex had walked the entire parade route with reporter's pad in hand, interviewing participants and members of the crowd, waiting for those freakish little bits of detail and incident which made a story sing. The march seemed barely gay at all, its revolutionary potential defanged.

Alex scratched his head that something which had once been so radical was radical no more; that things which his generation had thought would change the world had ultimately changed very little. Most people want to leave the world a better place; and his crowd had somehow assumed that through their outrageous conduct this was exactly what they were doing, pushing the boundaries, changing the spirit of the times, carving out a better, freer, more creative world for those to follow.

"They are without ancestors," he sometimes thought of the younger gay men he watched in the bars. "They have no history."

As it turned out, the world was born anew every day; and in a city like Sydney there was little thought for those who had gone before; the city's history irrelevant.

The Sydney Morning Herald reported: "The biggest cheers of the night were reserved for the Armed Services and Police float which featured a female officer booming out a fine rendition of Bruno Mars' Just The Way You Are.

"The Defence float was the biggest ever with high ranking officers and carrying the imprimatur of the armed forces, which have been marching since 2008, and in uniform since 2013." [115]

It would never have happened in his day. Back then the police were considered the enemy and anything to do with officialdom, including the military, was to be entirely distrusted.

The First Australians float was followed by the '78 float, with the surviving members of the first protest march.

Alex survived for reasons he didn't always understand; a shard of glass into the future.

To see a time when so many of those he had known would be labelled apostates.

And when the terror of social conformity had been replaced by a different set or terrors altogether.

****

Alex's daily walks invariably took him through the terrain of his own past; through what had once been Sydney's own demimonde, and now was nothing but empty, characterless streets. He always walked; he couldn't stay inside himself. And so he passed derelict street scene after derelict street scene, "My girlfriend's going to jail on Wednesday"; past men pissing on public streets, the smell of urine now growing in so many corners of an increasingly hapless, vagrant city.

One morning in early May of 2015 he walked past the old site of Brutus's, a gay cafe which, back in the late 1960s, opened at midnight and with which he had been entirely intrigued.

Most everyone on the scene at that time ended up at Brutus's after midnight; it had been lit with black strobe lighting and he promptly acquired a fluorescent shirt which lit up in the black strobe light; and if heads weren't turning before, they certainly were after that.

---

[115] Sydney Gay and Lesbian Mardi Gras floods the streets of Sydney with colour, Luke Malpass, The Sydney Morning Herald, 8 March, 2015.

The front entrance set off a little bell which everyone could hear; and every exit and entrance, every coming and going, was closely observed.

Brutus, as everyone called the middle aged "queen," as they were all called then, or "gay guy" as the more politically correct termed them now, was not particularly attractive, to be blunt, but his position as the owner of such a strategic late-night den gave him power.

The old cafe, set among atmospheric terraces, had long since been demolished and was now a six lane thoroughfare.

Brutus was shot straight through the heart at a distance of 100 meters in Rushcutters Bay Park, right next to those very same beats.

The perpetrator had been a rent boy Alex had known casually; but from the gossip had plenty of reason not to like old Brutus.

The boy went back inside "the big house."

"Good shot," they all thought.

Brutus's closed.

But back then, in the 1960s, they had all thought they were at the beginning of an enterprise, a freedom loving society, a place where the demimonde would flourish.

They would never have believed that half a century on the streets would be silent, barely any nightspots remaining open, that the Muslim ban on entertainment would be more or less in place, that the city would be an empty and dangerous place. And that their sexuality would be more loathed than ever; and place them at greater risk of assault than ever before.

In mid-2015, the Middle East Media Research Institute, better known by its acronym MEMRI, ran a compilation of videos and photographs of Islamic State's execution of gays under the heading: "ISIS Campaign Of Executing Homosexuals – By Stoning, Shooting, Throwing Off Roofs, Public Torture: In Accordance With Shari'a Law As Explained By Influential Mainstream Islamic Preachers, Scholars On Leading Arab Media Outlets, Including Al-Jazeera, Hamas's Al-Aqsa TV – WARNING – GRAPHIC IMAGES."

The preamble noted: "In recent months, the Islamic State (ISIS) has publicly executed men they have convicted of homosexuality in Iraq and Syria, including by burning them alive and by stoning them to death. The most common method of execution, however, has been throwing them off tall buildings; if they survive, they are usually shot or stoned, sometimes by the crowd of observers. This punishment for homosexuals was detailed, featured, and praised in the latest issue of ISIS's English-language magazine Dabiq, in an article titled 'Clamping Down on Sexual Deviance.'

"According to majority interpretations of Islamic Sharia law, homosexuality is indeed punishable by death; this has been clearly stated by well-known and highly influential Sunni Muslim authorities, sheikhs, professors, and Muslim Brotherhood leaders. These have included leading Sunni authority and head of the International Union of Muslim Scholars Sheikh Yousuf Al-Qaradhawi; highly influential Kuwaiti Islamic preacher and Muslim Brotherhood leader Tareq Al-Suweidan; Saudi cleric and Islamic University professor 'Abd Al-Qader Shiba Al-Hamad; and many others. Such punishments are also based on the Biblical story of Lot, which is often cited by both mainstream sheikhs and ISIS to justify the killing of homosexuals.

"These statements and teachings regarding the death penalty for homosexuality appear in Muslim school curricula, on mainstream television, and in mosque sermons across the Arab and Muslim world, and are also expressed by Muslim authorities in the Wes. They have also been expressed by jihadi leaders, including al Qaeda leader Ayman Al-Zawahiri, who was reportedly directly involved in the prosecution and death of a youth accused of homosexuality in the 1990s. Recent examples of executions of homosexuals by Al-Qaeda and ISIS using these methods – stoning to death, throwing off high buildings, and shooting – are documented in this report; it should also be noted that ISIS has continued to use U.S. social media, particularly Twitter, to disseminate to its supporters online images of its executions of homosexuals.

"To date, there has been very little discussion in the Arab media about these executions, and there has been no significant Arab or Muslim religious or political leader who has denounced them."

ISIS was not the only one calling for the death penalty for gays.

Leviticus 20:13 read: "If a man also lie with mankind, as he lieth with a woman, both of them have committed an abomination. They shall surely be put to death. Their blood shall be upon them." Uganda had instituted the infamous "Death to Gays" Bill, condemning so-called acts of aggravated homosexuality, while a number of Christian preachers across America advocated the death penalty. Sean Harris, pastor at Berean Baptist Church, for example, preached that gays should be put to death and exhorted his congregation to physically abuse their own children, punch them and even break their wrists, if they showed any signs of homosexuality.[116]

****

---

[116] Like ISIS, US Christians advocate killing gays, Jon Ponder, Pensito Review, 19 February, 2015.

To Alex, the absurdity of Australia's involvement in the alleged fight against Islamic State in Iraq could not have been better illustrated by the fact that in Australia, as elsewhere, Islamic State propaganda was so readily available online.

MEMRI, one of the best available sources for all the latest updates of the myriad of transnational and international jihadist groups coalescing under the banner of Islamic State, was possibly the world's most dangerous jihad site.

In Australia, with reasonable connection speeds, it was possible to access MEMRI, in 0.3 of a second. It was possible to find the Islamic State Twitter feed in 0.2 of a second. It was possible to find the Al Qaeda sites and their affiliates in much the same space of time.

The jihadists weren't in hiding anymore. It was impossible not to become disturbed by the visual violence: crowds lining up to watch homosexuals, adulterers and apostates being stoned to death, Christians being beheaded or shot, gay men thrown from roof tops.

"Support Our Spring Campaign" read a pop up banner on the site, seeking donations for a worldwide escalation of Holy War; or jihad.

MEMRI not only detailed all the latest Islamic State propaganda, it hosted some of the most vividly violent execution videos ever made, ritualistic killings designed purely to send fear into the hearts of unbelievers, to drive a mass conversion of the populace to Islam, to create a kind of awe.

These videos were all easily accessible to any disenchanted young Australian. Within seconds they could watch on their phones the beheadings, the blood from the severed necks of Christians flowing into the sea, the bodies of unbelievers shot in the head dropping in lines to the ground. The videos were all professionally and expensively produced with the highest production values courtesy of the media arm of Islamic State. And all facilitated by the United States of America's government.

MEMRI was based in Washington DC, had tax exempt status as an educational institution under US law, and had been established 17-years before.

It had a worldwide following.

Any Australian with an internet connection could access it.

Any Australian teenager could access the execution videos, including the stoning, murder and torture of homosexuals.

And many of the online videos ended with the words: "Download free to your app."

****

One morning, distressed by the world he had found himself in, Alex walked further on past the old site of Brutus's; out onto the narrow wedge beside Sydney's Rushcutters Bay, with the Sydney Harbour Bridge visible in the distance, and sat for a short time in much the same place he had restlessly sat all those decades before; his mind curling through the inside of the apartments on the other side, taking in the musty smell of sleep, the stirrings as the residents awoke into another day.

The park benches were new, but back 40 or more years before, when he had sat in more or less exactly the same spot, he rarely slept and had smoked more than 100 cigarettes a day.

Nicotine was an anti-hallucinogen.

As a distressed teenager it had helped; as part of himself, or so it had felt, streamed across the bay.

That morning in May he walked back up to the Cross, taking pictures of derelict shops on his smart phone, and bought the Saturday editions of the newspapers.

He might as well just quote the story in *The Daily Telegraph*, under the headline "Terror Teens": "POLICE and ASIO have foiled a teenage terror plot to detonate three bombs in an attack believed to have been planned for this Sunday in Melbourne.

"A 14-year-old was also targeted in a separate raid in Sydney.
"In Melbourne, the bomb squad and heavily armed police were used in a raid on a doctor's home, where his son was arrested.

"Three bombs were found at the upmarket home and a 300 metre exclusion zone put in place as they were detonated in a nearby reserve."[117]

Dozens of counter terrorism police swooped on the home while his mother was reversing out of the driveway. Police alleged the 17-year old who was arrested had been planning a terror plot aimed at a Mother's Day event.

AFP Deputy Commissioner Mike Phelan said: "The environment is changing rapidly. It is deeply troubling to police that young people in our communities are becoming so disaffected and alienated that they would consider engaging in acts such as this. We may not know exactly where it was going to occur or when it was exactly going to occur. But let me tell you, something was going to happen and as a result of Victoria Police and AFP intervention, some Victorians are going to be alive because of it."

---

[117] Terror Raids Target Teens, Simon Benson and David Hurley, The Daily Telegraph, May 9, 2015.

Online posts by the boy declared that Muslims should hate the unbelievers and that those from the Shiite sect "were not human."

His 21-year-old sister dismissed the posts as the writing of an emotional teen distressed by what was happening in his family's Syrian homeland. She described him as "kind, gentle and softly spoken." [118]

****

In July of 2015 the Australian Federal Police was forced to cancel an annual Eid dinner marking the end of Ramadan after Muslim community leaders vowed to boycott the event.

A group calling itself Concerned Muslims Australia set up an online petition calling for all community leaders, Imans, organisational executives and other key figures to boycott the dinner, saying it was being used by the government to create a false image of cooperation.

The petition, signed by a number of leading community figures, claimed that over the previous 12 months the Australian Government had executed a concerted and prolonged campaign of anti-Muslim hysteria, pulling out all stops to demonize, marginalize and victimize the Muslim community. Under the pretext of international developments and a supposed impending domestic threat, many tranches of counter-terrorism legislation have been passed that target Muslims specifically.

"I can't break fast with those who authorise flash bombs to be used against families," said Australian Muslim Women's Association spokeswoman Silma Ihram, who was one of 840 people to sign the petition. [119]

The petition claimed Federal and State Government bodies including the Australian Federal Police and ASIO had been key strategic components in the Australian Government's deliberate targeting of the Muslim community, used to execute phony raids that had often amounted to nothing. Where specific threats had been prevented, the raids had been dramatized beyond any reasonable measure to reinforce the notion of a Muslim threat.

The petition went on to claim: "Police raids and increased surveillance by intelligence agencies have created immense distress for families and entire communities, making victims out of those with no part in the Government's ill-defined "extremism." Police brutality is also

[118] Terror teen troubled by war in homeland, The Sunday Telegraph, May 10, 2015.
[119] Australian Federal Police cancel EID dinner, Rachel Olding, *The Sydney Morning Herald*, 13 July, 2015.

a serious concern, with increasing reports of physical violence being used against innocent Muslims.

"The creation of this atmosphere has also directly led to an increased backlash against Muslims, particularly the vulnerable, in all walks of life. An Islamopbobic atmosphere is directly resulting from the actions of police and government agencies.

"In its bid to shore up tokenistic support for the above and other measures, the Government, through its various agencies, invites Muslim leaders and organisations to dine with its policy makers and bureaucrats, attempting to create a false image of cooperation, harmony and trust which could not be further from the truth. We interpret these overtures as insult to injury: it is incredulous that the same agencies that harass, discriminate and target the Muslim community would expect it to break bread with them.

"We refuse to be treated like a national security threat and call on you to recognise such events as attempts by the Government to paint a false picture of cooperation between it and the Community. We thus call upon you to take the only action befitting as a response, and to refuse in principle to sit with the Government while it continues to treat Muslims in the most underhanded way possible."

Among the leaders who supported the boycott was Sydney lawyer Mariam Veiszadeh, who said previous efforts at community engagement had been disheartening and leaders felt like they were being used as a rubber stamp for draconian legislation: "We have been continuously echoing our communities' concerns to the Abbott Government but it largely seems to fall on deaf ears."

In a statement, Concerned Muslims Australia hailed the cancellation of the dinner as proof of the "abundant strength in the unity of the Muslim community."

An Australian Federal Police spokeswoman claimed the canceling of the dinner was a sign the organization was consulting with and responding to the Muslim community.

If only time could stand still, that inhaled breath before calamity.

But it would not.

SECTION FOUR: SOLDIERS OF GOD

EVEN NONLINEAR NARRATIVES required a set piece, a central point where the past and the present collided, where characters came out of hiding, themes were confirmed.

In those earliest days of the Australian winter of 2015, for Alex, haunted by scenes of violence and the feeling of disturbance everywhere, as if the fabric of the world itself was now sick, it was a conference officially titled "Australia's Regional Summit to Counter Violent Extremism: Challenging Terrorist Propaganda."

The conference was opened by the Prime Minister Tony Abbott and had many of the lead players in the game in attendance, including the head of ASIO, Australia's Foreign Minister, Julie Bishop and the Attorney General George Brandis; along with representatives from more than 30 different countries. There was a large Muslim contingent.

His worst fears were confirmed.
The political leadership managing Australia's terror threat were in large part wrongheaded, if not downright dangerous.

Or so it seemed to Alex.

He wasn't a terror expert. He hadn't set out to write a book about terror. His only objective had been to write a snapshot of Australia in 2015 called *Workers' Paradise Lost*. And one thing led to another; the story that was impossible to ignore.

The conference was held at Pier One, nestled under the southern flank of the Sydney Harbour Bridge, once a bustling wharf shipping wool out of the colony, in the latter decades of the 20th Century a bedraggled fun pier full of dilapidated slot machines, in 2015 an upmarket conference venue.

From its front windows the Pier had striking views of the Sydney's major landmarks, including the world famous Sydney Opera House and Luna Park; all of them now terror targets and graced with additional security.

Perhaps by coincidence, as he assumed his seat, Alex sat next to one of the senior figures in the NSW Islamic Council; a quiet man whose smart phone instantly translated his texts into Arabic, one of those men one saw on the edge of markets and crowd scenes, smoking a quiet cigarette, dignified, self-contained, a wise man who kept his thoughts to himself.

Except when he was directly asked.

"Sceptical?" Alex asked.

The man shrugged: "It's the situation on the ground."

The usual cluster of media waited outside Pier One for Abbott to arrive. Alex knew some of them and felt a stab of nostalgia for all those days he himself had spent as part of the media pack waiting for someone famous or infamous to arrive or depart from one venue or another.

On the way to the conference Alex had listened on the car radio to Abbott doing his morning rounds of media, answering soft questions from media supporters.

There would be no press conference at the Summit itself, no awkward questions to dodge or regret.

Pier One had already been of considerable interest to the city's jihadists and therefore of considerable interest to the nation's security forces. There was every reason to have security for the conference at the highest levels possible.

Already on camera and having passed by burly security guards, Alex joined the queue, had his identity checked and ticked off, and passed through a metal detector; not a common feature of news events in Australia.

Twelve years before, in mid-2003, an Islamist known only as Mansour J decided to treat himself and bought a boat.

Mansour J, later to face terrorism charges in Beirut, had come to the attention of authorities both for his associations with jihadists and for his criminal activities. By the late 1990s he was accused of being involved in at least three shootings. As Martin Chulov described in *Australian Jihad*: "He advocated the law of the streets in Sydney's south-west, where, among some sections of the Middle Eastern community, rough justice is regularly and ruthlessly imposed and turf claims are brutally enforced by stand over figures and their henchmen..."

Mansour J was particularly feared because of his sociopathic approach to work, he had a habit of laughing as he shot at people.

In 1998 it was alleged that Mansour J was the driver when another man shot up the Lakemba Police station.

In 2001 Mansour J was given his freedom by a District Court judge concerned at the delay in the case going to trial; and concerned that the prisoner had not been able to access regular Muslim prayer meetings or halal food.

Chulov recorded that Mansour J transformed from thug to man of God: "At 28 years of age, J left prison a radically different man from the one who had been incarcerated. During his time in jail he had gradually embraced the teachings of Salafi Islam – an almost identical doctrine to that underpinning the theology espoused by Osama bin Laden. It called for a pure interpretation of the Koran, and held that every Muslim had a duty to commit jihad.

"J says he had been awakened in prison through the teachings of imams who visited him. One was a prison chaplain…"

The further radicalization of Australian jihadists under Muslim chaplaincy schemes would later become a major issue.

J walked out of prison six weeks before 9/11 changed the world.

Australians linked to the ideology from which bin Laden's al Qaeda drew its inspiration were now fair game for scrutiny. In terms of grappling with the terrorist threat, in the early years of the millenium the AFP and ASIO were in their infancy.

They turned their spotlights, "such as they were," onto a prayer room in Haldon Street, Lakemba, run by fundamentalist preacher Sheik Abdul Salam Zoud; follower of the Wahhabi tradition. He had previously been accused of being Australia's chief recruiter for jihadist networks, an accusation he denied. He was also on an ASIO list of 23 people associated with al Qaeda preacher Anwar al-Awlaki.

The prayer hall was above a shopping mall in Haldon Street, Lakemba.

The group was a breakaway from the nearby Lakemba mosque; where Zoud was thrown out for his alleged extremist views.

Alex had been dispatched by *The Australian*'s News Desk to quiz its devotees; but never got very far. The site of an unbeliever on their doorsteps was almost too great an affront to bear; the hostility visible. Unlike the Lakemba Mosque, he was never invited inside.

Ethnic tensions broke across Sydney in several different ways during those first few years of the new millennium, and as a result well-meaning people who wanted to show their support for multiculturalism and the Islamic community made the trip out to Lakemba, middle class white citizens, mostly women, roaming in groups through the Middle Eastern style streets before finding a suitable local restaurant.

Oohing about how lovely the food was, they would then streak in groups back to their BMWs as fast as their social x-ray legs could carry them. Alex always thought it ironic that as they admired the food, upstairs was one of the country's most radical mosques, where everything those women stood for would be counted as apostasy.

In the Sharia those Muslims so longed for, these women would have been given the opportunity to adopt the veil, or be put to death.

The women disappeared back to the safety of their own white bread suburbs, where they could tell everyone how wonderful it was that Australia was such a diverse and tolerant society.

Of the prayer room Chulov recorded: "There were known to be men and women among them, and elsewhere in the Australian Islamic community, who were admirers of bin Laden and of the work of the terrorists sent to attack New York and Washington in his organisation's name."

Mahmoud J was one of them.

Not previously noted as a pleasure craft aficionado, by mid-2003 Mansour J began spending a considerable amount of time on Sydney Harbour in his nine-meter runabout; in particular checking out the Shell Oil Refinery at Gore Cove, the Opera House and Pier One at Walsh Bay.

"Police were in little doubt that what was taking place on the waterways amounted to the early stages of a terror planning mission," Chulov wrote. "Their suspicions were reinforced by several conversations picked up on phone taps. There were no specifics, just tough talk about attacking those who stood in Islam's path. As the 2003 holiday season approached, a response was ratcheted up, calling for a full anti-terrorism plan to be activated."

Others came to different conclusions, in particular ASIO, which concluded that nothing more was going on than a bit of chest-beating. Not for the first time, and certainly not for the last, ASIO's judgment would be called into question.

The objections of their senior operatives were set aside and the National Security Committee of Cabinet, led by then Prime Minister John Howard, was convened.

NSW Police were given carriage of what would become one of the biggest Australian police operation of the post-2001 environment. Counter terrorism detectives feared that Mansour J and members of his Lakemba brotherhood would choose a time of attack when there would be hundreds of thousands of revelers lining the harbor foreshore, New Year's Eve.

Chulov recorded that as New Year's Eve approached, police activated full command posts at the Sydney Police Centre and AFP headquarters in Canberra. ASIO's command center was also on high alert. A bomb unit was put on standby and sniper teams deployed. In total, close to 200 police were tasked to ensure that if Mansour J was up to something, he would be foiled before he had a chance to act. They also made sure he knew he was under surveillance.

In those years Alex almost always put his hand up to work New Year's Eve. They were easy shifts and his kids were usually away with relatives.

He would almost always be asked to go down to the Harbour foreshore, to get some feel good quotes from the revelers, families excited by the prospect of fireworks, enjoying a night out with their kids; he would jot down enough quotes to keep the News Desk happy, and move through the crushing crowds.

Inevitably, because of production deadlines, he would be asked to file copy on the midnight fireworks, before midnight. That was when imagination took hold. There was, as he discovered over the years, only so much you could say about fireworks, particularly when they hadn't yet gone off.

It always struck him that the thronging shores of Sydney Harbour on New Year's Eve constituted a prime location for massacre, mayhem, maximum casualties. But in 2003, and the years that followed, the explosions and massacres Alex was convinced would occur never came.

Perhaps because of the amount of attention he had attracted, Mansour J lost interest in boating. He was amongst the top five most watched men in the nation. Nonetheless, he managed to leave the country in 2004 on a false passport, heading straight for Beirut, and straight into further trouble.

****

At the Countering Violent Extremism conference, that morning in mid-2015, there would be none of the usual standing around grinning and gripping and welcoming guests for the Prime Minister, as was his wont.

Tony Abbott arrived after everyone was seated, only minutes before he was due to give the Opening Address. A busy man. Or a worried security team taking no chances whatsoever with their charge.

After the usual air pecks and handshakes the Australian Prime Minister settled quickly into his chair in the front row.

Abbott, and Alex, sat and listened to the Welcome to Country ceremonies, those well-meaning rituals practiced by the often blood diluted descendants of the ancient peoples, a ritual invoked by the invaders more to assuage guilt than show respect; while all around them could be felt the land, the spirits, the ancestors.

Alex felt as if, internally, Abbott's mind was scrabbling towards some ledge, trying to understand a new world order; either that, or he had been instructed to keep his mind blank.

Perhaps he was frightened that someone would find out the depth of his betrayals.

But already, in the progressive collapse of Abbott's Prime Ministership, too many people knew the depths of the government's incompetence, from senior members of the bureaucracy to the hunting media packs.

In one of those brief, sliding encounters which had once been a characteristic part of Sydney's remarkable social fluidity, where you could go out on the town and end up in the beds or on the couches of the filthy rich or the humble poor, a trait long since vanquished, Alex had breakfast in a Kings Cross cafe, sitting next to the handsome son of the head of the Foreign Investment Review Board.

Just as in every sector of society, it didn't take long to get to the subject of the parlous state of the nation.

Tastelessly perhaps, he quipped: "Who needs a terrorist attack? The place is dead already."

Although from different eras of Sydney life, they both lamented the passing of Sydney's inner-city demimonde.

In response to a few sharp questions, the good son let it be known that the country's most senior bureaucrats hated Tony Abbott.

Alex already knew that, but it was nice to have it confirmed.

It wasn't the left wing sentiment that ponded in various sections of the bureaucracy, social justice dreams which would remain forever unquenched because reality did not fit theory; it was a disdain of a professional caste for the unprofessional conduct of another.

Tony Abbott was a professional politician. He should have known better; he should have known to seek advice, not to fill his office with political hacks and religious warriors but with professional administrators, he should have known not to look back to previously failed administrations in the search for a future path.

Abbott remained in power solely because of the parlous state of Australian democracy; in a dual party system because the opposition was in such a hapless state and because his disenchanted colleagues had yet to work out how to get rid of him without wearing the electoral stain of political assassination, as had cursed the previous administration.

And then it was the Prime Minister's turn to give the Opening Address.

Sometimes, or so it seemed, Alex had an almost uncanny knack of knowing what people were thinking. He hadn't survived as a journalist for so many years, hadn't dived in and out of thousands of people's lives, without having picked up some powers of divination.

The thing that startled Alex the most about Abbott's entry into the conference was that the man was frightened, as if, despite the blanket security, he thought he was about to be blown up. It was not his usual jocular walk onto a field of hostile ideological opponents, which Abbott was used to, but something else entirely.

If the Prime Minister, blanketed by the best security the country had to offer, did not feel safe, who could feel safe?

No one.

Abbott, as a professional politician, with the same folksy down-pat palaver of any country spruiker, went into rote mode, got up and made his speech. For a conference titled Combating Violent Extremism: Challenging Terrorist Propaganda, stacked with international experts on terrorist messaging and with diplomatic representatives from some 30 different countries, many of them Muslim, many of them with no affection for the American crusader, the speech in itself was extraordinary.

Abbott began with a perhaps forgivable hyperbolic lie: "As everyone who has experienced the great city of Sydney knows, there is no more beautiful and easy-going large city anywhere on earth."

In 2015 many of the charms of Sydney had vanished: the city was trashed, dangerous, bleak, expensive, housing unaffordable for ordinary workers, the entertainment districts virtually shut down and there were increasing numbers of beggars on the streets; it was in the grip of an ice epidemic, deeply divided along ethnic, religious and class lines and in no way at all could be described as easy-going. The general population was simmering with resentment and frustration.

It took no time at all for the Australian Prime Minister to buy into a religious war: "This country has not flourished because success was inevitable or ordained by God; this country has flourished because people from the four corners of the earth have come here to work hard, to respect each other, and to build a better life for their children and grandchildren.

"This country of ours has an indigenous heritage, a British foundation and a multicultural character.

"Yet the tentacles of the death cult have extended even here, as we discovered to our cost with the Martin Place siege last December.

"We have all seen on our screens the beheadings, the crucifixions, the mass executions and the sexual slavery that the Da'esh death cult has inflicted, mostly on Muslims, in the Middle East.

"That is what the death cult has in store for everyone if it has its way.

"This is not terrorism for a local grievance; this is terrorism with global ambitions.

"The death cult now holds sway over an area as large as Italy in eastern Syria and northern and western Iraq.

"Its affiliates control parts of Libya and Nigeria; it is active on the Horn of Africa and parts of the Arabian Peninsula and it has ambitions to establish a far province in South East Asia.

"Its senior members are routinely calling on sympathisers to kill unbelievers wherever they find them, sometimes specifying Australians.

"In the past year, Da'esh and its imitators have carried out terrorist attacks here and in Melbourne, as well as in France, Belgium, Canada,

Afghanistan, Pakistan, Egypt, Nigeria, Jordan, Denmark, Kenya and the United States.

"At successive conferences such as this, the list of atrocities gets longer and longer.

"Daésh is coming, if it can, for every person and for every government with a simple message: submit or die."

That was one reference to a Christian God and three references to the "the death cult" aka Islamic State in about two minutes flat; in a room full of propaganda and counter terrorism messaging experts, many flown to Australia at taxpayer's expense purportedly so the country could take advantage of their expertise.

The Prime Minister had been repeatedly warned that the use of the phrase "death cult" was counterproductive, fuelling rather than detracting from recruitment, encouraging rather than discouraging Australian jihadists.

In a room full of some of the world's leading experts on terrorist propaganda, it was beyond inexcusable.

Dr Anne Aly, Associate Professor in the Faculty of Humanities at Curtin University, adviser to governments on terror messaging, had previously said: "Osama Bin Laden used to say, 'you love life, we love death.' Dying a martyr is their badge of honour, it's a huge push factor for young Australians and the Prime Minister is putting that front and centre.

"I don't know who he's talking to when he says death cult because the people who are thinking about going over there are laughing and walking away."

Abbott first coined the "death cult" phrase in September of the previous year while announcing Australia would re-enter Iraq.

"I refuse to call this hideous movement an 'Islamic state' because it is not a state; it is a death cult," he told the Australian parliament.

The Sydney Morning Herald managed to count 346 uses of the phrase "death cult" in press releases, transcripts, speeches and video recordings between September 2014 and May 2015. [120]

He even managed to weave it into 36 interviews and speeches that had nothing to do with national security, from press conferences with NSW Premier Mike Baird to doorstops in the Melbourne suburbs.

His record was 17 times in one press conference – a March 3 briefing on military operations in Iraq – and in parliament he had answered 20 questions without notice on "death cult" since September, compared to just one on ice, one on domestic violence and three on

---

[120] Counter-terrorism adviser: Abbott's IS 'death cult' label is counterproductive, Rachel Olding, *The Sydney Morning Herald*, 12 May, 2015.

Ebola. Questions without notice are those fired by friendly politicians to allow the government to boast about its achievements.

At least 22 other Australian government Members of Parliament had followed their leader and mentioned "death cult" in parliament using adventurous variations like murderous death cult, bloodthirsty death cult and apocalyptic death cult.

A spokesman for Mr Abbott said that he made no apologies – "because that's what it is: a cult that rejoices in death."

Sydney tabloid *The Daily Telegraph*, badged their terror pages with the logo.

The editors of *The Telegraph* should have known perfectly well that badging their pages Death Cult was inflaming the appeal of jihad to Australia's disaffected Muslims.

In the past Abbott had been one of a string of politicians making their way to the headquarters of News Limited in Surry Hills, determined to liaise with the *The Australian*, and *The Daily Telegraph's* senior editorial hierarchy. They would have high ranking meetings with the senior editors while Alex watched from his humble reporters desk. Every Australian politician liked to think they had News Limited in their pocket. Alex had seen them come and seen them go.

Abbott owed his election in part to the unabashed support of the Murdoch press.

It would continue to act as his loudspeaker.

In May of 2015 came the headline: "We've Jihad It With You."

Inflaming Muslim sentiment, as he had been so repeatedly advised not to do, a "defiant" Abbott declared he would not negotiate the cosy return of foreign fighters who had a change of heart and vowed to incarcerate them. Up to a dozen "death cult" deserters were, *The Telegraph* reported, now attempting to seek repatriation.

Treachery within and treachery without.

"If you go, and you seek to come back, as far as this Government is concerned, you will be arrested, you will be prosecuted and you will be jailed," Abbott said. "If you go abroad to kill innocent people in the name of misguided fundamentalism and extremism, if you go abroad to become an Islamist killer well, we're hardly going to welcome you back into this country." [121]

When Alex spoke to Professor Anne Aly after the speech and asked her what she thought she virtually rolled her eyes at the repeated use of the phrase "death cult" and of the Prime Ministers repeated references to a Christian God in front of a multifaith audience. She said she

---

[121] Defiant PM Tony Abbott threatens homesick Australian jihadists with jail if they try to return, *The Daily Telegraph*, 20 May, 2015.

believed that in his role as leader the Prime Minister's statements were a breach of the Australian Constitution, which made it clear that Australia was a secular, multifaith society: "He thinks he is speaking to people like himself."

Perhaps there was another interpretation, that Abbott thought he was speaking to the unbeliever and it was his destiny to play a higher role; to destroy the faith of Australians in earthly government.

Much about Australia of 2015 made little consistent sense. Nothing was impossible. There were days, with frequent references to God studding his speeches and displaying scant regard for normal political processes, when Alex began to think the Prime Minister was acting like one who truly believed the world had reached the so called End of Days, the prophesied Apocalypse; and mere worldly concerns like good governance were as nothing.

Abbott had access to highly qualified public administrators and professional media management experts, people who actually knew what they were talking about, how to build on strengths, eliminate weaknesses; but with his bumbling administration and mishandling of public perceptions, Abbott appeared to avail himself of none of them

He was marching to his own inner drummer, following his own higher calling, the destiny of the nation in his palm, and with the Ravishing upon the land.

****

Forty years before exactly, in 1975, in one of those peculiar twists of fate, Alex had met a then teenage Tony Abbott.

Alex was, even back then, one of the fastest typists anyone had ever seen, and he used the peculiar skill to help put himself through university, working at the Macquarie University Students' Council at the time.

The Students Council was always a hotbed of intrigue. Alex had run for President once, but got beaten out by a Trotskyist, Rod Webb. In those days of Vietnam War protests, you couldn't get far enough left.

In any case, that day he had been sitting typing away, doing all the normal clerical tasks.

And in had bowled Australia's future Prime Minister, Tony Abbott.

He was part of a group from that most elite of Sydney schools Riverview who were, in their final year, inspecting the tertiary institutions of the city which, as was their due as members of the city's upper class, they never doubted they would attend.

It was simply a matter of which one they would grace with their presence.

Abbott stood out because he was handsome, supremely fit, as he would be throughout his life, and had a certain smiling charismatic self-confidence, a self-assurance about his place in the world found only amongst the sons and daughters of the wealthy. Alex could remember the cocky walk of Abbott in 1975, that same fresh faced heir to the realm confidence you saw on the flushed cheeks of Eton's playing fields.

He also stood out because he was determinedly interested in politics, which is how he ended up at the Students Council offices, having made a specific request to see it.

What made him stand out even more, in that brief flurry of the lower ground offices, was that even back then he was avowedly interested in conservative politics. Alex, himself eternally beyond polemic, had asked, if memory served, which way Abbott the school boy leaned. He leaned right.

The memory stuck, as would so many others.

Alex leaned neither left nor right. If he leaned in any direction, it was towards the heavens. His favourite lines of the time had been:

In the forest, in the unexplored
valleys of the sky, are chapels of pure
vision. there even the desolation of space cannot
sorrow you or imprison. i dream of the lucidity of the vacuum,
orders of saints consisting of parts of a rainbow,
identities of wild things / of
what the stars are saying to each other, up there
above the concrete and the minimal existences, above
idols and wars and caring. tomorrow
we shall go there, you and your music and the
wind and i, leaving from very strange
stations of the cross, leaving from
high windows and from release,
from clearings
in the forest, the uncharted
uplands of the spirit.

Written by his contemporary, Michael Dransfield, who died of a heroin overdose at the age of 24, in 1973.

Just as Alex himself had done, Dransfield as a young man had sought the assistance and advice of Geoffrey Dutton, who had been a lion of Australian literature back in the 1960s and 1970s, a genuine light on the hill. As a teenager Alex had treasured Dutton's support, just as Dransfield had done. Geoffrey Dutton died in 1998 at the age of 76. Included in his books was the classic on early, indigenous Australia, *The Hero as*

Murderer. In the Australia of the era, for suburban boys, there was no such thing as an artistic path. And then there had been Geoffrey Dutton.

A naturally gifted writer, Dransfield would never see a day when all the hope, all the pioneering changes in consciousness and compassion that they thought they were delivering to the future would be vanquished in a heartless probity, a brutal, dysfunctional and ignorant age; an Australia Dransfield never hoped for.

A world so dysfunctional, so confused in its convictions, that it was about to be wiped away by the Sharia.

During those tumultuous times, and in the years that were to follow, many of Alex's friends died of what he referred to as the twin demons of the era, AIDS and overdoses.

That no human sympathy, no empathy, from these very different strands of Australian society, had filtered across lines of class, culture and sexual orientation to the people who had taken the Liberal Party hostage, their lives of rigorous rectitude, Tony Abbott, his mentor and predecessor John Howard and their ilk, was clearly evidenced by their actions and demeanor, their probity, their view of the way the world should be.

Their suits were their armor.

While for most students, going to university was the beginning of their explorations of the world and of their own potentialities, for finding themselves as the quaint expression went, Alex had, or so he felt, already lived several lifetimes before he got there. He had already written several admittedly unpublished books, had read everything from Joyce's *Ulysses* to Tolstoy's *War and Peace* and a great deal in between, had seen lovers die, acquired heroin habits in Penang and boyfriends in Berlin, climbed the Pyramid of the Sun in Mexico and hitch hiked across America, wandered virtually penniless through Franco's Spain and watched the famous troupe of blind singers on the main square of Marrakesh, the Jemaah al-Fnaa, walked through narrow back alleys and elegant boulevards, travelled all over Europe, been to Asia repeatedly, much of this hyper activity courtesy of the free tickets that flowed from his father's job as an airline pilot.

And had already been a part of the Sydney's inner city demimonde since 1960s, where he had quickly adopted the ethos of the street, never sleep with anyone except for money.

While Tony Abbott played Rugby on the clipped sports grounds of Riverview.

Who was he to tell anyone how to live? Who were these people, these sons of the good burghers of Sydney, these emissaries from the comfortable citadels of certitude and privilege, who thought they had the inner running on God?

Forty years on from that chance university encounter and Abbott's cock-of the-walk Eton strut was a very different story.

****

As someone who came within a hair's breath of becoming a Jesuit priest, a so-called Soldier of God, and whose Roman Catholic beliefs would determine his actions throughout his life, Tony Abbott could not have failed to understand the notion of Holy War.

Almost every single sentence of Tony Abbott's speech that conference day appeared to be tailor designed to inflame sentiment.

And it didn't take him long to swing straight into it:

"The declaration of a caliphate, preposterous though it seems, is a brazen claim to universal dominion.

"You can't negotiate with an entity like this; you can only fight it."

The declaration of a caliphate was anything but preposterous; it was an enormously successful religious, political and military strategy and was being taken very seriously indeed by millions of people around the world.

"We've sent a strong military force to the Middle East to hit Da'esh from the air and to train and assist the Iraqi army to retake their own country.

"We are talking with our friends and partners about how the air strikes might be more effective and how the Iraqi forces might be better helped.

"American leadership is indispensable here as in all the worlds trouble spots."

It was all very well to hold lunar right political positions in the privacy of your own home. To inflict them on the populace was an entirely different question.

In Alex's lifetime America's leadership had included the disasters of Vietnam, Afghanistan and Iraq.

If anyone doubted that Abbott was fighting a war of his own imagining, it was to come soon enough: "In the end, though, the only really effective defence against terrorism is persuading people that it's pointless. We have to convince people that God does not demand death to the infidel. Over time, we have to persuade people that error does have rights."

Over time, we have to persuade people that error does have rights.

What the…?

The Prime Minister was telling the Australian people, a country founded from the survival instincts of convicts, virtually all of whom had been brutally treated by their English overlords for in most cases minor misdemeanors, that error had rights? Over time, of course.

Alex had made mistakes all his life, done things instantly regretted, thrown himself, or so it sometimes felt, off the appropriate time line or over a cliff, abandonment, comfort in oblivion, from the high road to the low road. Like Moby Dick, diving into the ordinary to avoid detection. It didn't mean he was a bad person; or that he deserved to be put to death. It meant that he made mistakes, like every other human being.

"We need everyone to understand that it is never right to kill people just because their beliefs are different from ours," Abbott began his wind up. "Above all, we need idealistic young people to appreciate that joining this death cult is an utterly misguided and wrong-headed way to express their desire to sacrifice."

It was, in Alex's humble view, a thoroughly disgraceful performance.

Killing people because their beliefs were different to those of the average Australian was exactly what Australia was doing in Iraq.

Abbott closed his speech with a riff to a Christian God, to a mixed audience of Muslims, Christians, those of no faith and those of minority faiths, including a number of descendants of the first peoples.

"As the world gets smaller, the challenge to find common ground, and to build upon it, becomes more and more urgent. I thank God that more and more people are focussed on the things that unite us and invite everyone to join us in respect for the universal decencies of mankind."

Abbott had just sat through a Welcome to Country ceremony; its intent ignored by the nation's leading politician.

May you be safe while you are on our lands.

Safety on Aboriginal lands, as on the land of the vanquished Eora clan groups where he now stood, was a gift from the ancestors.

The ancient culture and profound spirituality which had held sway over Australia for tens of millennia had nothing to do with an Abrahamic God.

As the Prime Minister left the stage, puzzled by Abbott's peculiar stances, Alex listened as carefully to his own perceptions as he did to the exterior noise; and he thought one thing: "He knows, he knows what he's doing."

****

The truth of modern day Australia could be found far more easily on the streets than it ever would be in the corridors of power, grace more likely in extremes than in comfort; but there was no point in telling the rulers of Australia that in 2015.

In 2015, in the Land of Tony Abbott, there was no room for the fallen angels of the street. The Beloved of God. Once a surprisingly cheerful band, exhibiting all the black manic humour of crashed talents, they now looked out without hope; while an uncaring middle class drove past in late model cars. There was no way back across the bridge.

There should have been room for other voices, for the peculiar clairvoyance of the people on the street. There was not.

As far as Alex was concerned, those who failed to understand the fallen angels on the street were the true barbarians, the true failures.

He had always walked the streets in the predawn, and in those days of late autumn and early winter, the atmosphere chilly, distrustful and uncomprehending, he would see firsthand the consequences of the havoc Abbott and his ilk had wreaked on Australian society.

Opposite the Matthew Talbot Hostel, the largest hostel for the homeless in inner Sydney, he could easily count at least 20 people sleeping rough, the nightly overflow from the hostel, curled as mankind had done since the beginning of the species in little nests, clothes, blankets, things to soften, just slightly, the hard ground.

Every major city had people who slept rough, whose consciousnesses could not be contained within four walls, who preferred to sleep under the night skies, but now their numbers were multiplying, and much of it now was not out of choice. Urban decay, a society which had lost its way.

He watched the fallen, the poor, stir in the dark like fronds underwater, restless in those hours before sunrise, as, too, mankind had been throughout its history; and it was in these times, watching these people, that images of some of the worst of the Islamic State massacres would rise to the fore. As if, even in far off Australia, these events were ripping apart the normal fabric of time. He could hear the massacred, weeping through the wires; the dead, the injured, the grief and suffering studding the lives of the survivors. Increasingly, people at random offered up a feeling of disturbance.

It was impossible not to recall the massacre of the Yazidi, in large part due to the astonishing paintings of 31-year-old Yazidi artist Ammar Salim; remarkable in their vivid detail, agony writ large. Michelangelo or Leonardo da Vinci could not have done a better job given months to complete the task.

One painting showed smoke rising from a Yazidi town in the background, while in the foreground Islamic State flags hovered over a devastating scene, men in traditional black Arabic robes fighting over the spoils, for the young and pretty ones take into sexual slavery, other Arab raising swords to behead an old woman, while around her lie the dead.

The painting depicted the worst that men are capable of.

"We Will Kill you, We know where you live," Islamic State warned the painter.

Kill the artists. Kill the writers. For ignorance has always been the tool of tyrants.

The paintings held a remarkable similarity to the masterpiece *Massacre at Chios* by the painter Eugene Delacroix; another imprint of pain across time; another massacre of unbelievers; disease, death, cruelty against a desolate landscape, a child struggling to suckle on her dead mother. Twenty thousand civilians were killed in the attack by the Ottoman Empire, another 70,000 deported into slavery; all in the name of God.

Delacroix spoke of the spirits at the edge of sight, of paintings as a message from one soul to another. Sometimes, it seemed to Alex, he too could see those spirits hovering around the makeshift camps outside the Matthew Talbot, the ice tragics gathering on the corners, disturbed in an age of threat; waiting for the sun to rise, for a better time.

****

The Prime Minister lectured the people on God.

The Muslims lectured the people on Allah.

Yet it was the failure of the monotheistic faiths which had brought this disaster upon the world.

One of the peculiar things about this Holy War was that Islamic State was sweeping the world with barely a protest. As their members were being slaughtered or harassed into submission, leaders of the Christian churches had been remarkably silent, as if, it sometimes seemed to Alex in those inflamed early hours when his mind ran free, Christ himself had vacated the scene; evidenced by empty churches, the lack of fervor in the followers.

Well, he didn't want to offend the People of the Book, as Christians were often called, but that's the way it struck Alex; that we all make mistakes, that Christ, a clustered soul, had meant well, had aimed to lift the people up, and deeply regretted the excesses of the Early Church, the massacres and tortures, perpetrated in his name, which had been just as bad as those perpetuated by Islamic State.

But Christ having vacated the battlefield, another tide was sweeping the Earth, a far more powerful collector of souls had taken hold. The Lord of the Worlds. And with every soul offered up to join the millions already bowing down in waves of awe in his heaven, his power grew.

In his image populated fantasies, Alex had always loved the end of Empire, had been happy to return time and time again to the infinite loveliness of the Earth, a jewel suspended in the cosmos, entranced by the frailties and fascinations of its peoples, the lives through which he passed. "The world is so beautiful," as Buddha was reported to have said on his death bed.

Sometimes Alex would say out loud: "Look at all the trouble the saints have caused. Who would want to be a saint?"

He was drawn to the comments Frances Bevan had written in *Three Friends of God*, a book about a group of Catholic mystics from the 14th Century: "And so, dear children, there are great experiences, and beholdings of the Face of God, times of joy and adoration, so that we may feel ourselves in the third heaven like the blessed Paul, and yet so much may we be exalted by the very joy of God, that we shall need a messenger of Satan to buffet and beat us.

"Yes, we might be great prophets, and do great signs, and heal sick people, and discern spirits, and foretell things to come.

"In one word, children, we might have and do all things, and yet be worm-eaten apples after all. Therefore beware." [122]

Well, what would Alex know, but that was the way it seemed; as apocryphal imagery filled the internet; as the streets grew eerily, desolately quiet, with little but human wreckage filling them anymore, and fear corkscrewed into people's hearts.

****

At the Countering Violent Extremism conference Tony Abbott was followed by Julie Bishop, who had won widespread respect for her polished performance as Australia's Foreign Minister. She was one of the leading contenders to replace Abbott, when the time came.

Bishop was a professional to the tips of her fingernails.

All Alex sensed from her was dismay. The situation, and Bishop knew it, was sliding rapidly out of control.

She might have been good at hiding her feelings, but she couldn't hide her body language.

Bishop spoke to the country's cognoscenti.

On the streets and in the homes of Australia's suburbs there was barely any recognition of what was happening. People didn't want to know. The country had turned inward, because nowhere else made sense.

Jihad, Islamic State, the Sharia, they were all ideas; and unlike the simplistic Western parables of mujahedeen as barbarians, in fact it was amongst Islamic intellectuals and on the battleground of ideas that this war would be won or lost.

Bishop's speech was a partial reprise of an earlier speech she had given to the think tank the *Sydney Institute*, when she had stirred controversy by declaring Islamic State, or Da'esh as she insisted on calling them, to be

---

[122] Three Friends of God, Frances Bevan, Christian Classics Ethereal Library, 2005.

the most significant threat to the global rules based order to emerge in the past 70 years.

"This threat is a form of terrorism. more dangerous, more complex, more global than we have witnessed before, a pernicious force that could, if left unchecked, wield great global power that would threaten the very existence of nation states," Bishop had said.

"Through traditional and non-traditional means, this form of terrorism has combined the most medieval of constructs with a sophisticated use of technology in a way that challenges the very foundations of nations.

"Australia is not immune.

"Over the past 18 months in my discussions with numerous senior leaders and officials in the Middle East and Europe, many have expressed the fear that we are facing a generational struggle against Da'esh and like-minded extremists and the ideology that drives them.

"Da'esh must be stopped. There must be an international response to Da'esh to prevent a more rapid spread of its ideology and its attraction to people from across the world."

At the Countering Violent Extremism Conference, just as she had done at the Sydney Institute, Bishop referred to a book which had impressed her: Eric Hoffer's seminal work from the 1950s, *The True Believer: Thoughts on the nature of mass movement.*

With the foresight of prophecy, *The True Believer* contained extensive discussions of Islam and Christianity.

Hoffer argued that fanatical and extremist movements, religious and political, arose from identical wellsprings, and similar circumstances, when large numbers of people came to believe that their individual lives were worthless, that the modern world was corrupt and that hope lay in joining larger groups.

"The ideal potential convert is the individual who stands alone..."

Hoffer observed that highly ritualized dying and killing downplayed concerns among recruits about violence, as they saw themselves as part of a ceremony.

"This is grimly exemplified by the brutal murders by Da'esh, which they publish prolifically, and include beheadings, and crucifixions and mass murders portrayed in a way the makes them part of a ritual," Bishop said. [123]

Hoffer was himself a fascinating man; had attempted suicide, spent a decade on skid row, read widely despite the lack of a formal education and possessed a compulsion to write, saying his writing grew out of his

---

[123] Address to Regional Summit to Counter Violent Extremism, Speeches, Australian Foreign Minister, 11 June, 2015.

life as a branch from a tree: "My writing is done in railroad yards while waiting for a freight, in the fields while waiting for a truck, and at noon after lunch. Towns are too distracting."

He refused to label himself an intellectual, calling himself a longshoreman. He worked on the docks most of his life.

In *The True Believer* Hoffer wrote: "All mass movements deprecate the present by depicting it as a mean preliminary to a glorious future; a mere doormat on the threshold of the millennium. To a religious movement the present is a place of exile, a vale of tears leading to the heavenly kingdom,

"In the eyes of the true believer, people who have no holy cause are without backbone and character—a pushover for men of faith.

"All the true believers of our time—whether Communist, Nazi, Fascist, Japanese or Catholic—declaimed volubly on the decadence of the Western democracies. The burden of their talk is that in the democracies people are too soft, too pleasure-loving and too selfish to die for a nation, a God or a holy cause. This lack of a readiness to die, we are told, is indicative of an inner rot—a moral and biological decay. The democracies are old, corrupt and decadent. They are no match for the virile congregations of the faithful who are about to inherit the Earth.

"All mass movements generate in their adherents a readiness to die and a proclivity for united action; all of them, irrespective of the doctrine they preach and the program they project, breed fanaticism, enthusiasm, fervent hope, hatred and intolerance; all of them are capable of releasing a powerful flow of activity in certain departments of life; all of them demand blind faith and single hearted allegiance.

"There are vast differences in the contents of holy causes and doctrines, but a certain uniformity in the factors which make them effective. However different the holy causes people die for, they perhaps die basically for the same thing."

The True Believer concluded with a quote from a writer who by 2015 had largely lapsed into obscurity but with whom Alex and many of his generation had been fascinated by, J.B.S. Haldane, who counted fanaticism as among one of the few truly important inventions between 3000BC and 1400 AD: "It was a Judaic-Christian invention. And it is strange to think that in receiving this malady of the soul the world also received a miraculous instrument for raising societies and nations from the dead—an instrument of resurrection."

The birth of fanaticism.

A malady of the soul, a malady of the spirit.

So, to Alex, it most certainly seemed to be.

Take the words of the Koran and the Bible literally. Stone the homosexuals. Stone the adulterers. Execute the infidels.

It was the opposite of open mindedness, compassion, tolerance. And the West had welcomed it all into their midst.

****

One of the most fantastical, seemingly utterly baffling things about the Land of Tony Abbott Circa 2015 was that ever since he had come to power in September of 2013, from blatant to obscure, every single Counter Terrorism Operation, Police Taskforce and Police Strike Force had been named with what could be readily described as pro-jihad or pro-Islamic tags.

The names highlighted everything from the rising of Islamic State to the Centenary of the massacre of 1.5 million Christians in Armenia to the massacre of Muslims in Bosnia.

How could this possibly be true?

Of all the many things that did not make sense during Tony Abbott's Prime Ministership, this was to Alex's mind the single most astonishing thing of all, the thing that made the least sense of everything that had happened during Tony Abbott's entire dire stint as the country's 28th Prime Minister.

Alex, as an old news hound, counted 18 of them in all.

One, two, three, even half a dozen might have been discounted as coincidence or incompetence, but 18. Not possible.

Perhaps the issue could seem trivial; they were only names.

But in the heightened alert that was Australia 2015, it was all about messaging.

And the names appeared, on the face of it, to be a deliberate attempt to send a message; and the ones getting this message were not the dozing, hypnotized, disaffected, deluded, sports mad, television addicted majority of the Australian citizenry, but the ones most alert, awake and inflamed: the Muslim minority.

The message could not have been more clear: The Holy War had begun.

It was no wonder the Islamists had so little fear, and so little respect, for the authorities.

Jihad was coming, ably assisted by the Australian taxpayer.

To Alex there appeared to be only two conclusions to be reached: either Tony Abbott was as stupid as people liked to think he is; or he was complicit.

Few people in Australia had the will, the education or the internet skills required to decode some of the references. But Prime Minister Tony Abbott did. He had been to the best private Jesuit schools in the country.

He had been to Oxford University in England. He had studied at Australia's leading Jesuit seminary in preparation for his vows as a priest.

Most of his critics liked to dismiss Abbott by insulting his intelligence; and he was frequently called stupid.

Unfashionably, Alex never agreed. He had met Tony Abbott on a number of occasions, had watched him at numerous press conferences and knew perfectly well that the man might be many things, he might not run with the gobble turkeys of the latest intellectual fads, but he was not stupid.

Alex kept insisting: it doesn't make sense, his government doesn't make sense, Abbott doesn't make sense.

Alex had first picked up on the conundrum of the naming of counter terror and police operations when he noticed that the pre-Anzac day terror raids in April of 2015 had been named Operation Rising. In his research, he had seen the term everywhere; the Rising of Islam, the Rising of Islamic State, even the Rising of the Network Society, as those seeking enlightenment of a different kind were sometimes referred to.

The story got better when in response to questioning he was informed by the Australian Federal Police that the government had nothing to do with the naming of Counter Terrorism operations.

If the Australian government did not have anything to do with the naming of its own counter terrorism operations, then who did?

Perhaps what they meant was that the administrative wing of government had nothing to do with the naming of the operations but that it was in the hands of politicians. There would be no formal explanation.

Alex had dealt with too many incompetent government departments and officials over too many years to expect anything but dissembling from his inquiries as to exactly how 18 government operations costing many tens of millions of dollars and involving hundreds of officers came to be labeled with pro-jihad pro-Islamist names.

Before pestering the Australian Federal Police and the Prime Minister's Office with questions he knew perfectly well they would not answer, Alex, with increasing astonishment, began to track back all the names and to make a list, in approximate reverse chronological order.

They went as follows:

1. Counter Terrorism Operation Amberd: Reference to the centenary of the Armenian massacre in which 1.5 million Christians died.
2. Counter Terrorism Operation Rising: Reference to the Rising of Islam.
3. Strike Force Dawed: Digital audio workshop, you have been electronically snooped.

4. Counter Terrorism Operation Castrum: Reference to a style of fort used by the Crusaders.
5. Operation Duntulm: A castle on the Isle of Skye, where the Stone of Destiny is believed to have been held.
6. Eligo National Taskforce: The Knight of Reason or the Atheist Knight in crusades.
7. Operation Appleby. A well known radical Islamist preacher.
8. Trident Taskforce. The UK nuclear program opposed by Muslims.
9. Operation Coulter. American columnist and one of the world's most famous critics of Islam.
10. Project Tricord and Operation Polo. A musical notation from southern Iraq and a reference to Marco Polo, one of history's greatest critics of Islam.
11. Taskforce Jericho. A former Islamic Caliphate.
12. Operation Zanella. Most likely a reference to the Bosnian massacre.
13. Blue Line. After an American police information depository heavily criticized by Muslims.
14. Strike Force Raptor. A type of plane used in bombing Iraq.
15. Strike Force Duperry. A surname meaning perfect within and perfect without.
16. Taskforce Maxima. Another reference to a staunch critic of Islam.
17. Operation Hammerhead, a security service specializing in radical Islam.
18. National Task Force Attero, reference to a song about suicide bombers.

This was a nonlinear story in a linear format.

Alex could only tell the story as best he could.

Masterful ineptitude. Or destiny. Preordained, the dissolution of nation states. The Rising.

Let the cards fall where they may.

1. COUNTER TERRORISM OPERATION AMBERD.

This was name of the post-Anzac Day Counter Terrorism Operation, a Joint Counter Terrorism Operation conducted at a residence in the suburb of Greenvale in May of 2015.

Amberd is an area of what is now modern day Armenia; the site of the largest massacre of Christians in history. 2015 marked the Centenary.

An estimated 1.5 million died in 1915 at the hands of the Ottoman Empire. In memorial services the Pope declared it to be the first genocide of the 20th Century.

Turkey promptly withdrew its ambassadors from both the Vatican and Italy. The dispute made headlines around the world and was of particular interest to both Christians and Muslims.

The Armenians had been Christians since the year 301AD, making theirs the first nation to officially adopt Christianity, even before Rome.

The UK Daily Mail said the blood-soaked depravity exceeded even today's atrocities by Islamic State and began their story with the recollections of a young girl cowering in her bedroom in 1915 as she hears her father being dragged out of the house, and his shouts: "I was born a Christian and I will die a Christian."

Not until first light did the girl dare to creep downstairs.

She saw an object sticking through the front door: "I pushed it open and there lay two horseshoes nailed to two feet. My eyes followed up to the blood-covered ankles, the disjointed knees, the mound of blood where the genitals had been, to a long laceration through the abdomen to the chest. I came to the hands, which were nailed horizontally on a board with big spikes of iron, like a cross. The shoulders were remarkably clean and white, but there was no head. This was lying on the steps, propped up by the nose. I recognised the neatly trimmed beard along the cheekbones. It was my father."

2. OPERATION RISING

The AFP had called their pre-Anzac day counter terrorism operations The Rising.

Indeed it was.

This was a common expression amongst the world's estimated 1.57 billion Muslims and referred to The Rising of Islam or specifically The Rising of Islamic State.

Castle Rising was closely associated with Queen Isabella of France; a name that lived in infamy in the annals of Christian Muslim conflicts; for it was a different Queen Isabella, Isabella of Castile, who had initiated the Inquisition; and had accepted the surrender of the Muslims at Granada. The two were connected through the British royal family. Many Muslims and Jews were forced to convert or put to death during the Inquisition. The Roman Catholic Church gave Isabella of Castile the title of Servant of God in 1974.

3. STRIKEFORCE DAWED

The Middle East and Counter Terrorism Task Force operation in Sydney in May of 2015 was named Dawed.

This is internet slang for Digital Audio Workshop, and the term Dawed translates, to put it colloquially, as "you've been electronically snooped."

With listening posts across Western Sydney utilizing Arabic speakers to track the conversations and activities of suspected terrorist sympathizers, being "dawed" was a major issue for the Islamic community.

Strike Force Dawed comprised officers from the State Crime Command's Middle Eastern Organised Crime Squad and was established in February of 2015 to investigate the supply of drugs throughout Sydney. As the Australian Crime Commission confirmed, illicit drugs were a major source of income for gangs channeling funds in the hundreds of millions of dollars towards terrorist groups.

Police conducted extensive searches of 10 properties, during which they located and seized amounts of methyl amphetamine, heroin and cocaine; a pistol, a sawn-off shot gun and ammunition; and approximately $100,000 in cash.

Seven people were arrested and variously charged with supplying commercial quantities of prohibited drugs, knowingly dealing with the proceeds of crime, knowingly participating in a criminal group, shooting with intent to cause grievous bodily harm and discharging a firearm in a public place likely to cause injury.

4. COUNTER TERRORISM OPERATION CASTRUM

This was a NSW Joint Counter Terrorism Operation, also in 2015.

Two men were arrested on the 10th of February, 2015, at Fairfield in Western Sydney and charged with preparing or planning to terrorist acts. There is a town in Palestine known as Castrum, a style of Fort used by the "crusaders" throughout Palestine during the Crusades.

The ruins of Castle Castrum in Europe exhibit this style of crusader architecture.

Police alleged that the two men were well advanced in their preparations to undertake a terrorist act in Australia as revenge for incidents overseas. [124]

---

[124] AFP Media Release, 11 February, 2015.

5. OPERATION DUNTULM

The Castle of Duntulm on the Isle of Skye is believed to have been built on the site of a number of structures dating back to prehistoric times.

The site may in all possibility have been at one time a keeping place for the Stone of Destiny, the most significant stone in Christianity. Legend has it that it is made of the same material or may have once been a part of the same stone as the Kaaba in Mecca.

Exactly why the world's two largest monotheistic faiths regard a stone as sacred is lost in the early annals of both faiths, and is believed to predate the birth of both faiths.

Legend has it that it contains some of the oldest material on earth. The Isle of Skye is believed to have been the first point of contact between the Islamic world and the Celtic kings.

Operation Duntulm was an ongoing Joint Counter Terrorism investigation into alleged financial assistance for foreign fighters.

On the 10th of January, 2015, a NSW Police-led investigation with members of the Joint Counter Terrorism Team Sydney, NSW Police Tactical Operations Unit, Public Order and Riot Squad, Middle Eastern Organised Crime Squad and the Bankstown Local Area Command saw the execution of a number of search warrants across south western Sydney.

Commander of the Counter Terrorism and Special Tactics Command Mark Murdoch said Operation Duntulm had been running for more than a year and was focused on a range of support mechanisms being provided for those who had left Australia and were now fighting overseas.

"The operation today is about the gathering of evidence and intelligence to enable us to take action against those who think they can engage in these activities," he said. "Investigators this morning seized a range of items from the premises searched including documents and computers, and these will be forensically examined. The community is again reminded that fighting in or supporting overseas conflicts is illegal and extremely dangerous. It doesn't matter who you are or what you believe in, if you choose to illegally fight in an overseas conflict you are not only breaking the law, you are placing yourself in immense danger." [125]

---

[125] AFP Media Release, 10 January, 2015.

6. THE ELIGO NATIONAL TASK FORCE

Eligo was the Knight of Reason, or the Atheist Knight, from the Crusades.

It is also in more recent times the name of a prominent blogger who denies the existence of God, and also the name of a prominent organization Eligo International, which specializes in high-level diplomacy, including interfaith dialogues between leaders of the Muslim, Jewish and Christian faiths. Such dialogue is anathema to the Islamic State.

In Latin the word means to pick out or to choose; for instance in the phrase eligo ratio vel mortem, choose reason or death.

The Eligo National Task Force targeted money laundering, directly associated with the funding of terrorist organizations and had led investigations into the use of alternative remittance and informal value transfer systems by organized crime syndicates.

In 2014 the Task Force claimed to have seized $665 million of drugs and assets, $38.5 million of it in cash, and to have disrupted 18 organized crime groups and identified 128 criminal targets.

7. OPERATION APPLEBY

There were several Islamist connotations to the name Appleby. There was an Australian academic, critical of Tony Abbott's approach to terrorism, named Appleby. As well, a former AFP Manager of Serious and Organised Crime, Damien Appleby, came to public attention when he broke up a racket importing semi-automatic firearm components.

Operation Appleby, however, was most likely to have been named after Tariq Appleby of the Muslim Heroes Project. Based in Malaysia, it was a part of a worldwide effort to rediscover and resurrect Islam's past martyrs and noble warriors. Appleby's particular areas of interest were the education of youth and the encouragement of the institution of marriage.

Operation Appleby was an ongoing operation being conducted by the Sydney-based Joint Counter Terrorism Team which was investigating persons suspected to be involved in domestic terrorist acts, foreign incursions into Syria and Iraq and the funding of terrorist organizations. Sixteen people were detained on 16th of September, a day after Abbott announced military intervention in Iraq.

8. THE TRIDENT TASK FORCE

The Trident Task Force was likely to be named after the UK Trident Nuclear Missile program, the British nuclear defense system, which was opposed by Muslim groups.

Throughout 2015 the acquisition of nuclear weaponry by Islamic State had been a subject of increasing concern. A whistle blower claimed that the Trident Nuclear Missile security was so poor it was only a matter of time before nuclear submarines became a target for terrorists.

In 2003 UK Defence Secretary Geoff Hoon declared that the UK would use Trident in Iraq if chemical or biological weapons threatened British troops.

The Trident Hotel in Mumbai, part of the Oberoi complex, was the subject of terrorist attacks in 2008. There were other associations.

The Trident Taskforce disrupted a number of drug running operations; and seized large quantities of drugs, steroids and human growth hormones. The Taskforce consisted of members of the Victorian Police, the AFP, Australian Customs and Border Protection, Australian Transaction Reports and Analysis Centre, the Australian Tax Office and the Australian Crime Commission.

The Trident Taskforce also broke up some of the biggest organized illicit tobacco syndicates in the country's history, including rackets importing large volumes from Indonesia and the United Arab Emirates.

9. OPERATION COULTER

Ann Coulter was a famous, or infamous, conservative American columnist who declared after the September 11 attacks: "We know who the homicidal maniacs are. They are the ones cheering and dancing right now. We should invade their countries, kill their leaders and convert them to Christianity. We weren't punctilious about locating and punishing only Hitler and his top officers. We carpet-bombed German cities; we killed civilians. That was war. And this is war."

She also famously said: "Not all Muslims are terrorists – but all terrorists are Muslims" and "If only we could get all Muslims to boycott airlines, we could dispense with airport security altogether." [126]

Operation Coulter was also involved in disrupting drug syndicates.

---

[126] AFP Media Release, 17 April, 2013.

10. PROJECT TRICORD & OPERATION POLO

This was a joint agency operation in Western Australia.

The Islamist reference in Project Tricord was not clear, but could refer to a media organization Tricord Media, which has produced a CD series Burning Questions which relates to questions of faith and inter-faith issues, including the Islamic faith; interfaith dialogue anathema to fundamentalists. The series quoted Jews, Christians and Muslims and asked Which Religion is true?

It was also possibly a variation on the spelling of trichord, a musical notation found particularly in southern Iraq. There is no correlation in Western music.

In May of 2014 500 police were involved in executing 38 search warrants. Half a million dollars in cash and 21 firearms were seized and 19 people charged with drug related offenses, including dealing with proceeds of crime in excess of one million dollars. Some 130 foreign nationals working for the drug syndicate were questioned and detained.

Marco Polo, often referred to simply as Polo in the literature, was a famous early traveller.

While there were doubts over its authenticity, in a quote which had gained widespread currency on the internet Polo was reported as saying: "The militant Muslim is the person who beheads the infidel, while the moderate Muslim holds the feet of the victim."

Marco Polo was considered Islamophobic. Of the Muslims of Iraq, he wrote: "According to their doctrine, whatever is stolen or plundered from others of a different faith, is properly taken, and the theft is no crime; whilst those who suffer death or injury by the hands of Christians, are considered martyrs." He was repeatedly critical of Muslims, the enslavement of women and the murdering of infidels; including the caliph of Baghdad whose "daily thoughts were employed on the means of converting to his religion those who resided within his dominions, or, upon their refusal, in forming pretenses for putting them to death." [127]

11. JERICHO WATERFRONT TASKFORCE

Jericho in the Middle East repeatedly came under the control of Arab caliphates. It was known as the fertile City of Palms. Arab geographer Al-Maqdisis wrote in 985 that "the water of Jericho is held to be the highest and the best in all Islam." In earlier years it was part of

---

[127] *The Travels of Marco Polo*, Double Day & Company, 1948.

the Jund Filastin, the Military District of Palestine. Caliph Umar ibn al-Khattab exiled Jews and Christians to Jericho. The city flourished until 1071 with the invasion of the Seijuk Turks and the subsequent upheavals of the Crusades.

In Australia the Jericho Waterfront Taskforce was established to combat criminality on the Queensland docks, which were even more lax in their security arrangements than docks to the south. They were believed to be major transport hubs for drugs into Australia. In June of 2015 the Taskforce conducted 604 vehicle checks and 50 roadside drug tests as part of a blitz on the Gladstone Port in northern Queensland. Agencies involved included the Australian Federal Police, Queensland police Service, Australian Customs, Australian Crime Commission, the Australian Tax Office and the Australian Transaction Reports and Analysis Centre.

12. OPERATION ZANELLA

There are numerous Islamic associations with the name Zanella. The Piazza Zanella in northern Italy had been a focal point for Muslim demonstrations, with one in 2015 on the theme Islam and Immigration: the duty to defend ourselves.

There were also a significant number of prominent Islamic scholars with the name Zanella, including British Muslim academic Yusuf Zanella, a contributor to the magazine Islamica.

President Zanella of the Free State of Fiume, an independent state between 1920 and 1924, annexed by Italy and now part of Croatia. Alex's reading of the maps showed that it covered the area of the Bosnian massacres.

Zanella was also the name of an Italian politician who has spoken out in defense of free speech and condemned the attacks on the Islamic intellectual Ayaan Hirsi Ali, whose most recent book *Heretic: Why Islam Needs a Reformation Now* resulted in numerous death threats and the provision of 24 hour security.

Operation Zanella was the AFP code name linked to the Eligo National Taskforce which specifically targeted money laundering operations. In September of 2014 significant volumes of documentation believed to be related to the laundering millions of dollars out of Australia were seized in raids across four states.

13. BLUE LINE

Would appear to be based on the American operation known as The Thin Blue Line, which is accessible to past and present law enforcement officials in the US and described by American Muslims as extremely offensive to their faith; and whose material is reported to include advice on how to detect a jihadist, such as finding Muslim Student Association literature in a Person of Interest's car. There were other more offensive characterizations. In Australia it operated as a similar central source for information.

14. STRIKE FORCE RAPTOR

There were numerous news stories of ISIS members being killed by Raptors, a type of drone.

Raids by Strike Force Raptor were conducted in 2014, seizing firearms, drugs and cash, major sources of funding for Australian based terrorists.

The F22 being used to bomb Iraq was also known as the Raptor.

Strike Force Raptor was particularly associated with motorbike gangs, major distributors and suppliers of drugs within Australia. There was a strong Lebanese contingent within the Clubs. There were a number of major raids in 2014.

15. STRIKE FORCE DUPERRY

According to the online Urban Dictionary this is a surname which translates as: Someone who is extremely beautiful on the inside as well as the outside. Someone with this name has potential in everything and is born to make the world

On the face of it this is a reference to the Prophet Muhammad.

On the 20th of May, 2014 detectives investigating a drug trafficking syndicate seized 60 kilograms of precursor drugs for the manufacture of ice.

Strike Force Duperry was a joint investigation by the NSW Police Force's Organised Crime Squad, the Australian Crime Commission and the NSW Crime Commission, with support and assistance provided by the Australian Federal Police and the Australian Customs and Border Protection Service.

Four men in the early twenties were charged with large commercial drug supply. All were refused bail. Seizures included passports suspected of being counterfeit, mobile phones, cash and documents.

Previous seizures by the Strike Force included an assault rifle and ammunition, ice with a potential street value of $2 million, heroin with a potential street value of $870,000 and cash.

Joint intelligence analysis had previously indicated that members of the syndicate were involved in the importation of 42 kilograms of pseudo-ephedrine, a precursor to ice, in sea freight from China.

Australian Crime Commission CEO Chris Dawson said the operation led to the dismantling of a high risk, serious and organized crime syndicate that had been highly resilient to traditional law enforcement approaches.

16. TASKFORCE MAXIMA

Taskforce Maxima was established in Queensland as part of a crackdown on drug trafficking in Queensland, particularly motor cycle gangs.

There are a number of Islamic connotations for Maxima, including the Mecca Maxima cosmetics company, established in October 2013 and with a branch in Tony Abbott's electorate. Their recent most advertised brand was Urban Decay.

There were also waves of Muslim protests in Indonesia over the release by Maxima Pictures of a movie by a porn star.

An early Christian female saint of the same name was flayed to death.

The most important reference however is to Queen Maxima of Holland, who had been active in the debate over whether Muslim immigration was destroying the traditional way of life in Holland. Author Ayaan Hirsi Al had been under 24-hour guard ever since the Dutch film maker Theo van Gogh was killed by Islamists because of the film Submission, in which she highlighted the plight of millions of Muslim women. She was forced to return to Holland after America refused to provide her with protection.

Ali claimed that Dutch multicultural polices which encouraged large Muslim intakes had been a mistake which was destroying the country. "In no other modern religion," Ali wrote, "is dissent still a crime, punishable by death." [128]

There were still other government Operations which could be easily interpreted as having pro-jihad tags.

---

[128] Ex-Muslim author and activist Ayaan Hirsi Ali calls for reform of Islam, News, 23 March, 2015.

17. OPERATION HAMMERHEAD

Operation Hammerhead appeared not to be a reference to the Hammerhead shark, common off the east coast of Australia, but to a security group targeting radical Islam.

The riot squad, traffic patrol and mounted police formed part of the high visibility operation on Sydney's streets to guard against potential revenge attacks and other conflicts following counter-terrorism raids in September of 2014 and the announcement that Australia was re-engaging in Iraq. Some 220 police officers covered transport hubs, landmarks and public areas.

18. ATTERO NATIONAL TASK FORCE

The Attero National Task Force appeared to be a direct reference to the third album of Swedish heavy metal group Sabaton. Songs on the album involved considerable glorification of the Nazis, with whom the Muslim world sided in the Second World War; and song titles included Rise of Evil, The Final Solution and In the Name of God, about suicide bombers in the Middle East.

The lyrics for In the Name of God ran in part:

Hide from the public eye, choose to appear when it suits you
Claim you're just, killing women and children
Fight, when you choose to fight, hide in a cave when you're hunted
Like a beast spawned from hell, utilizing fear

Chosen by god or a coward insane?
Stand up and show me your face!

Suicidal, in a trance
A religious army
Fight without a uniform and hide in the crowd
Call it holy, call it just
Authorized by heaven
Leave your wounded as they die, and call it gods will

The names were beyond coincidence, from the celebration of massacres to right wing columnists.

When he first raised the issue with terror message expert Professor Anne Aly she said: "That's no coincidence."

None of it engendered confidence.

What next, Alex thought, Operation Sharia.

Might as well.

As was the nature of journalism in contrast to reportage, questions forged the story.

So although he did not expect any coherent accounting, he asked the questions of the Australian Federal Police's Media Office in any case:

1. What is the traditional way in which Counter Terrorism Operation names are chosen; who is responsible, what vetting is done by senior members of the AFP over the use of these names to ensure that they do not give inappropriate signals?
2. Has the process changed since the Abbott government came to power?
3. Has the Prime Minister's Office, the Prime Minister himself or anyone in his office directed the AFP as to the choice of names since he came to office in September of 2013?
4. Has the Prime Minister or anyone in his office expressed any concern whatsoever to the AFP over the choice of names for the country's counter terrorism operations? Has anyone within the AFP at any time ever been directed by any member of parliament, or anyone at all outside the organisation, as to the choice of names?
5. Has there at any time been any concerns raised by any community, judicial or parliamentary group over the choice of names?
6. Has any public servant, senior departmental head or anyone else within the public service ever expressed concerns to the AFP over the naming of the counter terrorism operations?
7. Has the AFP at any point in time expressed any concern to the Prime Minister's Office over the naming of counter terrorism operations since Tony Abbott came to power? Has the AFP ever felt under any political pressure to name the operations in one way or another?

The response: that the Australian government had nothing to do with the naming of Australian counter terrorism operations.

An answer so bizarre it was instructive within itself.

He asked a similar set of questions of the Prime Minister's office; had the Prime Minister or anyone in his office ever made any directions as to the naming of police and counter terrorism operations?

There was no answer.

In a land of ailing democratic institutions, where there was no accountability, where those who ruled had forgotten they also served, there would be no answer.

The average Australian might not have known that Operation Amberd was a direct reference to the largest massacre of Christians in history; but the Prime Minister would have. The average Australian might not have known that Operation Coulter was a direct reference to one of the world's most famously barbed critics of Islam, that Operation Zanella a was a direct reference to the Bosnian massacres of Muslims, or that Operation Polo was a reference to one of history's greatest critics of Islam, that Taskforce Maxima was a direct reference to one of the world's leading academic critics of Islam, a woman who had famously written: "Tolerance of intolerance is cowardice."

But the Prime Minister would have.

And so should the nation's security organizations to which he had gifted more than a billion dollars in additional funding, the Australian Federal Police, the Australian Security and Intelligence Organisation, the Australian Secret Intelligence Service and the Australian Signals Directorate.

The fact that not one good Muslim pointed out to the nation's security authorities that they had been naming their counter terror operations with pro-jihad tags showed how deeply, totally the security apparatus was compromised.

The public was entitled to ask, if a simple matter like the naming of operations in a manner so as to avoid sending counterproductive messages could not be got right; what other things were going wrong in these administrations almost entirely immune to public scrutiny?

Alex had once lived next door to Philip Knightly, the famous journalist. They would meet on their respective doorsteps sometimes. Alex couldn't have been a bigger fan. Knightly, a true gentleman of the old school of journalism, was the author of that brilliant book, "The First Casualty."

As in, The First Casualty In War Is Truth.

And so, so terribly, it remained the case.

No truer a phrase, no better a truism.

****

The Prime Minister did not stop long enough to hear the next speaker, Muslim Abdul-Rehman Malik, a London-based journalist who contributed regularly to the BBC and was program manager for a group calling itself the Radical Middle Way. He decried the use of "death cult" rhetoric as unhelpful.

Then he demanded of the audience, in a kind of pantomime he had clearly done before: "What do you see in this picture?"

He held up a well-known picture of a man with graying hair, his hands bound behind his back, blindfolded, being held by two Islamic State captors on the ledge of a tall building. The man was accused of being a homosexual. For the crime of loving in a different way, he was about to be shoved to his death.

In the well-known incident, when it became apparent that the man had not died on impact, the crowd below stoned him to death. Ironically, it was an image frequently used because it was less confronting than many others.

In the name of Allah The All Merciful.

In the name of the Merciless Prejudices of the Mob.

"What do you see in this picture?" Malik demanded again.

"A mobile phone," one of the audience volunteered.

"That's right," he said. And went on.

The thing that was most striking about the scene was not that yet another homosexual was being killed by Islamic State, but that the scene was being filmed from both sides, the two perpetrators both had mobile phones, were both filming, and the footage would be up on the internet via Twitter within a blink.

Just as with executions filmed on Mobile Phones, so the facing of Network Seven onto Martin Place, once deemed a terrific marketing ploy, with curious onlookers gathering in shots behind morning hosts and the glassed in Seven Studios becoming a Sydney institution, had now made Martin Place one of the most dangerous places in Australia.

The Seven studios were exactly like a mobile phone.

They amplified through their cameras actions of symbolic import.

The nightmare that was now visiting Europe, the death of the old cultures, the institution of Sharia, restive, dangerous, alienated and growing Muslim populations convinced of the divine rightness of their cause, had well and truly arrived in Australia.

There were now many hundreds of jihadists within Australia who would gladly gift their souls to Allah.

In the night, in the morning, thoughts came unbidden in some sort of heightened state.

"You are under attack."

Alex didn't know how reliable they were; he couldn't know, for every moment changed in decaying, corporeal forms, these bodies of the flesh, unfounded of spirit.

But he issued the advice, as if someone was listening: "Triple the watch on Martin Place. It has all the symbols, a secular place without a mosque; the cenotaph, deemed a celebration of previous invasions of Muslim lands, the banks, the Post Office, law firms, insurance companies, an upmarket hotel. nearby Parliament House and the law courts where a number of Muslims had now been tried; all of them are now targets, all of them are now profoundly unsafe."

How they would do, when they would do it, these things could not be easily divined; that was the point of terror. No one knew where. No one knew when. Everybody was frightened. The agents of chaos, with their lone wolf calls and ceaseless plotting, had made the situation totally unpredictable. The only way out was the worship of Allah. The Lord of the Worlds. The All Merciful.

After the Prime Minister had given his speech Alex stood off to a distance and watched the glad handing of various conference attendees, many of whom Abbott would have known or recognized from the diplomatic circuit. His large-boned Chief of Staff, the oft hated Peta Credlin, hair dyed a not very fetching shade of blonde, hovered nearby, clipboard in hand, worried expression across her brow, shepherding him along.

She couldn't get her boss out of there fast enough. The pair of them left Pier One as quickly as dignity would allow. There would be no sitting around listening to the experts. And no talking to the media.

The Prime Minister was shepherded through the protective arms of his security detail, back into his busy life. While Alex went back into the fabric of Sydney, a city full of ghosts.

After leaving Pier One Alex walked through the historic alleyways of Millers Points, past some of the oldest surviving buildings in the colony, climbed back into his car, thankful he hadn't got yet another parking ticket, and drove back into what for him was an increasingly unforgiving place. In what seemed like an instant, but in fact had been a long time brewing, Sydney had become an extremely dangerous, unsafe city.

SECTION FIVE: THE PONDING OF IGNORANCE

THROUGHOUT THE EARLY months of 2015 Australia was gripped by the sad debacle of the execution of two members of the so-called Bali 9; Andrew Chan and Myurna Sukumaran.

If the Prime Minister of Australia Tony Abbott still thought it would be a good idea to assist America in the invasion of Muslim lands, then President Joko Widodo of Indonesia, the world's most populous Muslim nation, was about to teach him a lesson in the Art of Holy War.

Indonesia had a population of more than 252 million people, with an estimated 87 per cent of them being Muslim.

An archipelago of islands, there had been an increasingly fundamentalism and radicalization of the population since the 2002 Bali bombings.

The decision to answer President Obama's call to invade Iraq soured Australia's relationship with its northern neighbor.

Now two Australians would make "the ultimate sacrifice."

The Bali 9, as they were known, youthful drug smugglers who took advantage of a market created by ill-advised legislation and tried to make some money on a heroin importation scheme.

The scheme came badly undone after the Australian Federal Police passed on the information they had on the scheme to the Indonesian police, no doubt causing great embarrassment. As was customary, the chances of the Indonesian police not having already been bribed for the transaction was remote.

An extremely minor kerfuffle in world terms, major in Australian terms, was the question of whether or not the Australian Federal Police had "blood on their hands," whether they were responsible for the deaths because they had informed the Indonesian authorities, thereby insuring the young Australians would be arrested on Indonesian soil, and face the death sentence.

One of the many ironies of drug legislation had always been that the authorities knew all about drug smuggling schemes, from one end of the supply chain to the other. While the politicians made their laws, the authorities took their take and looked the other way, from the poppy fields of Asia to the streets of Sydney. The chance that the Indonesian authorities did not already know about one of their own countrymen selling kilograms of heroin to a foreigner was zero.

Alex had seen it all before, on a different assignment; the narrow backstreets where he was the only foreigner for miles; the large comfortable house, the not-so-discretely well-armed guard.

He had been ushered into one of the house's exterior living rooms by a maid and the ever attendant security, where after a short time a man had emerged and graciously asked him to make himself comfortable, would he like a cup of tea?

Yes, thank you.

The man had explained that his grandfather had set up the business more than 60 years before. As he laid out sample ounces of various brands, he boasted that in contrast to his rivals he always had the best quality and range, from China White to Indian Brown, could supply in any quantity whatsoever, and was happy to help establish new conduits to the West.

It was all an easy matter. Everyone would be paid. Discretion was paramount. Guitars were a favourite smuggling instrument of the time.

If anyone thought that everyone from the rickshaw driver to the neighbors to the local police hadn't noticed exactly where he was going, and knew exactly what business that house was involved in, and if they didn't think the local authorities and custom agents were not all paid handsomely for their cooperation, then they were naive.

Not one journalist asked the obvious question: what happened to the Indonesian suppliers?

Why weren't they facing a firing squad? Were they still selling kilos of heroin to foreign drug networks?

Of course they were.

Not to mention the fact that while it was hard to find alcohol, you could find hashish on virtually any street corner across the Muslim world; they just didn't regard it as a drug.

They two Bali 9 facing the death sentence, along with victims from several other nationalities, made perfect fodder for a spectacle that would rivet Indonesia, sadden and horrify the Australian public, and should have at last woken up the Australian government to the dire danger their foreign policy was putting their country and their citizens into.

Whatever misinformation the Abbott government fed the Australian public, it was not lost for a second on either the Indonesian government or the Indonesian people that Australia was now directly involved in murdering Muslims in Iraq and Syria.

In the weeks preceding the executions President Widodo had not even bothered to answer Tony Abbott's calls. Why should he talk to an infidel who was killing innocent Muslims in far off lands?

Never forget: my brother is my brother.

The idea that the executions were about paying the penalty for drug smuggling was a nonsense.

Widodo had given clemency to three convicted murderers in the preceding months; and his country sought clemency for Indonesians caught in similar situations around the world.

On 4th March, 2015 Chan was transferred from his Bali jail to Nusa Kambangan, also known as Execution Island.

That these were no ordinary executions was obvious from the start.

A massive display of state power, including heavy, ostentatious security, an armada of vehicles accompanying the prison vans, and planes flying overhead were all part of what would normally been a quiet, secretive middle-of-the-night transfer from a prison to an execution site.

Hundreds of helmeted police in full riot gear formed lines outside Kerobokan Prison and lined the route, while planes flew overhead.

The two Australian prisoners were placed inside an armored paramilitary police vehicle called a Barracuda for the transfer. The men were dressed in straight jackets, handcuffed and manhandled on to the plane for the transfer from Bali to Java.

Their immediate security detail wore not just black helmets and black riot gear, they also wore black balaclavas, a characteristic of Islamic State executioners.

Australia's Foreign Minister Julie Bishop described her shock at the force used during the transfer from Kerobokan prison to the execution site Nusa Kambangan Island. "I just cannot comprehend it," she told media. "They are two men who are described by their own prison governors as model citizens, two gentlemen who pose no risk to anyone. I cannot comprehend the manner or the method of their transfer." [129]

The Foreign Minister would come to understand all too well all too soon; as the shock and grief driven into her face in the wake of the executions testified.

It wasn't about force. It was all about spectacle.

Indonesian authorities refused those facing the death sentence the right of a pastor of their choice to witness the executions. There would be no mercy for the Christians.

Nor were the relatives of the unbelievers, those outside the faith of Islam, treated with even a modicum of respect.

Families of the condemned arriving at the port of Cilacap to take the ferry to the execution site, only to be faced with lines of security guards and snarling dogs, an out of control media pack and a baying public.

---

[129] Australia lodges complaint over Bali transfer, CNN, 6 March, 2015.

It was an old trick, to let those you did not like face a media mob, personnel with cameras, microphones and notepads jostling frantically for position. Alex had seen the Australian authorities do it themselves. It added to the ignominy, the distress; and the theatre.

Fairfax Media's Indonesian Correspondent Jewel Topsfield reported: "The Sukamaran family arrived first, and the media scrum was so intense they could not move. They were literally trapped on every side. Myuran's sister collapsed. One of male members of the family was screaming with terror. They were really distressing, frightening, chaotic scenes. It seems extraordinary that they were not driven into the port, that they had to face this media maelstrom." [130]

Peter Fray was an old colleague from his days on *The Sydney Morning Herald* wrote in a front page story: "We've seen the firing squad gathering on the island, smiling and joking. A guard outside the prison was seen giving the thumbs up sign. And we've seen a sign-writer putting Chan's and Sukumaran's death dates on crosses."

Many in the media mob were Indonesian journalists, following the story in triumphant detail. Footage showed security guards with Doberman dogs in the midst of the melee; adding to the heightened sense of panic.

When news of the Bali 9 arrests first broke, Alex, as a general news reporter, had been tasked with finding the families of those who came from Sydney; in particular, Andrew Chan, whose family other reporters were finding difficult to locate. What struck him was how little family he had.

Born in 1984, Chan had only been 21 years old when he was arrested at Denpasar Airport in 2005. He was described as a ring leader of a heroin importation gang, a ludicrous accusation against someone so young.

Chan was born in Sydney to first generation Cantonese speaking migrants. He had an older brother and two older sisters, but from what Alex could determine only one remained in Sydney.

It took quite some diligent research tracking down Chan's family; with a name like Chan and with a population cohort which spoke little English.

After several hours working every technique he could think of, Alex spoke to Chan's father; but the man had limited English, and the conversation was difficult.

And in any case talking to the Chinese, who had long been importers of some of Australia's best heroin, about heroin smuggling

---

[130] Bali nine families make final desperate pleas, Jewel Topsfield, The Sydney Morning Herald, 28 April, 2015.

was in itself not a subject on which they were likely to be very forthcoming.

Very few people have the criminal contacts necessary to facilitate the purchase of kilos of heroin. Chan's community contacts no doubt facilitated the purchase.

The Chinese had always had a healthy distrust of the media; and of all the ethnic groups Alex had encountered and reported on, they were the least forthcoming of all.

No use trying to tell them that the Fourth Estate was a vital component of a modern democracy. They had already learnt in their own country: trust no one. And in particular trust no one in a position of authority. It was usually not that difficult to establish an instant rapport and convince someone that telling their version of events to a journalist they could trust was a positive thing to do. But the Chinese perceived journalists as authorities rather than as independent scribes because they came from a country where the media outlets were government owned.

In 2006 Chan was sentenced to death by firing squad.

After a decade in prison the pair had spent so long on death row they were approaching the ten year point where Indonesian custom allowed for sentences to be commuted or reviewed.

They weren't going to reach the 10 year mark, and the President of Indonesia Joko Widodo had no intention of letting them.

Chan worked an unglamorous job in a catering company in Western Sydney. In an interview he said: "I don't think I was really going anywhere in life. I don't think, you know, I was achieving too much, even though I had a stable job and all. Yes, I don't think I was really heading anywhere, to be honest, you know, I've used drugs myself, I was a drug user. You know, I know what it feels like to - to be, you know, one of them junkies walking on the street I guess... You don't think too much about - I didn't anyway. You know, most people think yeah, you would, but I didn't. It wasn't - more or less for me it was just quick pay day, that's it. Just think to yourself quick pay day, that's it - nothing more, nothing less." [131]

In the sequence of events, on the transfer flight to Central Java a smiling Denpasar police chief posed for photographs with the condemned men.

Australia made an official complaint over the photographs, which would do about as much good as had their legal appeals.

---

[131] Bali 9: Andrew Chan revisits his past, Deborah Cassrels, The Australian, 4 March, 2015.

Although clearly posing for the photograph while placing his hand on Chan's back, Commissioner Djoko Har Utomo claimed he did not know the picture was being taken and was simply trying to cheer up the condemned men. The image was distributed to local and international media.

While the police officer may have been smiling, Chan indeed looked grim.

But there was to come one sunny, final, utterly poignant day.

Chan would marry his fiancé Febyanti Herewila on Execution Island, in the final 48 hours of his life, despite the inevitability of what was to follow. The wedding was officiated by Chan family friend and Salvation Army Minister David Soper.

The wedding was documented by officials from the Attorney Generals and Prosecutions Office.

****

On the same day that the final countdown to the executions turned into its final hours, Alex discovered that he could not get into his own car, that the lock had been damaged after someone tried to break into it.

"It's crazy," said the mechanic said who came to fix the lock; a lament that could be heard just about everywhere. "It's all happened in the last ten years," he said. "You can't get ahead anymore. I blame the GST."

"Used to be a great country," Alex replied. "Not anymore."

Yes, well the GST had been another pack of lies from the political class.

"Never, ever," Tony Abbott's mentor, former Prime Minister John Howard, had declared in the lead up to one election; promptly changing his mind afterwards.

The tax was a direct attack on the small business operators who voted for Howard in droves; while the billions of dollars it raked off the people had been entirely wasted.

The legacy of the tax could be seen in the empty shops of Australia's shopping malls; the deathly pall, the lack of vibrancy in local economies, and the consequent depression of the populace.

Screwed by the left and screwed by the right.

In those final hours before the Indonesian execution, outside the Stonewall Bar where he had taken on the habit of sitting and relaxing after work, Alex had been watching, as was his wont, the ludicrous consequences of the country's over-regulation.

As usual, security guards were trying to tell punters that they had to sit on one of the few available chairs if they wanted to have a cigarette; the regulation being that you had to be sitting at a table in order to have a smoke.

That the chairs were already occupied didn't matter; the security guards had to do their job in complying with another absurd regulatory restriction. The security guard was having no luck with a rather large lesbian, who was pointing out the obvious that there were no seats vacant, but a gay man was more compliant, and managed to sit down long enough, while its occupant went to the loo, to get a few puffs down his throat.

That was when one of the derelict humans who occupied the area, this one a woman he had spotted over the years, sat down, stole his drink and then brazenly pretended it was hers.

Alex was in research mode, not conflict mode, got up, went to the ATM and bought himself another.

Sitting down again, he asked Old Reg, a regular at the tables, for a cigarette. "It's difficult to maintain grace under pressure sometimes," Alex said, and made sure the woman knew he knew.

Not that she could care. She had won the day and had a beer in hand.

They were small incidents, but you could tell a lot about a society from the behaviour of the people on the street.

Australia had turned into a nation of thieves. The underclass had always been a little light fingered, the five-fingered discount as the Australian expression went. But the situation was getting patently worse; people on the street more visibly desperate, more devolved.

It was a society in collapse.

Uncomfortable sitting next to someone who had just stolen from him, Alex stood up and went home; to that 14th floor apartment at the bottom of Oxford Street where he had briefly dwelt and where he had felt nothing but lonely in the sky; and where he heard all too much from the surrounding apartments.

There would be worse to come.

****

By morning Andrew Chan and Myuran Sukumaran were dead in what as far as Alex was concerned was the greatest jihad spectacle ever mounted by Indonesia.

The subjects of execution sang Amazing Grace and refused to wear blind folds as they faced their executioners:

Amazing Grace, how sweet the sound
That saved a wretch like me,
I once was lost but now am found,
Was blind, but now I see.

Yea, when this flesh and heart shall fail,
And mortal life shall cease,
I shall possess within the vail,
A life of joy and peace.

That the murders drew international attention was entirely the point.

Some local spectators laughed while playing videos on their phones of coffins and police leaving the execution site.

There were numerous tweets along the lines of Nicki@OzzeeLady: "Unintelligent uneducated third world people! Need to STOP SENDING Indonesia money! Australians need to STOP GOING THERE."

Of course they needed to stop going there. If they didn't think there was another Bali bombing coming, they couldn't read the tea leaves. Or take note of the flaming obvious.

That Australia had been sending a wealthy country like Indonesia a billion dollars a year in foreign aid, money raked off the backs of ordinary Australian taxpayers who could barely afford to pay their own electricity bills, was one of those anomalous travesties of Australian governance that desperately needed reform; and for which the Australian Department of Foreign Affairs and Trade was almost entirely to blame.

Australian aid money went to the construction of schools teaching what bureaucrats termed moderate Islam. Funding Islamic schools in the hope that fundamentalist teachers such as Bali mastermind Abu Bakir Bashir could be eliminated from the Indonesian education system had always been a poorly conceived idea. And as the state of present day Indonesia amply demonstrated, had failed.

Garbage in garbage out. There was no religious freedom in Indonesia. There had been numerous incidents of attacks on Christian churches and the homes of Christians across Indonesia in the preceding years; yet Australian taxpayers, many of whom could not afford to give their own children a proper education, had been supporting this expensive debacle.

Australians might have been saddened by the executions of their countrymen, but the Indonesians were not. The leader of the world's most populous Muslim nation Joko Widodo was clearly pleased by the course of events and the cautionary killings of the unbelievers.

"Do not ask me this again," Widodo snapped at a reporter who had the temerity to ask him about the international backlash.

"The executions have been successfully implemented, perfectly," declared Indonesian Attorney General Muhammad Prasetyo. "All worked, no misses."

There was an unusual silence from Australia's normally outspoken Muslim spokesmen in the days following the execution.

It did not bode well.

Abbott was keen to put the story behind him; just as, it would appear, were the country's news editors. In the days following the executions of Chan and Sukumaran the wallpaper of the soul that was Australian television drifted quickly away from the drama that had moved so deeply, if briefly, the country. The world had just witnessed one of the largest ever spectacles of jihad by the world's most populous Muslim nation, and Australian news editors turned a blind eye.

Two days after the executions Seven News, the highest rating television network in the country, led with a story about Sydney house prices, a perennial for the 25 years Alex had worked as a general news reporter on Sydney's leading newspapers; followed by the Duchess of Cambridge's admission to hospital and the impending birth of a new Royal, a sports events in Brisbane rained out.

Some if not most of the coverage in the wash up after the executions focused on the evils of the death sentence.

Indonesia had deliberately and ostentatiously, with a massive and expensive display of state theatre, killed two Australian citizens, shown contempt for the condemned and caused massive distress to family members; and repeatedly snubbed the Abbott government.

All those journalists had all seen what he had seen, or could easily access what he had seen, they had all witnessed one of the most dramatic and expensive jihad spectacles in history.

They had all watched the balaclava clad security guards, the jeering crowds, the planes flying overhead, the streets lined with heavily armed police officers, the manhandling and humiliation of the captives, the families thrown without mercy to out-of-control crowds.

But no politician and none of the media coverage in the wake of the executions mentioned a Holy War; although nothing could have been more obvious.

In the days that followed the executions Prime Minister Tony Abbott covered himself with ignominy, demonstrated why the public instinctively disliked him and why his colleagues were increasingly determined to get rid of him.

Unlike most Australians Abbott had access to internet that actually worked.

He had just had a birds-eye view of one of the most spectacular and expensive jihad exercises in history; and he either did not know what he saw, chose to ignore it or deliberately set out to mislead the Australian people.

Alex leaned towards the latter.

Muslims believed that a body should be disposed of within 24-hours of death. That the corpses were sent days later, after excuses over bureaucratic processes, was an insulting gesture by the Indonesians to the stinking kafir of the south.

Four days after the deaths Abbott condemned the Australian Catholic University's decision to offer scholarships in honor of the recently slaughtered as open to "profound question"; inappropriate for an institution which was supposed to stand up for the best values.

Abbott told 2GB, one of the few media outlets in the country whose staunchly pro-Liberal on-air announcers were still barracking for him, that forgiveness was part of the Christian faith, but another part called for people to be their best selves.

"We know they were repentant, we know that they were rehabilitated, we know that they seem to have met their fate with a kind of nobility and all of that is admirable," he said. "But whether that justifies what has apparently been done is open to profound question."

At the time of the statement, the bodies of the two Bali 9 victims were only just arriving home.

Their grieving families were yet to bury them.

That didn't stop the unseemly scene.

The University had taken the relatively unusual step of issuing a statement from its Vice-Chancellor, Professor Greg Craven.

It read in part: "Our thoughts and prayers today go out to the family and friends of Andrew Chan and Myuran Sukumaran.

"Australian Catholic University joined thousands of Australians in a campaign advocating for mercy for the two men.

"We did this because ACU is committed to the dignity of the human person, and that applies equally to all human beings: victims as well as to those who have been convicted of crimes. As a Catholic university committed to promoting a culture of life, we stand opposed to the death penalty.

"And while our calls for mercy for Mr Chan and Mr Sukumaran were ultimately rejected, we strongly believe that hope remains for prisoners around the world who face a similar fate. The death penalty is a violent, cruel and immoral punishment that has no place in our society. And yet it persists. In memory of Mr Chan and Mr Sukumaran, each of us can take action to end this punishment.

"As a recognition of these two young men and their supporters, ACU will introduce two scholarships open to international students from Indonesia to study undergraduate degrees at any one of ACU's campuses.

"These will be awarded to academically qualified applicants upon the submission of an essay on the theme of 'the sanctity of human life'.

"In a small but deeply symbolic way, the writing by Indonesian students on the sanctity of life would be an ongoing contribution toward the eventual abolition of the death penalty in Indonesia; the scholarships a fitting tribute to the reformation, courage and dignity of the two men.

"ACU will also hold memorial services to commemorate not only for Mr Chan and Mr Sukumaran, but all those affected by capital punishment, victims, perpetrators and their loved ones."

The Catholic University's magnanimity, their reflection that human courage and decency lay as a trait in those who fell fowl of the law and those who did not, that grace was far more likely to be found in extremes than in comfort, fell on deaf ears.

Abbott's public relations hacks could not have devised a more offensive response if they had spent a decade trying.

The Prime Minister declared there could be no truck with drug trafficking and the university's proposal sent a very unusual message.

The very man whose ignorant policies and refusal to listen to expert opinion had helped create the situation in the first place.

Abbott governed for all Australians, for radical theologians and old ladies in the pews, for transsexuals plying their bodies on the street and the greener than green socialite doctor's wives, not just those with a similar strain of Christian rectitude as himself.

Just as assuredly as he governed for the middle class families of Sydney's North Shore, he governed for the ice raddled gay lads of the wanton demimonde screwing themselves stupid in the tawdry backrooms of Oxford Street, for the hapless citizens of the city's housing estates, for Buddhists, Muslims, Sikhs, Hindus, and for the many Australians of no faith at all.

Abbott governed for those with unblemished criminal records, and those who were in and out of "the Big House" every other day.

He came from the right side of the tracks, came from a wealthy migrant background, and according to reports had not even taken out Australian citizenship until his 20s. He was not a first generation immigrant trying to make his way in a culture not his own. He came from a stable family; had been to Sydney's most expensive private schools and his family were firmly within the top few percentile of the country's wealthiest citizens. He had been to the country's most elite tertiary institution, Sydney University. And he had been to Britain's even more elite Oxford University; a privileged education unattainable for virtually all Australians.

Abbott was not the one who had just faced a firing squad and a jeering Muslim mob, singing "Amazing Grace" with his eyes wide open as he waited in mind-numbing fright for the moment when his blood splattered body would fall to the ground; and his consciousness cease in a streak of agony.

He was not the one who had spent a decade on death row, and made something of himself in difficult circumstance.

He was not the one who, having grown up in the often scrabbling urban decay of Western Sydney, operating in an economy where, thanks to grotesque over regulation there were few natural markets, who was thus prepared as a young man, at a time of life when a normal sense of danger isl absent, to take advantage of drug laws which artificially inflated the price of opiates and provided opportunities for everyone from enterprising individuals to criminal networks and corrupt police to enrich themselves.

But Abbott was the one who had, both in the present and previous governments in which he had served, overseen the social collapse which was driving the demand for illicit drugs; had overseen or participated in the economic policies which had turned a once vibrant, optimistic, happy country into a ghost town; implemented or sustained laws which almost all drug policy experts said did not work and could not work; and had overseen the escalating disillusionment with politics, the social, cultural and economic free-fall spiral of much of the populace into a defeated, severely depressed, inward looking state of mind which was also fuelling demand.

Abbott, a politician who could not keep his own election promises and had thereby repeatedly lied to the Australian people, had neither the integrity nor the humanity to lecture anyone on being "their best selves." But that's exactly what he did. Before the bodies were even in the ground.

In the end he was simply unctuous, cruel and dismissive. There were no other words for it.

****

Alex had had been busted back to Australia in 2013, entirely against his wishes.

Like the convicts of yore, he had done his time. But the extreme levels of invasive and incompetent surveillance he had endured while writing a book on the so-called Land of Smiles, *Thailand: Deadly Destination*, and the mafia inspired howling of the Thai mob which resulted, had left him wounded, fragile, hunted to the edge of extinction.

Incensed, harassed month in and month out, Alex had begun to act in a peculiar and offensive manner in what should have been the privacy of his own home; his deteriorating self-confidence burnt at the fraying edges of nervous collapse.

"We're done here, he thinks it's funny," one of the investigative team declared, packing up after having watched his house all day.

He didn't think it was funny. He thought it was stupid. Why were they wasting time and public resources on him, on the say of the Thai mafia, corrupt police, bought journalists.

Not once had they bothered to ask him.

Under surveillance he had felt he had no choice; and returned to Australia from Asia. It was nice to see his kids; but that was about it.

Let it go, let it go, commonsense cried, but he just wanted to be somewhere else. He didn't know why he had let his guard down. Why he had handed his will and his life over to South East Asian demimondaines and the mafia bosses of Bangkok. Why he had been fascinated by things he should have ignored. Why he had thought he could write about the milieus of another country without consequence. Why everything had come crushing down.

Not to put too fine a point of it, back in Australia Alex was in a place he did not want to be, as depressed as he had ever been. He stared out the front door of his mother's house as if her front lawn was the bleakest landscape on Earth. Short lives. Futures destroyed. Paths not taken. Things that would never be. He continued to pine for places that would be forever gone from his life. An unblinking gaze, he had once written, but there was nothing unblinking about the way he felt. About the way places and people lingered in memory; things that should never have been, impossible things.

On long walks Alex could still hear them, the people he had come to know in the City of Black Eyed Angels, and wished he could not; those lives lived too fast.

There are some people in life you will always miss, he told a friend. And that was all. These things were cast on a barren sea.

"Bad boys," read the graffiti scribbled in black on a brick wall down at Shellharbour Beach.

There were no welcoming signs. At the Oak Flats pool in the Illawarra south of Sydney there was a metal display: don't dive, don't drink alcohol, don't smoke, don't swear, don't bring your dog, watch your children, don't crowd the lanes, no boisterous play. Twenty four instructions in all. Nothing that said welcome to your local pool.

He didn't have any illusions that kindness ran in a cold climate; that there would be a warm place here for him; that there would be a future worth embracing in this infinite embrace of normality, of ordinariness, cold wind, cold light.

In the fine winter dawn he heard a car door slam nearby. Instantly his mind turned back to being hunted; and haunted. Their only regret was that they hadn't killed him already.

So he remained uncomfortable. Morning treks became evening walks. Distance curled into even greater distance. Years passed in other people's lives, while he was still nomadic. And shadows ran across the rocks.

Just when he had become convinced there was a law governing virtually all forms of human behavior in the Great Socialist Republic of Australia, he read a news report of a teenager being charged with "conducting an unregulated activity." Just in case the legislators had accidentally overlooked anything, they had made up a charge to cover that as well.

Alex always walked, and as he lingered through the Illawarra Memorial Gardens, gazing at the last remnants of people's lives, the last memories of loved ones, he saw the signs forbidding the leaving of vases of flowers by the grave sites.

Even to leave flowers for the dead was now against the law.

Occupational health and safety; layer upon layer of rules.

The single triggering factor which had determined his return had been his elderly mother telling him it was so cold she had been sitting over a single bar heater crying.

Pensioners everywhere in Australia were struggling to pay the power bills and many daren't turn on their heaters, no matter how cold the nights. While Australia had the reputation as a hot place of deserts and stinking heat, in fact, as the Great Southern Land, much of it was cold during the winter months.

Outlandishly, the price of electricity had tripled in the almost four years he had been away, imposing huge burdens on businesses and individuals alike.

The frequent reassurances by politicians that privatisation of the electricity networks would be good for consumers, introducing competition and driving down prices, had proven to be outright lies.

In contrast to the dynamic societies of Asia, from the astonishing beauties one of the world's most fascinating city Bangkok to the swarms of children running beneath the ancient mango trees of Nepal, Alex was shocked by the decrepitude into which Australia had sunk.

Virtually every second shop in the main street was closed. For Sale signs were everywhere. There was very little money in circulation. Dreams had contracted. Once proud workers were no longer to be seen.

And he arrived slap bang in the middle of an election campaign; the interminable battle between left and right, the signature tune of Australian politics. But what was left and what was right? It meant nothing anymore. The right, which old motifs determined stood for individual enterprise and small government, massively expanded government intervention into the business and private spheres. While the left brought on ever grander plans to sped the money of the people they purportedly represented; and redistributed wealth to largely futile causes.

Thus it was that at the age of 61 Alex found himself huddled up under a blanket on his mother's couch watching the 2013 Australian elections.

****

In his first National Security Address, in February of 2015, the Prime Minister Tony Abbott, flanked by representatives from the Australian Federal Police, the Australian Defence Force, ASIO and other agencies including Crimtrac, introduced his speech by saying that these were testing times for all the authorities, for everyone sworn to protect democratic freedoms. Already at least 110 Australians had travelled overseas to join the death cult in Iraq and Syria. At least 20 of them, so far, were dead.

"The terrorist threat is rising at home and abroad – and it's becoming harder to combat," he said. "We have seen on our TV screens and in our newspapers the evidence of the new dark age that has settled over much of Syria and Iraq. In Australia and elsewhere, the threat of terrorism has become a terrible fact of life that government must do all in its power to counter.

"We have seen the beheadings, the mass executions, the crucifixions and the sexual slavery in the name of religion. There is no grievance here that can be addressed; there is no cause here that can be satisfied; it is the demand to submit, or die.

"We have seen our fellow Australians, people born and bred to live and let live, succumb to the lure of this death cult.

"We have heard the exhortations of their so-called caliphate to kill all or any of the unbelievers.

"And we know that this message of the most primitive savagery is being spread through the most sophisticated technology.

"By any measure, the threat to Australia is worsening. The number of foreign fighters is up. The number of known sympathisers and supporters of extremism is up. The number of potential home grown terrorists is rising. The number of serious investigations continues to increase."

The Prime Minister said when the National Terrorist Threat level was lifted to high, which meant a terrorist attack was likely, critics had said they were exaggerating.

"But since then, we have witnessed the frenzied attack on two police officers in Melbourne and the horror of the Martin Place siege.

"Twenty people have been arrested and charged as a result of six counter terrorism operations conducted around Australia.

"That's one third of all the terrorism-related arrests since 2001 – within the space of just six months.

"The judgment to lift the Threat Level was correct. Not only has Australia suffered at the hands of terrorists – but so have Canada, France, Denmark, Iraq, Egypt, Libya, Nigeria, Japan, Jordan, the United Kingdom and the United States."

Abbott said the tactics of terrorists had evolved. In the decade after 9/11, Australian security agencies had disrupted elaborate conspiracies to attack electricity supplies, the Grand Final at the MCG and the Holsworthy Army Barracks in western Sydney. In addition to the larger scale, more complex plots that typified the post 9/11 world, such as the atrocities in Bali and London, sick individuals were acting on the caliphate's instruction to seize people at random and kill them.

"Today's terrorism requires little more than a camera-phone, a knife and a victim," the Prime Minister said. "These lone actor attacks are not new, but they pose a unique set of problems. All too often, alienated and unhappy people brood quietly. Feeling persecuted and looking for meaning, they self radicalise online. Then they plan attacks which require little preparation, training or capability. The short lead time from the moment they decide they are going to strike, and then actually undertake the attack, makes it hard to disrupt their activities.

"This new terrorist environment is uniquely shaped by the way that extremist ideologies can now spread online. Every single day, the Islamist death cult and its supporters churn out up to 100,000 social media messages in a variety of languages. Often, they are slick and well produced. That's the contagion that's infecting people, grooming them for terrorism."

Abbott said even if the flow of foreign fighters to Syria and Iraq stopped, there was an Australian cohort of hardened jihadists who were intent on radicalizing and influencing others. The number of Australians with hands-on terrorist experience was, he warned, several times larger than the number who had earlier trained in Afghanistan and Pakistan.

"Of that group, two-thirds became involved in terrorist activity back here in Australia," he said. "The signs are ominous. ASIO currently has over 400 high-priority counter-terrorism investigations. That's more than double the number a year ago."

As well many of those involved in the Bali attacks early in the millennium were now being released from prison—some neither reformed nor rehabilitated.

With rhetoric that he would rephrase and repeat in different settings, Abbott tapped into public sentiment: "Over recent months, I spent many hours listening to Australians from all walks of life. Clearly, people are anxious about the national security threats we face. Many are angry because all too often the threat comes from someone who has enjoyed the hospitality and generosity of the Australian people.

"When it comes to someone like the Martin Place murderer, people feel like we have been taken for mugs. Australian citizenship is an extraordinary privilege that should involve a solemn and lifelong commitment to Australia. People who come to this country are free to live as they choose – provided they don't steal that same freedom from others. We are one of the most diverse nations on earth – and celebrating that is at the heart of what it means to be Australian.

"We are a country built on immigration and are much the richer for it. Always, Australia will continue to welcome people who want to make this country their home. We will help them and support them to settle in. But this is not a one-way street.

"Those who come here must be as open and accepting of their adopted country, as we are of them. Those who live here must be as tolerant of others as we are of them. No one should live in our country while denying our values and rejecting the very idea of a free and open society.

"It's worth recalling the citizenship pledge that all of us have been encouraged to recite:

I pledge my commitment to Australia and its people; whose democratic beliefs I share; whose rights and liberties I respect; and whose laws I will uphold and obey.

"This has to mean something. Especially now that we face a home-grown threat from people who do reject our values. We cannot allow bad people to use our good nature against us."

Abbott announced the impending appointment of a National Counter Terrorism Coordinator, the prosecution and monitoring of foreign fighters returning to Australia, new measures to strengthen immigration laws, suspension of citizenship privileges for those involved in terrorism, access to welfare payments and consular services for those fighting abroad and a clamp down on so-called hate preachers and organisations that incited religious or racial hatred.

Abbott ended his first National Security speech with a rhetorical flourish:

"Organisations and individuals blatantly spreading discord and division – such as Hizb ut-Tahrir – should not do so with impunity. I've often heard Western leaders describe Islam as a 'religion of peace.' I wish more Muslim leaders would say that more often, and mean it. Everybody, including Muslim community leaders, needs to speak up clearly because, no matter what the grievance, violence against innocents must surely be a blasphemy against all religion."

The Muslim community could not have spoken more clearly. Dropping drone bombs in the Middle East, as Abbott was responsible for doing, was, as far as they were concerned, terrorism against innocents; plain and simple.

At the same time Abbott released a report titled Review of Australia's Counter Terrorism Machinery which found that Australia faced a new, long-term era of heightened terrorism threat.

It was blunter and more precise in its language than the Prime Minister himself: "All of the terrorism-related metrics are worsening: known numbers of foreign fighters, sympathisers and supporters, serious investigations. We are not 'winning' on any front.

"There are an increasing number of Australians joining extremist groups Overseas. There are an increasing number of potential terrorists, supporters and sympathisers in our community. There is a trend to low-tech 'lone actor' attacks which are exponentially harder to disrupt: there may be no visibility of planning and no time delay between intent and action. There is now an inter-generational dimension, with the families of known terrorists increasingly radicalised and involved. The international forces driving terrorist ideology and capabilities are stronger, and extremist narratives have increasing appeal in the Australian community.

"Reflecting this environment, there is an increasing requirement for early disruption of terrorist plans to best ensure public safety. This comes at the cost of securing sufficient evidence to prosecute. This leaves potential terrorists at large. It also erodes trust, confidence and relationships with at-risk communities. It may also undermine public confidence in national security agencies and the Government generally.

"The Martin Place siege and the Melbourne attack on police are examples of a global trend: we face an increasing number of potential terrorists who are hard to detect and often willing to attack using quickly implemented, low-tech tactics. National security agencies are significantly bolstering their capabilities to detect and disrupt the threats we face. Every dollar must be spent wisely. National security agencies must come together seamlessly around shared priorities. A restructure or reshuffle of national security agencies is not the answer. But more must be done to strengthen cross-agency coordination and leadership.

"It is almost inevitable that we will have more terrorist attacks on Australian soil." [132]

It took no time at all for the Hizb to hit back, with a release dated the same day and headlined "Abbott Government Scapegoats Islam and Muslims For Consequences of Western State Violence."

The release read in part: "The overall lack of any new substance in the statement confirmed the view that this was little more than a cheap exercise in fear politics.

"The statement continues the disingenuous approach of western states of seeking to alter the victim-aggressor paradigm. The aggressors – powerful states whose violence is responsible for the blood of millions – are duplicitously painted as the victims. In truth, the wrong reactions of some to neo-colonial brutality does not change the fact that that brutality is the original aggression and the fundamental problem. Preventing the action would prevent the reaction. Continuing the aggression is a recipe for perpetuating the problem, which is all we've seen in the last 14 years of the 'War on Terror.'

"In claiming that no grievances or causes are behind the violence, it is the Abbott Government who excuses and justifies terrorism. It excuses and justifies the 'primitive savagery' inflicted on entire populations in Iraq and Afghanistan by its allies. It excuses and justifies the systemic violence inflicted on entire peoples by the despotic regimes it supports such as the regimes in Egypt and Saudi Arabia.

"The emphasis on revoking citizenship, restricting immigration and denying welfare is indeed 'window dressing' playing to right-wing racist opinion on these subjects. Otherwise, it is rather plain that those intent on doing the wrong thing will not stop based on considerations of citizenship or welfare. Indeed, these measures continue to build on the now well-established two-tier legal system in this country: one set of laws for Muslims and another for everyone else."

---

[132] Review of Australia's Counter Terrorism Machinery, Department of the Prime Minister and Cabinet, January, 2015.

The Hizb said the Prime Minister's painting of the Australian establishment as good-natured, tolerant, decent, and accepting did not apply to the children of Iraq killed first by heartless sanctions and then war.

"Who does Tony Abbott think he is fooling? If the 'terrorist threat' is rising at home and abroad, as claimed, the current 'counter-terrorism' approach, more laws, more surveillance and more soft-power intrusion in the Muslim community, applied consistently for 14 years now, is surely a failed approach. The Prime Minister should admit this, instead of offering more of the same.

"Hizb ut-Tahrir rejects the charge of preaching hate or spreading discord and division. It is those in the political establishment and media who constantly demonise Islam and Muslims and partake in a cheap politics of fear that spread discord and division. War creates hatred, not speaking against it. Blind support for an unjust and brutal invasions like "Israel" which has pushed three generations of a people into slums creates hatred, not speaking against this. Dictating and imposing religious beliefs create hatred, not speaking against this."

The Hizb claimed the call for Islam to be reformed and Muslim leaders to do more was a continuation of the heaping of collective blame for violence on Muslims.

"It is not Islam that needs reformation. Islam has a thousand year history of different peoples living peacefully together under the Caliphate, with prosperity and safety for all. In sharp contrast, liberal democracies cannot point to even one example in a 300-year history where minorities were not abused and/or scapegoated for the systemic failures of the state and society – precisely what is occurring in our present case. At its essence, what we are seeing is a slow but sure move in western states towards authoritarianism – poignantly symbolised by the Prime Minister's choice of venue and introductory celebration of the AFP, ADF and ASIO – to preempt the inevitable and growing unrest caused by systemic failures. Fear of Muslims is just a convenient scapegoat." [133]

****

It had become a sign of the socially progressive to dismiss Abbott as stupid; and to express an intense dislike for him.

But fed up with the group think of the gobble turkeys, Alex had not been one of those; and initially hoped that the advent of a

---

[133] Abbott Government Scapegoats Islam and Muslims For Consequences of Western State Violence, Hizb ut-Tahrir media release, 23 February, 2015.

conservative government would bring some common sense to the story of Australia's poor governance; a story stretching back far too many years. For a brief illusory moment, Abbott appeared to represent the aspirations of the citizenry.

The shambolic previous six years of Labor government had left the country rudderless, hostage to noble and impossible causes, incapable of telling its own story, depleted and defeated. The people had lost faith in their politicians and faith in their government.

Kevin Rudd had been swept in on a tide of popular support in 2007, the country sick to death of his predecessor, the "conservative" John Howard.

Hated in his final years, with the shambles that were to follow history quickly rewrote Howard into a successful conservative leader who had provided long and stable government.

In fact as far as Alex was concerned he was a man of narrow views who had been hostage to process and bureaucrats. He squandered the country's mining boom and set up many of the circumstances which made Australia so ungovernable in 2015.

It was Howard who had led the country into the Iraq War, against the wishes of much of the population, and had promoted hysteria over so-called Weapons of Mass Destruction.

Howard had betrayed his socially conservative base by two of his worst appointments, the choices of left wing personnel for two of the country's most significant institutions, The Australian Broadcasting Corporation and The Australian Family Court, dictating the course of the country's social and cultural history.

The appointment as Managing Director and Editor in Chief of the ABC of Mark Scott, a stolid and unimaginative bureaucrat, had been a disaster for the nation's ability to tell and listen to its own story. He was largely responsible for the narrow toggle of stories that dominated the public broadcaster, and because of its dominance drowned out alternative voices; and more importantly, the voices of much of the population.

Australia had one of the worst family law systems in the world and the appointment of feminist Bettina Bryant as Chief Justice of the Family Court in 2004 had, as far as Alex was concerned, also proved a disaster for the country's social policies. Those who thought the jurisdiction's historic antipathy towards fathers would be reformed under a conservative government were bitterly disappointed.

The nation had been happy to see the back of Howard.

But if Howard had been bad, his successor Kevin Rudd was even worse.

Alex had been out of step with his largely left leaning clique of aging friends when he had warned that Kevin Rudd was not the wunderkind they thought he was.

A naturally left leaning country with a strong anti-establishment streak as a result of the modern state's origins as an English penal colony, Australia had embraced Kevin Rudd and his multiple causes, from global warming to Aboriginal reconciliation, with all the zealotry of a religious conversion.

A blabber mouth of immense proportions, a product of the self important public service management culture of the 1980s, Kevin Rudd had managed, through an adoring media, to convince the Australian people, "working families," "the folk out there," that he was on their side.

But Alex had watched him, as he had watched so many other politicians, at press conference after press conference and could see exactly what he was like. It came as no surprise to see the euphoria of the Kevin '07 election, after an initial run of stratospheric opinion polls, fall victim to Rudd's blathering ways.

Rudd always thought he was the smartest person in the room; a sure sign that he was not.

"A once in a century egomaniac," as the intellectually lively political commentator Mark Latham so aptly put it.

Alex couldn't stand Rudd, and it was not a sentiment he held alone. Just as they could hardly wait to get rid of John Howard, now the Australian people could hardly wait to get rid of Kevin '07.

So it was, as he sat huddled on his mother's couch, that Alex came to be barracking for a conservative politician, Tony Abbott, as he watched the election campaign of 2013 unfold.

As the polls swung his way Abbott kept up the mantra: "Stop the Boats. Abolish the Carbon Tax. No New Taxes."

National security was never mentioned, was on nobody's radar.

Five days before the election, Rudd was increasingly shrill, disbelief, defeat already in his eyes. He had made the same mistake as his predecessor, to assume the people loved him, to fall for his own story.

And then Kevin Rudd was finally gone, trailing with him the same peculiar circumlocutions of thought, the same baby talk and the same Canberra bureaucratic babble that had infested his brain throughout the campaign. Gone were the glory days of signing Kyoto, of national reconciliation, disability insurance schemes, saving the nation from the global financial crisis, laptops for every child.

And for one brief illusory moment it felt as if common sense, the aspirations of ordinary people, had finally been restored to Australian governance.

****

Tony Abbott particularly endeared himself to Alex one Sunday, when he had been sent out with a photographer by *The Australian's* news desk to get a picture and hopefully a comment from Tony Abbott re a particularly difficult personal circumstance the yet-to-be Prime Minister had found himself in.

The news, which in the end turned out to be false, that Abbott had sired a love child in the 1970s was a deeply difficult one for a man who had once aspired to be a priest, and a gift of manna to a media always happy to stick it to Tony; a man they painted as a paragon of evil because of his socially conservative views and his tenure in a series of senior portfolios in the Howard government.

Most Australians were rather broadminded when it came to matters of sexual conduct.

But for a zealous Roman Catholic, married with three growing daughters entrenched in a rigidly conservative Christian tradition, it was an entirely different manner.

Alex and the photographer were bored with stakeouts, they always were.

At the behest of the Chief of Staff you sat outside the house of someone who did not want to be photographed; and waited and waited. The hours rolled by, the boredom mounted, and the victim, trapped inside, became more and more agitated. But they couldn't stay inside forever. He just wanted to tell them: surrender and be done with it.

Alex knocked on the door of Abbott's home in Forestville, a neat house on a well kept block, the fulfillment of a suburban dream; surprisingly unimposing for a man of such fame. Abbott's home, in contrast to the expansive mansions of some of his colleagues, exemplified, or so Alex theorized at the time, the very ordinariness of his dreams, a nice home in a tidy street, and it was this ordinariness which gave Abbott so much power, the ability to understand the aspirations of his fellow countrymen.

His wife Margaret answered the door.

Back then there were no minders, no security details.

Alex apologized for their presence and explained their mission; that they would sit there for the entire duration of their shift, embarrassing them and provoking the ire of their neighbors, at which point another shift would take over for the night.

The Australian, as the nation's paper of record, was determined to get the shot of the day.

"I will see what I can do," Margaret said. "Come back in five minutes."

Which is what he did, sitting in the news car looking at the suburban scene around him.

Tony knew more than enough, as a former cadet at the same newspaper where Alex worked, of the ruthlessness of News Limited to know that what he said was true; unless they got what they wanted they would stay outside his house indefinitely.

Five minutes later, as arranged, Alex went back and knocked on the door

Margaret explained that Tony could not possibly be seen to be posing for a photograph over such difficult and deeply personal issue, but he did at some point have to go and get something from the boot of his car.

There would be no comment.

If we promised not to speak to him, to take our shots from a distance, and be gone, that is what he would do.

Alex promised.

They each kept to their side of the bargain.

And within minutes Alex and the photographer were gone from the future Prime Minister's suburban street.

Saved from the tedium of an extended stakeout, Tony had won Alex's heart forever.

Well, until the promise of his government collapsed under the weight of hopelessly bad decisions, compromises, hypocrisies, poor management, sleights of hand, outlandish moralising and straight forward betrayal of the Australian public.

****

That Australia was already inextricably linked into the international jihadist network was evinced by Musa Cerantonio, a 30-year-old man resident in Melbourne who researchers had identified as one of the two most important "new spiritual authorities" guiding foreigners to join the Islamic State. For three years he was a televangelist on Iqraa TV in Cairo, but he left after the station objected to his frequent calls to establish a caliphate. Later he took to preaching on Facebook and Twitter.

In 2014 Cerantonio and his wife tried to emigrate, but they were caught en route, in the Philippines, and deported back.

Australia had criminalized attempts to join or travel to the Islamic State, and confiscated Cerantonio's passport. In 2015 he was stuck in Melbourne, where he was well known to the local constabulary.

As American journalist Graeme Wood wrote in *The Atlantic*: "If Cerantonio were caught facilitating the movement of individuals to the Islamic State, he would be imprisoned. So far, though, he is free—a technically unaffiliated ideologue who nonetheless speaks with what other jihadists have taken to be a reliable voice on matters of the Islamic State's doctrine.

"Cerantonio ... has the kind of unkempt facial hair one sees on certain overgrown fans of The Lord of the Rings, and his obsession with Islamic apocalypticism felt familiar. He seemed to be living out a drama that looks, from an outsider's perspective, like a medieval fantasy novel, only with real blood."

Cerantonio explained the joy he felt when Baghdadi was declared the caliph on June 29 and the sudden, magnetic attraction that Mesopotamia began to exert on him and his friends. "I was in a hotel [in the Philippines], and I saw the declaration on television," he told me. "And I was just amazed, and I'm like, Why am I stuck here in this bloody room?"

The caliphate, Cerantonio said, was not just a political entity but also a vehicle for salvation. Islamic State propaganda regularly reported the pledges of allegiance rolling in from jihadist groups across the Muslim world. Cerantonio quoted a Prophetic saying, that to die without pledging allegiance is to die jahil (ignorant) and therefore die a 'death of disbelief.'

Wood conjectured: "Consider how Muslims (or, for that matter, Christians) imagine God deals with the souls of people who die without learning about the one true religion. They are neither obviously saved nor definitively condemned. Similarly, Cerantonio said, the Muslim who acknowledges one omnipotent god and prays, but who dies without pledging himself to a valid caliph and incurring the obligations of that oath, has failed to live a fully Islamic life."

To Cerantonio Islam had been reestablished.

Under Australian law, giving allegiance to Islamic State was illegal. But he agreed that Islamic State leader Baghdadi fulfilled the requirements to be declared the caliph.

To be the caliph, one must meet conditions outlined in Sunni law—being a Muslim adult man of Quraysh descent; exhibiting moral probity and physical and mental integrity; and having authority. This last criterion, Cerantonio said, was the hardest to fulfill, and required that the caliph have territory in which he can enforce Islamic law. Baghdadi's Islamic State achieved that. [134]

---

[134] What ISIS Really Wants, Graeme Wood, *The Atlantic*, March, 2015.

****

Sexy Night at the Lakeside Hotel in the Illawarra, or tit night as the local lads called it, was their big night out of the week. Girls in bikinis wandered through the clusters of working class men, where Alex would remain forever an outcast. Always passing through. If there was anything to be said, he wasn't saying it, and they weren't asking. "You're not gay?" someone asked; and the red rain kept falling down. Wind whipped across the Illawarra, and a great fragment of life, of time, drifted away as the gums churned with each new gust.

"They're very beautiful trees, gums," he commented to a pleasant enough old soak in the corner as they both looked at the wind whipped trees.

"I like the apple gums," the man said.

"They're not gums, they're angophoras," he said. "You mean the ones that curl around a lot?"

"Yes."

"They're coastal angophoras. There's desert ones as well, big. Beautiful trees."

They contemplated this for a moment, as another gust churned through the branches.

The few friends he had seen were old, cold and grumpy; and he missed company, as he would always miss company, as if in the bubble stream of bars and outrage there could be genuine communication; for someone such as himself. He missed company, as he would always miss company, as if in the bubble stream of bars and outrage there could be genuine absolution.

Empath by nature; an urban synapse; a river through which many things flowed. He longed for more silken climes, for better stages of life.

Earlier in the year, while in Nepal, Alex had watched footage of houses crumbling into swollen rivers during the monsoon rains. Hundreds of people had been washed down the Ganges; and in most cases people had no idea who the victims were. Bloated bodies rushing to the sea. On the edge of great adventure.

"You a little depressed?" the man asked.

"A little," he said. "Nothing. I didn't expect to be here."

Man mountains gathered on the veranda for a smoke. They all knew each other. He didn't know anyone.

An eternal loop. You are here because you were there.

The day crawled into evening and he took a thousand steps home, cold wind whipping around him, gripped by a dread of the ordinary, counting the rhythm of his steps, everything at odds. Archers across the sky.

And played the Jeff Buckley song The Last Goodbye:

This is our last embrace
Must I dream and always see your face
Why can't we overcome this wall
Well, maybe it's just because I didn't know you at all.

****

A video seized from the home of two Sydney men arrested in February of 2015, in the same month Tony Abbott was to give his first National Security address, showed a self-described "soldier of the caliphate" brandishing a knife and pledging to begin "stabbing the kidneys and striking the necks" of Islamic State's enemies.

"We will carry out the first operation for soldiers of the caliphate on Australia," one of the men said in Arabic, declaring they would seek retribution "for our sisters, brothers, fathers, mothers in the name of the caliphate." [135]

Omar Al-Kutobi, 24, and Mohammad Kiad, 25, were allegedly about to kill or harm members of the public with a knife as part of a terrorist attack but were arrested at a property in Sydney's west hours before the planned attack. Authorities acted after the pair bought a large knife at a Western Sydney store.

Al-Kutobi, from Iraq, was believed to have arrived in Australia in 2009 using another person's passport and given a protection visa before being granted citizenship in 2013.

In the national parliament Prime Minister Tony Abbott gave a graphic description of the video, which he was shown at a counter-terrorism briefing in Canberra. "Kneeling before the death cult flag with a knife in his hand and a machete before him one of those arrested said this: 'I swear to all mighty Allah, we will carry out the first operation for the soldiers of the caliphate in Australia.'

"He went on to say: 'I swear to almighty Allah, blonde people, there is no room for blame between you and us. We only are you, stabbing the kidneys and striking the necks.' I don't think it would be possible to witness uglier fanaticism than this, more monstrous fanaticism and extremism than this, and I regret to say it is now present in our country.

---

[135] Soldiers of the Islamic State death cult, The Daily Telegraph, 12 February, 2015.

"I want to stress that we are a decent and tolerant people. We are a compassionate and free society but we will never allow evil people to exploit our freedom. It is absolutely vital that we maintain our vigilance because obviously there is a different kind of terror threat today to the one that we faced just a few years ago. It is, it seems, a metastasising threat and the influence of our agencies at every single level, at all levels, is more important than ever." [136]

"Evil in our midst" ran the headlines.

Australian Federal Police Commissioner Andrew Colvin said low-level, simple attacks that unfolded rapidly, were "our worst concern and the ability for people to move very quickly from an idea to an intention through to action is what law enforcement in this country is dealing with every day now."

In an official message released by the Prime Minister via YouTube at the same time Abbott declared: "It's clear to me, that for too long, we have given those who might be a threat to our country the benefit of the doubt. There's been the benefit of the doubt at our borders, the benefit of the doubt for residency, the benefit of the doubt for citizenship and the benefit of the doubt at Centrelink. And in the courts, there has been bail, when clearly there should have been jail." [137]

****

Hizb ut-Tahrir was far from the only Islamic group in Australia stridently calling for the introduction of Sharia law in Australia and condemning Australia's involvement in military adventures in Muslim countries.

Firebrand preacher Ibraham Siddiq-Colon, representing a group calling itself Sharia 4 Australia, described in widely broadcast comments those who criticised him as "skippies, retards, ferals, Westies and bogans."

"Who is a terrorist? Was George Bush a terrorist? Were American soldiers in Iraq terrorists?

"Any Australian soldier who trains, who hates Muslims, who gets on a plane, who invades another country, Muslim country, deserves the worst of treatments, that is the treatment under Sharia.

"If you don't want to get hurt, stay out of Muslim lands."

He said he undoubtedly wanted to see Australian soldiers hurt if they were going overseas to fight the Muslims.

---

[136] Sydney 'terror plot': Suspect 'used false documents to enter country,' Jared Owens, Dan Box, *The Australian*, 12 February, 2015

[137] A message from the Prime Minister, YouTube, 15 February, 2015.

"They are not going over there to make cakes," he said. "They are going over there to kill Muslims. I want Islam for Australia. I want to take you guys, the people, the Aussies, to heaven. One day it will be an Islamic country, whether you guys like it or not. If you die as a non-Mulsim you are eligible for hellfire.

"Look at the rise of Islam in Australia. We pray to God, our heads on the ground, purifying ourselves, waiting for the moment when Islam takes over the world. So be careful, we are on the way, look out." [138]

Some Muslim groups claimed he did not represent them, and Siddiq-Colon was told he was not welcome at Australia's largest mosque in Lakemba.

Former imam of the Lakemba mosque, Sheik Taj Din al-Hilali, who Alex had interviewed on a number of occasions over the years, was one of those in 2015 was warning of the perilous course on which the country had embarked.

Sheik Hilali had long been a controversial figure in Australian society and a staunch critic of Australia's involvement in Iraq and Afghanistan.

Once seen as a firebrand, he had been eclipsed by a new generation far more outspoken in their determination to bring the caliphate to Australia.

He warned that there were thousands of young Australian Muslims ready to join Islamic State and claimed to have warned the Howard government about the "ticking time bombs" of hard line Muslims in the community. He said radical preachers should be stopped from entering Australia. Efforts to spread Islam and make its followers aware of its background did not effectively present the moderate path among youths: "So the voices of extremism became louder than the voices of reason, and the rigid extremists succeed in attracting some youths under the appeal of jihad and martyrdom to gain paradise."

Sheik Hilali said the Australian government's harsh police powers terrorised innocents and children.

"This creates division and hatred among some Australian citizens towards their nation as it also stoked the fires of enmity among young people, and the evidence of this is the exit of tens of youths to join ISIS and other fighting groups in Iraq and Syria and, if more opportunities were open for more youths to travel, the numbers might reach the thousands," he said. "These youths were nurtured and educated in Australia, so who made them think like this and transformed them into

---

[138] SHARIA4AUSTRALIA: Ibrahim Siddiq-Colon, A Current Affair, Channel 9.

time bombs? I place the blame on the Australian government alongside Muslim organisations." [139]

There were numerous cases of cultural conflicts and misunderstandings dating back years; from child brides to the advocacy of polygamy. In one instance, four men were convicted and jailed for assault after administering 40 lashes with a cable to a man who had confessed to using drugs and alcohol on two separate occasions. After each ten lashes the man was allowed to go to the bathroom, where he vomited from the pain. Ibraham Siddiq-Colon said he would have administered 80 lashes.

In a well known piece of footage, two Islamic men with fulsome beards stand nearby a Western nightclub and marvel that the unbelievers appear to be enjoying their sin. "Avoid this place, fear Allah," they say. "Dancing, music, they walk by us asking if the food is halal. This is Islam. The homeland is bleeding. Shame on you. Do you not know that Allah is watching you? We see here people mocking our beards, mocking our dress. Making of Islam a mockery. We have music, we have drugs, we have dancing and and and ... Dancing and music and disobeying. People are becoming proud and happy with their sin. They are actually dancing in the street. Save yourself the punishment of Allah. Go back to your homes. Get out of this street, before the time is too late. Pack your bags and go home; repent, repent. Fear Allah and go home." [140]

****

In a country which had spent billions of dollars promoting the creed of multiculturalism, there was no more contentious issue in the Australia of 2015 than race.

The Australian Broadcasting Corporation ran a three part series called A Great Australia based on the book by News Limited journalist George Megalogenis's *The Australian Moment – How We Were Made For These Times.*

The country's intelligentsia, or so it seemed to a jaundiced Alex, went into an orgy of self-congratulation. Megalogenis told one interviewer: "We know we're the greatest people, but we don't want to admit it. We have a brilliant story to tell ourselves and the world. But

---

[139] Imported radicalism has snared thousands: Taj Din al-Hilali, Rick Morton, *The Australian*, 28 May, 2015.
[140] Ban the Islamic Extremist Group Sharia4Australia, Facebook, 31 May, 2015.

we don't tell it to ourselves. I really wanted to show people how to have a big conversation again."

Promotional stories recorded how Megalogenis and a film crew returned with former Prime Minister John Howard to his old school, Canterbury Boys High in Sydney's south-west, and captured a snapshot of Australia's longer story.

Howard, who almost derailed his own political career in the 1980s when he suggested Asian immigration to Australia was growing too fast, a view he later recanted publicly, found himself surrounded by students of Asian, Pacific and other regional multicultural heritage.

There was just one Anglo face among the students.

Megalogenis recalled the former prime minister asking one of the boys where he was born. "Westmead Hospital, sir," responded the young fellow. As a reviewer recorded: "Westmead is one of Sydney's largest hospitals. The boy's descendants may have been Asian, but he was Australian, born and bred. Here was middle Australia's man, whose formative years were the 1950s and who led his nation from the 20th century into the 21st, face to face with the future." [141]

The road to hell was paved with good intentions.

In a strange way the Australia of old had been a tolerant, welcoming place. Most people hadn't care where you came from, just as long as you worked hard and repeatedly declared how much you loved Australia.

Alex would once have instantly agreed; that that the breakup of crusty old Australia and sticking it up a conservative politician was exactly the right way to go.

Now Alex was entirely unconvinced; and no longer saw the fact that Australia's historical narrative had been superseded as a subject of celebration.

Alex often enough felt like screaming at the social engineers who thought Australia should be open to anybody and everybody: "It's not your country to give away. It is not your place to invite people on to these sacred lands; in order for them to acquire and destroy. It shows no respect, no respect."

But give it away they did.

Like so many others, instead of voicing his doubts Alex just watched the increasingly dangerous babble; the sad destruction of the land that was.

The Australia of 2015 was a polyglot nation of conflicting interests; the Muslims who wanted to impose the caliphate, the English who

---

[141] George Megalogenis delves into Australian history, Tony Wright, *The Sydney Morning Herald*, 14 March, 2015.

wanted to impose their arid spiritualities and their brutal class system, the voluble Indians who just wanted to make money, the Chinese who did make money, serious money, to the great resentment of many, the Thais who ran the brothels, the Lebanese who ran the drug trade.

One evening outside the Stonewall, watching the new phenomenon of Chinese tour groups flowing up and down the street, one disenchanted observer commented: "They're looking to see what they haven't bought yet."

As a reporter Alex had been to quite a number of the town hall meetings that Pauline Hanson, former leader of the party One Nation, had held around the country.

Her populist anti-multicultural platform had seen her derided as a racist redneck, although she was saying much what many people in the community thought. Alex had been in the taxis of many recently arrived immigrants, glad to be in the country, and they would say as if with one voice: "I don't understand, why do you let everybody in?"

In its 1990s incarnation One Nation called for zero net immigration, an end to multiculturalism and a revival of Australia's Anglo-Celtic traditions.

As could be readily heard on talk back radio, she was not without her supporters. Callers repeatedly demanded to know where the idea of multiculturalism came from and why it had never been put to the vote.

But both major parties saw Hanson as a threat. She attracted almost a quarter of the vote in the 1998 Queensland election. In 1998, Tony Abbott established a trust fund called Australians for Honest Politics Trust to help bankroll civil court cases against the One Nation Party and its leader Pauline Hanson. He was one of the major political figures leading the destruction of the party.

Alex, as was the inclination of his profession, tended to lean left on most issues. Caught up in the anti-Hanson fervor, he expected her public meetings to be grim, racist affairs.

They were anything but.

He had been surprised to hear the heavily accented English of many of those who attended her meetings.

There was no one more critical of the devastation wrecked on Australia than earlier waves of migrants. They believed the country had become almost totally communist in nature, that there were now few freedoms, individual effort was no longer rewarded, and that the ever expanding welfare state and the creed of multiculturalism were a disaster.

As Pauline Hanson quickly discovered, to suggest that multiculturalism and high immigration rates had been mismanaged by government and was destructive to the nation's identity got you howled down as racist.

So much for an open minded, diverse, tolerant society. All you had to do was disagree with the prevailing orthodoxies; and the howling began.

It wasn't intelligent debate, which the country so desperately needed. It was pack mentality at its worst.

Alex had spoken to and interviewed more than enough of them to know that the vanquished, those on the wrong side of history or the wrong side of a debate, never felt heard; and were increasingly angry.

Certainly the noble media warriors for a new Australia never spoke to, or airily dismissed, those many ordinary Australians who disagreed with them.

They never spoke to the few remaining Anglos, Greeks, Italians or Eastern Europeans in places like Lakemba, those hard working and successful immigrants who had embraced their adopted country; which in turn had embraced them back. They never spoke to the people who had been born and grown up there; and been forced, as they most certainly felt, to abandon their homes as the suburb became increasingly like a part of the Middle East. Their simple fibro working class cottages, humble though they might be, were enveloped with the affections for parents, for children, for family life, wreathed in memory; and they inevitably felt embittered as almost every single house around them became a Muslim household.

These were the same working people who, rather than be labeled racists, had learned to keep their mouths shut and their opinions to themselves. Except when they thought they were talking to someone who agreed with them. And he was good at that; letting people think he agreed with them, letting them talk, it had been a part of the chameleon nature of journalism which allowed for multiple points of view.

Australia had been sleep walking slap bang into a disaster zone for years.

It should have been obvious to anyone with eyes and ears that the country was coming apart at the seams, that a once proud, vibrant, optimistic and egalitarian country was no more.

Far from a socially and sexually tolerant multicultural paradise well intentioned social engineers believed they were creating, Australia was a country riven with ethnic and class tensions; the rising wave of Islamophobia was instantly mirrored by a rising tide of distaste for the unbelievers; and far from the wealthy and self-confident society of myth its people were financially and intellectually impoverished, withdrawing inwards and bitterly resentful towards those who had taken the spoils for themselves.

Progressive journalists, academics, bureaucrats, lawyers and their duped mouthpieces, politicians; in his increasingly jaundiced view it seemed to Alex that these people wrote the canon and filled it with their own texts. As Alex had once proclaimed on radio in a different context: "The liars, the lawyers, the bureaucrats and the social engineers have won the day."

If reality did not fit, it was ignored or its messengers derided.

Educated savants with no eyes to see.

In their triumphalism, could these people never hear the voices of the vanquished?

Those they dismissed as outside their intellectual milieu, and clearly unenlightened.

Through good intentions and blindness to consequence, a disregard for the country's history and a deafness to those less educated than themselves, the country's intelligentsia had helped to create the story Alex saw on the streets every night: a society without a core, a country in serious trouble.

The march of tertiary education, the broadening of its reach, had led to a self-congratulatory professional class; over-impressed with their own degrees and the radical ideas their lecturers had so enjoyed throwing at them. They were all foot soldiers in a greater mission, the transformation of Australia.

As one of Alex's former editors on *The Australian* Nick Cater wrote in his book *The Lucky Culture and the Rise of an Australian Ruling Class*, much of what was being seen in contemporary Australia was a result of the rapid spread of tertiary education in the 1970s, the same time Alex had gone to university. A time when the Frankfurt school dominated the thinking of university lecturers, a time when anything to do with old ways of being deserved to be deconstructed, where they all had a moral obligation to overthrow a tradition bound, oppressive society.

"For the first time there were people who did not simply feel better off but better than their fellow Australians," Cater wrote. "They were cosmopolitan and sophisticated, well read (or so they would have us believe) and politically aware. Their presumption of virtue set them apart from the common herd: they were neither racist nor sexist, claimed to be indifferent to material wealth, ate healthily, drank in moderation, and, if they were not gay themselves, made a show of solidarity with a lot of friends who were. Their compassion knew no bounds: the vulnerable of the world could rely on their support, in principle at least. They were plastic bag refuseniks and tickers of carbon offset boxes, for they knew what the science was saying, and it could not be denied. People like them should be running the country, they thought, or more accurately ruling it.

"Anyone who had behaved like this in the Australia I arrived in would have been told bluntly to pull their head in. Their ridiculousness would have been ridiculed, their pretensions pilloried and their conjectures countered by common sense. Today, however, they call the shots, since their voices represent the majority view in the media, education, the law and the political class. On an ABC TV discussion program, dissenting voices are sometimes outnumbered five to one; unpopular panellists face jeers and boos from the inner city audience as mocking tweets scroll across the bottom of the screen. This was not the classless society I had signed up to join...." [142]

The problem with putting only one side of touch button issues was that the monochromatic cultural and intellectual landscapes thus created excluded the voices of many Australians.

And sooner or later, in one way or another, those voices, as unfashionable as they might be, would be heard. In 2015 demonstrations by ultra-nationalist groups including Reclaim Australia and the United Patriots Front turned violent.

****

In May came news that 19-year-old Irfaan Hussein from Dandenong North on the outskirts of Melbourne had been killed, either beheaded or killed in a bomb blast as he attempted to flee a battlefield. Hussein became the fourth Victorian to be killed while fighting for Islamic State in the previous three months.

He was reported to be trying to flee home.
One friend said she made the discovery that Hussein had joined Islamic State when he posted a photo of himself wearing military gear and carrying weapons in the desert.

"I'd never seen violence from any of those guys," the friend said.

Neighbors remembered him as a "good kid" from a "lovely family."

Hussein deleted his social media accounts, but in a YouTube post in April 2014, under a clip of British Muslims dancing to Pharrell Williams' Happy, he wrote: "Here we are dancing whilst the rest of the world is bleeding, fear Allah." [143]

The Dandenong North teen, who used the nom de guerre Abu Sufyan Al Australi, attended school with Numan Haider, who was shot

[142] *The Lucky Culture and the Rise of an Australian Ruling Class*, Nick Cater, HarperCollins, 2013.
[143] Melbourne Teen Irfaan Hussein dies fighting with jihadists in Middle East, *Herald Sun*, 18 May, 2015.

dead in 2014 after stabbing two Melbourne police officers. The pair went to Lyndale Secondary College together. Shortly after graduating they began attending the al-Furqan Islamic Centre in Springvale, subsequently shut after being linked to extremism.

Another Melbourne teenage terror suspect, Harun Causevic, had Hussein's international phone number when he was arrested for allegedly plotting attacks on Anzac Day.

Of the Irfaan's death Prime Minister Tony Abbott said: "We know that the death cult is reaching out to us. We know that the death cult is attempting to brainwash young people online. Sadly there are some people who have succumbed to this brainwashing. If you go, you are likely not to come back because it is a very dangerous place. Do not go; that's my message.

"If you do go and you do to try to come back, as far as I'm concerned, you will be arrested, you will be prosecuted and you will be jailed because there is no place in our society for people who have been radicalised and brutalised by participation in these terrorist movements." [144]

Inshah'Allah.

God Willing.

There was no clear path. There was no clear truth. There were simply multiple contradictions; and that was a very dangerous path.

In the end everybody stopped listening. Turned on the football. Dreamt of a world that actually made sense.

****

From the discarded of the street to the salons of the rich, from Australia to the world, everything was connected.

Alex walked past pools of what passed for happiness, drunkenness, and said hello, as was his want, to the inner-city area's prostitutes.

"How are the punters?" he asked one usually ice-addled girl, well past her prime, if there had ever been one.

She shrugged dismissively. "They're all the same."

For once she wasn't stoned; and had cigarettes of her own.

He said a cheerful hello to the Vietnamese woman at the take-away, and she smiled back. "Every time I see you I wish we were in Vietnam," he said; and she, he knew, could not have agreed more. Many immigrants missed their societies, their friends, their families, they were appalled by the vagrant society, the lack of personal pride, the lack of

[144] Irfaan Hussein: Melbourne Teen killed fighting for Islamic State, Jared Owens, *The Australian*, 18 May, 2015.

communal pride, the expense and lack of communality they saw everywhere around them.

She told him that some Vietnamese said they were happy in Australia, and did not want to go home. But she did not believe them. "How can they be happy, their friends, their family?" Their culture.

A homeless man bummed a cigarette off him; and he agreed on condition he find a light, which he did, asking another person on the street less than two metres away, a man wrapped in a blanket against the cold. Alex looked in sadness at the damaged people on the streets, and shook his head.

"Bless you," he said, as if it was in his purvey to do so, for if anyone needed blessing, it was these. Sometimes he got a bit Biblical, he didn't know what it was.

The clairvoyance of the people on the streets, the fallen angels who looked out from fallen faces, the policy makers never saw these people. They lived sheltered behind suburban walls and suburban certitudes, and would never understand the consequences of their own actions.

But so bad had the situation on Sydney's streets become that even *The Daily Telegraph*, rarely an organ to empathize with people on the street, had taken up the subject.

"Homelessness crisis in Sydney at 'war zone' proportions and drugs, violence to blame," a story in The Daily Telegraph trumpeted of the vagrants cluttering the city streets, having just discovered a story which any person could see, any politician, any policy maker should have seen.

NSW Community Services Minister Brad Hazzard said: "The increase in the number of people who are homeless reflects a substantial increase in family breakdowns.

"There has been a clear message that often it is safer on the streets than it is in a 'homeless' person's home. Young people particularly are seeing increased levels of violence due largely to the drug ice, and domestic violence has increased due to drugs."

Hazzard said the state government had increased homeless service funding to $168.3 million — a 34 per cent increase on the previous government/

In the City of Sydney alone, there has been a 23 per cent increase in people sleeping on the streets in the last nine months, with homeless services in the city at an average occupation rate of 92 per cent. [145]

What anyone with eyes to see could now witness on the streets of Sydney were not caused by drugs and violence; they were symptoms,

---

[145] Homelessness crisis in Sydney at 'war zone' proportions, *The Daily Telegraph*, 23 March, 2015.

not causes, but in the financially, culturally and intellectually impoverished Australia of the 21st Century, it would be fortunate if anyone even knew the meaning of the word aetiology, the philosophy or study of causation. Ponds of ignorance indeed.

Derived from the Greek word aitiologia, meaning "giving a reason for," in medicine the term was used to denote the study of the many causes coming together to create illness. He was looking now, everyone was looking now, not just at sick individuals on the street, but at a sick society.

The Sydney City Council had been merciless in its sanitization of the city.

Unless you were a winner, you were a loser.

Unless you lived a quiet life in an upmarket terrace; you really were nobody.

Henry Lawson had been right; all the greatest thieves were on the outside.

"Pack Up Your Tents" ran one headline. "Council Warning to Rough Sleepers: Move Your Belongings Or We'll Do It."

Miniature shanty towns were beginning to form across the city; outside Sydney Town Hall, outside Central Station, outside the Matthew Talbot Hostel.

A group of rough sleepers in Wentworth Park in the inner-Western suburb of Glebe had made their own little community underneath the arch of a viaduct style rail bridge. The Council insisted that if the residents did not comply their meager belongings, their haphazard structures and improvised furnishings, would be forcibly removed.

The newspaper *Central Sydney* painted the atmosphere: "Despite adversity and hardships, some of Sydney's most vulnerable homeless people have branded together and set up makeshift homes under the viaduct. From brightly coloured tents, plush rugs, a refrigerator and even wind vanes, the group of rough sleepers have done their best to create a home under the circumstances."

Alex had done numerous stories about rough sleepers over the years. What often surprised him was how human they were, how cogent, and in a way how cheerful they were about their situation. The rest of the city might look on at their situation with derision; but many of them found their own equilibriums.

Charities were always mocking up studies and surveys to attract media attention and demonstrate that the homeless situation was worse than ever before. In 2015, it was genuinely true.

A national Salvation Army survey of 2406 people visiting 262 Salvation Army community centers showed:

Median $125 per week to live on after accommodation – $17.86
    per day
This fell to $9.57 a day if they were on the Newstart benefit
59 per cent delayed or were unable to pay utility bills
57 per cent had gone without meals
68 per cent went without dental treatment
36 per cent went without prescribed medicine
63 per cent were women
57 per cent reported physical or mental health issues that were
    barriers to them looking for work
13 per cent were homeless.[146]

Some of the first stories Alex had ever written for the mainstream media, decades before, had been about the homeless. But in 2015, it was a different story. The rough sleepers weren't just the usual characters who didn't like to sleep inside boxes, as they thought of rooms; they were not only significantly more numerous; they were more desperate, more erratic. As a long time observer of the underclass; Alex had never seen things so bad. There was a feeling of disturbance in the air; as if there was something wrong with the fabric of things; time out of kilter. Wild shouts. Peculiar bursts. An incoherence he had never seen before.

One of the rough sleepers, using the name Jimmy, said he was 67, had raised his children and grandchildren, and now faced the prospect of losing what little he had left.

"I am a pensioner. How would you feel if you worked hard your whole life, raised a family, paid your taxes and looked forward to retirement only to end up spending your remaining days living like this. We have been told if we don't clear our stuff out the city and the police will take it away. It is wrong, this is my stuff, it's all I have."

A Sydney City Council spokesman said in destroying the rough sleepers' homes they were responding to a complaint about unauthorized camping.

That was the Sydney of 2015.

Alex walked the streets; and just wanted out. If he could, in his physical form, have been "fluid in time," a phrase that kept recurring in his mind for no accountable reason, he would have gone back 50 years, to a wilder, kinder, more tolerant and far more fun loving place. But it was not possible. Not in this life. [147]

---

[146] Salvation Army survey reveals thousands living off less than $10 a day, John Dowling, *The Age*, 27 May, 2015.
[147] Pack Up Your Tents, James Gorman, *Central Sydney*, 11 February, 2015.

****

"I wonder what would happen if you let it out of the cage," Alex said out the back of a house in a small town on the edge of the Liverpool Plains in Central NSW, a regular stop on his ceaseless wanderings. "I suppose it would not survive."

He was referring to a sulphur-crested cockatoo.

"No," came the reply from one of the local residents. "It's been in a cage all its life."

Every time Alex came near the bird, it would stare at him quizzically, tilting its head sideways and looking him straight in the eye. They had a long life span, 70 years or more, three score and ten, equivalent to that of humans, and were said to be amongst the most intelligent of birds. It was a long time to spend in a cage.

He tried the "Hello Cocky" mantra that many captive sulphur-crested cockatoos could imitate, and got no response.

But often enough the bird sounded as if it was talking, in peculiar little streams. Alex could not make out the words, although they seemed to make some kind of internal sense.

The cage would have been large enough for budgerigars perhaps, but sulphur-crested cockatoos are large birds, and there was nowhere for it to fly. If it had ever flown.

Each morning the wild cockatoos which added so much beauty to the surrounding farmlands and the last edges of the cypress pines of the Pilliga forests of central NSW would gather at the cage, as if providing their captured friend with some companionship to last the day.

Perhaps they were just picking up stray seed, but there was barely any seed to attract them, and they stayed for a considerable time, just sitting on top of the cage or on fences nearby, as if keeping a silent vigil for their imprisoned cousin.

What did they talk about? What did they say to each other?

As the heat of the day set in, the bird's wild companions would fly off into the local scrub, staying in the area for a time before letting off their raucous cry and heading over to the nearby grain silos to check on the available pickings.

Later the same day Alex watched them from the veranda of the local tavern, gathering on the telegraph lines and stunted gum trees; nearby a ramshackle old railway house leftover from the previous century when this had once been a place of activity; behind the birds the flat of the Liverpool Plains stretching into a hazed distance, the checkered fields brown from the recent dry, a windmill in the distance. The dust adding atmosphere.

"What are you doing in this part of the woods?" he asked a couple who had wandered down from the caravan park, clearly visitors. Because all the locals were farmers or farm workers.

"Escaping the Muslims," the man said, with his not so diminutive wife in full agreement.

"From where?" Michael asked.

"Brisbane," came the reply.

"Didn't know they had even got that far," Alex said in what was meant to be a jocular tone.

"Oh yes," they said. "And the Indians. There's not a corner store they don't own. Them and the Chinese. They work all hours. They're taking over. We just want to get away from them."

Another triumph of social engineering, the voices, the politically incorrect voices, of the vanquished.

Soon the couple were gone, they didn't like his attitude, his failure to agree to everything they said, and Michael went back to staring at the darkening fields, the sulphur-crested cockatoos, the old farm buildings.

He had once owned a little farm just nearby; a place he had dearly loved.

As he had written about everything, he had also written about it, in a feature for *The Australian* which began: "All my life I've wanted somewhere to escape: somewhere I could be secure. Finally I've found it: Tambar Springs, a village in the middle of nowhere between Gunnedah and Coonabarabran in northern NSW.

"How corny to have become a tree-changer; to fit into a recognisable demographic, baby boomers searching for sanctuary a half century after they were young. Its claimed population of 103 is probably an exaggeration. 'This could be the beginning of a very happy life,' said the real estate blurb. Clever.

"My teenage children shriek in horror at the mere thought I might take them there, into a primitive place without computers, parties, movies or mobile phones. I usually go alone.

"The last time there was any real money in Tambar was last century during the wool boom. Now, everything is in flux; much of it is decaying, paint peeling off the walls. A few of the worker's cottages have been renovated. The bowling club, with views across the Liverpool Plains, one of Australia's richest agricultural areas, is long abandoned along with the crumbling tennis court next to my house.

"My children are used to the consumer luxuries of the age. They argue over which is the best of the half dozen Thai restaurants in walking distance of home and pester for chocolate gelato from Bar Italia in Leichhardt, which they maintain is the best in Sydney.

"To them the idea that their grandparents may not have worn shoes to school is nothing but a rustic fantasy. But in Tambar Springs, echoes of tougher times are everywhere, in humble houses and sensible vegetable gardens; in simple tastes and low expectations.

"Sometimes, in the sparse few streets that constitute the village, people just stand in their front yards, beers planted in stubby holders, staring at the distant hills, listening as if there were a message in the wind. If you ask what they're looking at, they reply truthfully enough: 'Nothing.'"

He had gone on to explore his increasing disenchantment with Sydney life.

"In Sydney, 10,000 people walk past my inner-city home every day and the street outside is packed with cars. I have begun to wonder if it's worthwhile. The population is preyed upon by parasites, politicians and parking cops, their daily working lives an unending grind.

"Sometimes I fantasise that one day the whole city will stop; that the government will impose one more toll or tax and everyone, sitting in those endless traffic jams, will step out of their cars, throw up their hands and yell: 'It's not worth it any more.'

"The country has gone to the dogs, as my peers are apt to say, escape is the only solution. Find a place of your own far away, and stay there."

But he had not stayed. He had lost the farm in the personal and financial maelstrom that had been his Thailand experience, and while he had walked out of it alive, he had not walked out of it the same.

As the sun disappeared and the sky darkened through ribbons of pastel orange, pink and mauve across the plains and the distant hills, the flock of cockatoos took flight to their nightly resting place; nearby their caged friend, keeping him company even through the night hours.

SECTION SIX: THE END OF DAYS

ALEX WENT TO Vietnam twice that autumn and winter.

That country which Australia had assisted the Americans in carpet bombing; in one of the country's most shameful foreign expeditions. The horrors of the Vietnam War had been seared guiltily into the consciences of his generation; The American War as the Vietnamese called it.

He had always been reluctant to go there, assuming they would, justifiably, hate on sight any representative of the nation which had participated in such unjustifiable atrocities. The quagmire of Vietnam.

America was all in to the world's trouble spots, as it should be, Australian Prime Minister Tony Abbott had declared.

Australia had been on the wrong side of history in Vietnam. Just as it now was in Iraq.

No thanks to Australia, Vietnam was now a remarkably successful society, proud, industrious, socially cohesive.

There was money in circulation, businesses were thriving, the people were industrious, women and men worked easily alongside each other, there appeared to be high levels of individual freedoms, people were free to practice their religions and their sexualities without harassment, and there was a high degree of individual happiness.

People smiled in the streets, and gathered in the evenings to gossip, to celebrate the simple things in life.

Children were fiercely well cared for, and as equally fiercely loved.

That most basic indicator of a society's well being.

In Australia failed social policies of the past had inhibited traditional family formation, led to a high number of incidents of child abuse, and brought natural population growth to below replacement levels, helping drive the push for high immigration levels.

Above all, Vietnam had gained what Australia had lost: the dignity of labor.

Whether their station in life was high or low, most people appeared happy in their work.

In Australia, large swathes of the welfare dependent and unemployed populated housing estates and whiled away their days with soap operas, disputes, intrigues or drug habits; the ice epidemic now visited on the country thus, through the lack of social cohesion, allowed to run riot through the nation's underclass. One of the most popular shows of the year had been *Struggle Street*, a fly-on-the-wall look at a collapsing society. Australians were supposed to be shocked by the fowl language, the unending streams of abuse, the sight of a pregnant 21-year-old woman in the final stages of her third pregnancy smoking marijuana and cigarettes. As some put it: "Why do I need to watch it? All I have to do is walk outside my own front door?"

You could learn a lot from people on the street.

It was called bottom up journalism.

In Vietnam he had not so much as been short-changed; although he almost came close once.

At a corner street stall selling drinks an old man, of an age to remember The War, and therefore with every right to hate Westerners, had charged him 20,000 dong, double the local price, for a "soya dah," soy milk with ice.

His wife promptly stepped in, scolded him sharply, and handed over the correct change.

As Alex prepared to return to The Dead Zone, as he had begun to think of his own country, came the news that police had arrested five teenage suspects on Islamic State inspired terror charges. [148]

"I hear something, Australia, terror," his friend said, at the cafe in the heart of District One of Old Saigon where he went each evening to relax after a day's work.

"Five," he said, having already followed the news. "Two in jail. You have this problem in Vietnam?"

"No," came the reply. "The police in Vietnam very tough. They not put up with this."

"You have no Muslim?" Alex asked.

"No," came the reply. "They would tell them to go."

"This a very very very big problem in Australia now," Alex said. "Very very very sad for the country. They bring it on themselves."

"Why they do like this?" his friend asked.

"Because they are true believers. Because Allah tell them to do. Because they are prepared to die for their beliefs."

Alex looked up and down the street from where he sat, opposite the National Citizen Bank tower. Century old trees 11 stories high formed a canopy down the wide, straight street. It was instantly easy to imagine an old Saigon of coolies and rickshaws, of Somerset Maugham and Graham Greene, of the upper classes and the coolies in a constant bustle of activity.

It was a Sunday evening, and in contrast to the rest of the week it was quiet.

---

[148] Australian teenagers held over alleged Melbourne terror plot, BBC News, 18 April, 2015.

But beside him, the rudimentary plastic tables and chairs set up each evening on the pavement were still full with the locals who gathered each evening to relax, just as he was doing, to talk, drink, exchange gossip, to while away the time before they began work again the next day.

One of the favourite games of the old men with whom he had become friendly was to produce banknotes from their pocket, and then bet on who had the highest number. Depending on the amount of money involved, the exuberant winner might shout all his mates a drink.

With the jihad within and the jihad without mentality that was Australia today, all of it would have been illegal in his home country. The health authorities would have shut down the rudimentary kitchen for some health infraction or other, the cheap plastic chairs and tables on the street would also have been illegal, breaching every Council ordinance imaginable. Much less the grievous sins of smoking, drinking and gambling on the pavement.

Back on Oxford Street, if a single leg of a single chair went from private property to public pavement, the fine was $600. Per leg.

It was no wonder Sydney was dying.

Nobody gathered in the streets and cafes of Sydney each evening to relax. It just wasn't possible; the restaurants and bars that did function were prohibitively expensive, reserved solely for the bourgeoisie.

With his return imminent, his mind flashed to the daily hustle over the seven chairs allowed outside the Stonewall Bar in Sydney; the way the bar's security staff struggled to ensure punters were sitting when they smoked, that they could not hang easily, laugh, relax.

Alex was not looking forward to returning.

As the days rolled by towards his departure, the pace of the streets in Ho Chi Minh City quickened as it prepared for Independence Day, Victory Day or Liberation Day, as it was variously known.

Groups practiced patriotic songs in the nearby park, children lined up in groups to practice their routines; and red flags blazoned with yellow stars or the communist hammer and sickle appeared along boulevards.

April 30 marked the day when the hated Americans were finally expelled from the country; with unforgettable pictures of the final debacle seared into the minds of a generation of Westerners, who to the present day felt guilty about what had happened. The hasty evacuation by helicopter from the roof of the American embassy, the desperate crowds outside the gates, a naked screaming girl covered with napalm running down a road, all were images people of his generation would never forget.

There was one thing about the Vietnamese, they were enormously patriotic.

"I want you to see, how intelligent are the Vietnamese people," one of the bellhops at his hotel had said, offering him a free tour of the Cu Chi tunnels outside the city on the back of a tour of paying customers he was conducting.

Alex was never a very good, or in any case very typical, tourist. He had been to Toledo in Spain four times before he bothered to climb the short few hundred metres from the main square where he liked to spend his time to the Alcazar at the highest point of the town, the reason most tourists went there.

It was a stone fortress used as a Roman fortress in the 3rd Century. In 1521 Cortez was received there by Charles I following the conquest of the Aztecs. Franco took the garrison in 1936, two days later being declared Generalissimo and shortly thereafter the leader of Spain. Franco was still in power when Alex had first began visiting there in the early 1970s.

Never one to turn down the offer of a free trip anywhere, Alex took up the bellhop's offer.

"First we see off the Chinese," the bellhop said, referring to a long ago war, "then the French, then the Americans. We only show you a little bit of the tunnels, in case the Americans come back."

The Cu Chi tunnels, now a major tourist site, were in themselves astonishing.

Craters from the 30 tonne load of explosives dropped by B52 bombers could still be seen; and the forest, as the guides point out, was new, because the Americans destroyed all the vegetation.

The tunnels, which underlined much of the country, were in several layers, because the bombs could destroy the first level. The remarkable ingenuity, determination and strength involved in building them, despite only primitive resources, and the complexities of fighting a war from underground, was a sign of the Vietnamese character.

Vietnamese were known as the Prussians of South East Asia, proud, militaristic. You could see it everywhere, in their everyday stance, their toughness, their wide, healthy faces. They were not obsequious to foreigners. They were sure of their place in the world. And confident in themselves. Just as Australians had once been.

You could say to any Australian "the country's fucked" and they would instantly agree, "Yeh mate, the country's fucked." A once proud nation was proud no more.

In contrast, everyone in Vietnam was a nationalist.

Or as one of the old men he would gather with in the evening put it, "everyone in Vietnam is a soldier."

In Australia any overt display of nationalism was decried as jingoistic, or racist.

The very occasional Australian flag that flew in front a suburban home might as well be a staked sign reading: "I am a redneck."

At the beginning of that most difficult of years, 2014, an illustrative controversy blew up over T-shirts which were emblazoned: "Australia Est 1788" in the lead up to Australia Day celebrations on the 26th of January. Social media went feral, deeming the t-shirts to be offensive against the original, traditional occupiers of the land.

The date referred to the arrival of the First Fleet and the establishment of the colony; or as the indigenous rightly enough saw it, the beginning of a cruel and barbaric invasion and the dispossession from their sacred lands.

"Good on you Big W for listening to common sense and withdrawing those T-shirts which were so offensive to the original, traditional owners of the land," wrote one Facebook user. You might have upset a few bogans who couldn't afford to shop at your store anyway but the silent majority salute you."

"Since when was PATRIOTISM deemed as RACISM?" another user posted.

The supermarket chains Woolworths and Aldi apologized to customers for any offense caused by the T-shirt and withdrew it from sale. [149]

Alex's sojourn in Vietnam came to an end.

On the return flight he watched the sun rise over Central Australia, those flat flat water shaped deserts, once again amazed that Australia's ancient peoples, the nomads who had dwelt there for many tens of thousands of years, had been able to survive, the ingenuity of mankind.

In the news, a report showed that Australians spent more than four hours a day getting to and from work, and were more dispirited than ever. Decades of mismanagement, at every level. Even basic infrastructure, like the road system.

On Oxford Street, the dismal state of affairs was even more evident. He passed beggars, ice addicts; another shop had shut.

On the corner of Oxford and Crown two particularly unattractive police officers, everybody loved a man in uniform but nobody could love this pair, were fining people $220 a pop for jay walking; as if there weren't larger crimes afoot.

Those particular traffic lights were excruciatingly slow, centuries could pass by inside your skull while you waited for them to change,

---

[149] Big W follows Aldi in recalling controversial "Australia Est 1788" shirt, News, 9 January, 2015.

and they were poorly designed, no safety reason not to cross, while pedestrians waited and waited for the lights to turn green.

$220 for jay walking. In Ho Chi Minh old ladies had helped him through the flotillas of motor bikes that marked the notorious Saigon traffic.

In Sydney they'd rather fine you if you made the common sense decision to cross against the lights before you died of old age.

Perhaps it was true. Karma came back quickly. Australia had helped the Americans attempt to destroy Vietnam; and Vietnam was now a far more prosperous, successful, happy and socially cohesive society than Australia. The First World had become Third; the Third the First.

Alex waited patiently for the lights to change, rather than risk a fine, watching the police harass ordinary citizens; and when they finally did change, indeed it felt as if centuries had passed by inside his skull. The number of chairs outside the Stonewall had been reduced to six.

****

Australia had seen anti-Muslim rallies before, but nothing on the scale of those in 2015.

In July the group Reclaim Australia held 18 rallies around the country; including in Sydney, Melbourne, Hobart and Perth. The Reclaim Australia rallies were often accompanied by No Room for Racism rallies, leading to scenes of jostling, angry crowds, heated exchanges and numerous brawls; thrown bottles, violent affrays and numerous arrests.

The Reclaim Australia protestors waved placards reading "Yes Australia No Sharia," "Stop Islamic Terrorism," "Say No To Sharia Law," "More Mosques More Terror," "Reclaim Aboriginal Australia," "No Islam No Sharia No Islam" and "All Girls Must Finish Kindy Before Marriage" and "You Pay for Halal In Your Groceries So You Fund Terrorism."

Supporters included the United Patriotic Front, Rise Up Australia and The Party for Freedom.

On the countering side protestors waved placards reading: "Stop Racism," "Nazi Scum Off Our Streets," "Stop Islamophobia" "Racists Go Home," "Racism is the Refuge of Ignorance' and "Fight Abbott, Fight Racism," all the placard wavers facing phalanxes of police.

Reclaim Australia protestors sang renditions of Advance Australia Fair or Waltzing Matilda while anti-racism protestors chanted "immigrants are welcome, racists are not" and "Off the streets, racist scum." [150]

In April 3,000 people had jammed Federation Square in Central Melbourne and police were forced to form human barricades to keep protestors apart.

In Brisbane there had been a tense standoff between between opposing groups in King George Square. Pauline Hanson addressed the rally, saying she was a proud Australian fighting for the country's democracy, culture and way of life. "I am not a racist, criticism is not racism," she told the crowd.

A 30-year old man was arrested for assault in Hobart.

Sydney rally organizer Sally Spearpoint denied Reclaim Australia was racist, saying protestors had a problem with Islamic extremists who wanted to live by Sharia law.

In their hundreds anti-Islam protestors waved flags and chanted "Aussie, Aussie, Aussie, Oi, Oi, Oi." Opposing groups, separated by police, faced off near the Lindt cafe, scene of the December siege.

The melees repeatedly led to violence; and were costing the authorities increasingly large sums to police. Yet it was in the intellectual and media spheres, on the battlefields of ideas, where the trouble first began. The stifling of dissent, of unfashionable or politically incorrect views, was one of the drivers of these increasingly ugly scenes; because when people felt their views were not being heard or respected, they took to the streets.

President of the NSW Anti-Discrimination Board, Stepan Kerkyasharian, said: "We are probably facing the worst possible scenario, and regrettably, what is happening internationally now has made it fertile ground for people to exploit that situation. When you've got a community which is fearful that they'll be targeted because of their religion, and on the other hand, you've got another section of the community which feels that someone amongst them might blow them up, you've got a formula which spells catastrophe."

Tellingly, there were a number of aboriginal people involved in the Reclaim Australia rallies. Addressing a crowd in Martin Place Rise Up Australia Party leader Daniel Nalliah received a warm response from the crowd. "They call it a racist rally and here I stand, guest speaker and the official speaker — I'm not white mate, I'm black," he said.

The crowd was outnumbered by an anti-racism rally a couple of blocks away.

---

[150] Reclaim Australia and No Room for Racism rallies clash across Australia, NEWS, 5 April, 2015.

The previous day there were 400 police in attendance at similar demonstrations in Melbourne, with dozens of arrests. In wild scenes, police in full riot gear and police on horseback attempted to keep protesting groups apart, repeatedly spraying the crowds with capsicum spray as the situation ran out of control.

Ambulance officers treated dozens of people.

In July Liberal National Party MP George Christensen addressed a rally in Mackay in Far North Queensland: "That culture of appeasement to radical Islam dictated that I should not speak here today for fear of giving you credibility, as if your voice would otherwise have no credibility. Well, I've got to say, you've got a very credible argument. You people have credibility. We will not sit idly by and watch the Australian culture and the Australian lifestyle that we love and that is envied around the world, we're not going to see that surrendered and handed over to those who hate us for who we are and what we stand for."[151]

Five people were arrested at the rally in Sydney and one 40-year old woman was charged with assaulting police. One man suffered head injuries and was taken to hospital. Placards included "Immigration Is The Elephant In The Room," "Say No To Sharia" and "No Bacon! No Boobs! No Beer! No one will Be Happy!."

Hundreds of people gathered in Perth's Central Business District, with police separating the opposing groups at Solidarity Park. Many Reclaim Australia protestors draped themselves in the Australian flag.

Rally Against Racism organizer Miranda Wood said they were there to challenge the ideological violence of Reclaim Australia: "Hate speech is not welcome and we will be there to challenge it."

In the nation's capital Canberra police blocked roads near Parliament House as anti-racism and anti-Muslim protestors clashed.[152]

With emotions at tinder point, Reclaim Australia protestors marched to the nation's Parliament House, but were ambushed in the car park, where they had assembled, by some 100 anti-racism protestors.

Anti-Islam protestors outnumbered anti-racism protestors in central Brisbane.

In Adelaide there were tense scenes as the opposing groups converged on Parliament House.

---

151 Reclaim Australia rallies: Racial cohesion facing its greatest threat in 30 years, Angela Lavoipierre, ABC, 20 July, 2015.

152 Police out in force as protestors converge in more rival rallies, ABC, 19 July, 2015.

As part of a national tour titled Fed Up, Pauline Hanson called for calm as police again separated protestors. She said the demonstrations were not about violence but about people being able to have their say. "I am against the spread of Islam," she told a cheering crowd. "We have other different religions that have never been a problem in Australia. I see divisions happening in our country and it's purely based on Islam. I'm not targeting Muslims, I'm targeting the ideology, what Islam stands for; and it is very different to our culture and Christianity." [153]

The Reclaim Australia website proclaimed: "WE are losing our democratic freedom to speak openly and honestly, we are losing our voice and our NATIONAL character. I am an Australian. If I say I love Australia and Australian values I am now labelled a racist.

"If I criticise Islam I am labelled both a racist and a bigot.

"Since when did speaking the truth about an ideology or practice become illegal in Australia. When did we agree to stop calling a spade a spade?

"Political correctness cannot take the place of informed discussion or the Truth.

"Democracy requires open and free debate."

On the opposing side, anti-racism protestors frequently decried Reclaim Australia as fascists.

One No Room for Racism participant Tony Iltis said of Reclaim Australia protestors: "Basically they are neo-Nazis who are able to not look like neo-Nazis because the mainstream has become so racist, think the Muslim community needs to know that not all Australians are racist. I think they feel intimidated and how the Jews felt in the 1930s."[154]

More rallies were planned.

****

The day after five teenagers were arrested in Melbourne for plotting an attack on Anzac Day celebrations, ISIS released a video showing the massacre of Ethiopian Christians in Libya. They were crossing the country in the hope of finding a better life in Europe.

The video, titled "Until There Should Come To Them Good Evidence" mirrored a previous video showing 21 Coptic Christians being beheaded by a beach. Their blood had stained the bay red

[153] Pauline Hanson calls for calm, NEWS, 19 July, 2015.
[154] Reclaim Australia rally: nationwide anti-Islam protests turn violent, SBS, 4 April, 2015.

Islamic State billed the killings as "a message signed with blood to the nation of the cross."

The title came from the Koran, 98.1: "Those who disbelieve from among the people of the Scripture (Christians and Jews) and among the Al-Mushrikun, were not going to leave (their disbelief) until there should come to them clear evidence."

The video, produced by Islamic State's media company Al Furqan, was subtitled in five different languages: English, Russian, German, French and Arabic. It explained that Christianity was a deviation from true monotheism and started with a history of Muslim Christian relations, followed by scenes of militants destroying churches, graves and icons. Just as in the days of Mohammad, they said Christians either had to convert to Islam or pay a special levy known as the jizya tax. [155]

It was made available online for anyone who wanted to watch through jihadist linked websites; a vivid display of extreme violence which was having exactly the desired effect, instilling fear into the hearts of non-believers.

"You will not have safety, even in your dreams," the balaclava clad conductor of the ceremony, speaking in British accented English, said in the video. "Our battle is a battle between faith and blasphemy, between truth and falsehood,"

Carefully orchestrated, with high production values, including fear instilling Arabic chants playing as the victims are marched to their death, prior to the mass executions the man issued a warning to Christians everywhere: "The Islamic State will spread, with Allah's help, and will reach you, even if you are in your strongholds. Whoever converts to Islam will be safe, and whoever pays the jizya tax will be safe. But whoever refuses will receive from us only specified by Muslim law: the men will be killed, the women and children will be taken captive, and the homes and property will be taken as booty."

Ethiopia had long drawn the ire of Islamists for its attacks on neighboring Somalia, whose population was almost entirely Muslim. The video switched between two groups of captive Ethiopian Christians in different parts of the country, those in the east being beheaded and those in the south being shot dead.

The final sequence of the video showed the executions, a line of men, having been shot in the head, falling into the sands, and on the beach the brutal be-headings of the Christians, their severed heads placed on their bodies, the blood flowing from their necks into the sea.

---

[155] ISIS releases video purportedly showing killing of Ethiopian Christians in Libya, Fox News, 20 April, 2015.

The video ended with the message "Download Free to your App."

A video any Australian teenager could access.

Alex had watched the video while still in Vietnam; it was impossible to watch without being emotionally affected. Back in Australia it kept playing through his head, an impossible horror. More videos, more horror, more massacres would follow.

****

In May of 2015 outspoken president of the American Freedom Defence Initiative outspoken campaigner Pamela Geller organized a Draw Mohammad cartoon contest in Garland, Texas.

Two attackers, Elton Simpson and Nadir Soofi, were killed by a policeman. A security guard was also injured. The attackers were equipped with assault rifles and body armour.

There was an Australian connection.

Days before the cartoon contest a Twitter user known as 'Australi Witness' shared a map of the community centre where the event was being held and shared calls for Islamic State supporters to attack "with your weapons, bombs or with knives." [156]

The SITE Intelligence Group said the Melbourne tweeter had a prestige position in online jihadi circles and was "part of the hard core of a group of individuals who constantly look for targets for other people to attack" and actively seeks recruits for Islamic State." Executive Director Rita Katz said: "They are working non-stop to incite other attacks."

Asked if she knew if American government agencies were following the man's activities, she said they struggled to keep track of American activity, let alone follow global chatter. "The Australians are having trouble following their own guys, you want the Americans to follow them too?"

Soon after the attack a man calling himself Australi Witness tweeted: "May Allah reward the Garland mujahedeen with a seat right next to the Prophet in Jannah." This was followed by: "May Allah exterminate all those who insult the Prophet & give Jannah to all those who defend the Prophet's honour."

He also posted a guide on how to join Islamic State.

---

[156] Australian Twitter user encouraged Islamic State fighters, Nick O'Malley, *The Sydney Morning Herald*, 4 May, 2015.

His Twitter account AustraliWitness3, subsequently suspended, carried a prominent picture of Islamic State leader Baghdadi and declared that he had been a member of Amnesty International before joining the mujahedeen.

Neil Fergus, Chief Executive of Intelligent Risks and head of Security for the 2000 Sydney Olympic Games, said Australi Witness was illustrative of the fact that apocalyptic jihad groups had the capacity, skills and money to put out high quality social media material on a daily basis.

Fergus said the groups had sophisticated teams working on their behalf to raise revenue and gain support for them philosophically, theologically and in encouraging people to carry out terror activities on their behalf.

Footage of a Jordanian pilot being burned alive, "the most horrific footage you can ever imagine seeing," was repeatedly taken down and repeatedly put back up again. "The people they have working in their media centres are very adept, very polished, at getting around blockages and promoting material online," he said. "This latest incident with a supporter of ISIL in Melbourne encouraging people to attack an art exhibit facility, could potentially have had a direct link in these people taking up arms and doing what they did."

Islamic State claimed the attackers as "two soldiers of the caliphate" and issued a statement: "We tell America that what is coming will be will be even bigger and more bitter, and that you will see the soldiers of the Islamic State do terrible things. The future is just around the corner." [157]

Geller said the event was entirely about freedom of speech and said the West was abridging their freedoms so as not to offend savages.

To *The Hollywood Reporter* Geller said: "The death penalty for insulting Muhammad is just one aspect of Sharia. There is much, much more of infidel behavior that violates Sharia. If we refrain from drawing Muhammad, more demands to adhere to other aspects of Sharia will follow. If a group will not bear being offended without resorting to violence, that group will rule unopposed while everyone else lives in fear, while other groups curtail their activities to appease the violent group. This results in the violent group being able to tyrannise the others."

In early June police killed a knife wielding Muslim man whose alleged aim was to behead Geller in revenge for the competition. Days

---

[157] IS claim US prophet cartoon attack, Radio New Zealand News, 6 May, 2015.

later a British Islamic State jihadist tweeted Geller's private New York City address, including her apartment number.

****

There was an old saying in journalism, the louder they squeal the closer you are to the target.

Finishing his book *Thailand: Deadly Destination* Alex had been spooked by the ability of the Russian and Thai mafias to pursue him across borders, those viciously deadly mobs from the so-called Land of Smiles. And squeal they had.

During the writing he had done his best to remain invisible, a has-been on the way to a train wreck. On its release he wanted to get as far away as possible, to go somewhere they were unlikely to follow.

So he went to what was once one of the remotest outposts in NSW, the outlaw town of Lightning Ridge; known for being one of the world's only sources of the prized gem stone opal.

In the past a trip to Lightning Ridge had been like visiting a colony on Mars, the landscape flat, the skies large, the landing strip beyond imagination.

Opal was famous as the only gem stone not mentioned in the Bible, and indeed there were different spirits in this part of the country.

Alex had been there a number of times over the decades, sometimes just passing through, mostly for work. He had been sent there with a photographer by *The Sydney Morning Herald* in the 1980s to do a story on the discovery of a new field of the rare and highly prized black opal.

News that a journalist was in town spread quickly. Miners had leant out of the windows of their battered, dust-covered trucks and shouted: "Hey mate, you want my tax file number?"

Because, of course, no one paid tax in Lightning Ridge. It was a cash only economy.

Old money trees, imported as good luck charms by the Chinese working on the neighboring pastoral properties early in the previous century, were normally only ever seen as small potted plants outside suburban houses. In that summer when the temperatures regularly soared into the 40s, the large money trees bushes were in bloom, replete with profuse sprays of tiny lavender-pink flowers.

Scattered through the flat red earth scrub were flowering prickly pears, their pretty yellow, hibiscus-like flowers adorning branching cacti.

Swarms of white butterflies covered stunted desert trees; while flocks of the particularly attractive bird known as Happy Families, or Apostle Birds, foraged through the scrub; their dark dusky grey coloring and brown wings making them seem like the archetypal bird, the bird from which all others had descended; or ascended.

The white clay tailings of old, depleted mines were dotted through the landscape; while above the last whispers of the Asian monsoon swirled in broiling clouds through the over-heated air, occasional squalls of rain barely settling the dust.

In the 21st Century Lightning Ridge was by no means as isolated as it had once been.

The roads into town were paved, suburbs had sprung up, and these days the landing strip no longer had potholes, in fact almost resembled an airport.

And with progress had come all the state-perpetrated evils of the time. Nowhere was the evidence of what was happening in Australia clearer than Lightning Ridge. The jihad within and the jihad without; it was all there.

"The biggest thieves in Australia are the government," the Muslim owner of one of the local garage said after they had become friendly.

Lightning Ridge was often called Australia's largest open-air asylum, the last refuge of God's ragged army.

It had been a place for misfits; for those who could not function in the strictured, structured environments of the country's suburbs. Adventurers had become opal miners because it was an uncontrolled frontier, a place and an occupation where the normal rules of polite suburban life, of nine to five office hours and the torment of bosses, did not apply.

Many Eastern Europeans, damaged by their experiences with communism in their home countries, moved to Lightning Ridge, a place where they could be free and accepted.

These old renegades and eccentrics, long after they were too old for the grinding hot hard dirty work of opal mining, lingered on in the district, on the edge of scrub, in makeshift patched together houses.

Every last one of those Alex spoke to was disgusted by the drift of Australia into a country of excessive, inane bureaucracy, to a country where the ability to fill out forms ensured survival, where it was communist in everything but name.

In the not-so-distant past no one had bothered to register their cars, and rough-edged opal miners gathered to drink in the evenings at the Diggers Rest Hotel, where the goings on had been the stuff of Outback legend. The men, they were almost invariably men, came into town after long days or weeks in the mines, to drink away their cares, celebrate their successes, mourn their failures, catch up with their mates. And to get thoroughly, shamelessly drunk.

The Diggers Rest burnt down in 2006, and with it went a whole swathe of Australian social history.

Fast forward to the present, and the town's one pub and one club were empty; everyone was too afraid they would be caught by the ever marauding police for being over the limit. And besides, any sign of intoxication ensured they would be shown the door; Responsible Service of Alcohol legislation.

Not everyone liked to take advantage of the pensioner's option, the hotel courtesy bus.

Not everyone liked everyone else to know their business, where they were going, when they were going, how much they had drunk, whose door they might be knocking on in the middle of the night.

Instead of getting together in what had once been the haphazard, character filled clubs and pubs, many of the miners, or those just eking out a living in the bush, who thought they had found a place where they didn't have to conform, now came into town only to pick up their slabs of beer and supplies and went straight back to their camps, where they could drink and smoke in peace; growing more and more isolated, and with the errant, erratic temperaments that drew many of them to these places, depressed and thereby suicidal. Deaths were common; even in the month Alex spent there.

Police on motorbikes toured the dirt back roads searching for anyone who might be growing a marijuana plant at their backdoor. As if anyone could care less, in a place like this, whether someone had a joint or not. Fifty years after the sixties.

The police were not serving the people. They were terrorising them.

One Saturday morning, as Alex walked the main street, he observed paddy wagons on both sides of the strip, pulling up every passing vehicle.

Just as he was contemplating the absurdity of such a show of authoritarian force in a place without even a single traffic light, two police in full tactical response riot gear walked past him.

Miners complained they were being booked for having dirty back windows, or too much shopping on their back seats.

One woman was charged for leaving her handbag on the front seat. Unsecured load.

Another was charged for leaving the window of her car open outside the front of her own house while she reversed another car out of her garage. In a place where temperatures could hit 50C, and window screens blow out from the heat.

Alex had been there when, upset, she came into the Lightning Ridge community. He had the documentation to prove it.

Another man was charged for leaving his keys in the ignition while he sat and had a smoke leaning against his own bonnet.

Insanity piled upon insanity.
That was Australia, 2015.

****

The grandiloquent dreams of both the left and the right of Australian politics had much to do with the state of the nation.

Curiously, the two colossus of Australian politics, Gough Whitlam from the Labor Party and Malcolm Fraser from the Liberal Party, the so-called progressives and the so-called conservatives, died within months of each other, like an old squabbling couple who despite all their fighting could not bear to live without each other; in 2014 and 2015 respectively.

As advocates of high immigration rates and a multicultural Australia, they had more to do with the creation of the demographic circumstances feeding directly into the nation's domestic terror threat than any other two men in the nation's history.

The policies were implemented by the political class; and never presented to the Australian people, who were eternally suspicious of high immigration rates. By 2015 there were suburbs in Sydney where 70% of the population were born overseas, and English spoken in barely a quarter of homes.

Both men came from privileged backgrounds, Fraser from the rural squattocracy, Whitlam from the city; and had never experienced personally the lives of the nation's workers and shopkeepers they purported to represent.

Both men had strode the national stage in the 1970s, when Alex, like most of his generation, had been aflame with political belief.

Alex had booed himself hoarse at rallies Malcolm Fraser, who was considered conservative, had held in Martin Place, while Whitlam had won his heart for ending conscription to the Vietnam War.

One of the slogans of the day had been that it would be impossible to sleep with someone who was right wing or conservative, nothing could be more awful; but spiral across the decades and nothing could seem more ridiculous. In the end what was left and what was right, what was progressive and what was conservative in Australian politics, and what, ultimately, were the best policies for the nation became entirely confused.

While much that was wrong was corrected, much that was wrong was created. For every upside, there was a down; for every action, an equal and opposite reaction.

Every step forward came to seem like a step backward. The progressive social creeds of an earlier time had in many cases turned on their most ardent advocates; and had come to seem by the 21st Century more like traps than enlightened agendas; breaches of common sense.

Alex had been one of those who had benefited from the massive expansion of tertiary education which had begun in the late 1960s, but had ultimately led to an entire generation corralled into another track of group think; impressed by their own superiority and disparaging of the redneck, racist, homophobic, prejudiced, ignorant working classes. On subjects to which most workers had largely been indifferent; or, in a sense, more tolerant than their tertiary educated accusers. The traditional tolerance of Australians vanished into an overarching canopy of political correctness. In the past Australians hadn't much cared where you came from, as long as you worked hard and repeatedly declared how much you loved Australia.

By 2015 bureaucratic edifices preached harmony in diversity, and sowed discord.

"Gough Whitlam has a lot to answer for," one middle aged woman said to another as he sat one morning by Lake Illawarra.

Off shore, black swans gathered, those ancient emissaries of the protective spirits. He could have sworn they were looking at him, surprised someone recognised them.

The death of Gough Whitlam led to outpourings of praise from the left, and a few drowned voices from the right.

Much of what had gone seriously wrong with Australia, its sense of identity, its ruptured political culture, its strangling, overlapping jurisdictions, local, state and federal, its vast spread of bureaucracies, the entrapment of millions of its citizens on welfare benefits and other government payments, the restriction of free or unfashionable speech, the disparagement by the chattering classes of working class sentiment, all had their origins in the 1970s.

The Labor Party which purported to represent the workers had done more to impoverish them and ridicule their core attitudes than anyone else. The party which purported to represent small business and the virtue of individual enterprise had done more to strangle them in red tape than anyone else.

Fraser had been a staunch proponent of a "big Australia"; and dreamt of a time when the country would have a population of 24 million.

The dream was almost achieved by the time of his death.

Those who thought governments should stick to fixing the roads and picking up the garbage were disparaged as ignorant, uneducated barbarians.

The same people who endlessly touted open-mindedness, multiplicity, diversity and tolerance could not bear for someone to hold a less enlightened view than their own.

Whether or not a big Australia and the abandonment of its traditional narrative was a good dream for Australia; many agreed and many disagreed; but those who disagreed, with the public media captured by the country's intelligentsia, were never heard.

Until they rioted in the streets.

As Nick Cater wrote in *The Lucky Culture and the Rise of an Australian Ruling Class*, the first decade of the 21st Century was a testing time for public debate. The intellectual renovators had torn down the Old Australia without staying to build a new one. Patriotic notions which had stoutened hearts of former generations had been declared ugly and offensive, but there were no new ideas to replace them. The grand narrative of progress that had served for 180 years had been destroyed, but the renovators walked away without clearing up the rubble.

"On the issues of Aboriginal Reconciliation, asylum seeker policy, the wars in Iraq and Afghanistan and, later, climate change, it was impossible to sit on the fence.... There were two distinct clans rallying around different totems: the insiders and the outsiders.

"A culture imposed from the top, however, is not culture at all; it is ideology, and the lesson of the twentieth century is that ideology is short-lived, since it rubs against the grain of human nature. Its power to influence human behaviour has been greatly exaggerated. Culture cannot exist independently of a a community, for it is the sum total of the principles on which a community agrees." [158]

By 2015 the country which Fraser and Whitlam had done so much to form was becoming increasingly ungovernable.

As the formidable public intellectual Paul Kelly wrote in his excoriating book *Triumph and Demise: The Failure of a Labor Generation*, vast green bureaucracies had been built on the high moral ground of climate change and a human rights industry championed asylum seekers while ignoring issues of national interest including security and border protection.

There had been a decline in self-reliance, the development of a culture of complaint, the rise of social envy, a growing dependency on government, and the development of a political system based on competing parties bidding up expectations about government's capacity to satisfy more and more needs.

---

[158] *The Lucky Culture and the Rise of an Australian Ruling Class,* Flamingo, 2013.

"The process of debate, competition and elections leading to national progress has broken down," Kelly wrote. "The business of politics is too decoupled from the interests of Australia and its citizens. This decoupling constitutes the Australian crisis.

"Australia's worst delusion is that because it has no immediate economic crisis, it has no political crisis. That would constitute the response of a stupid country ignoring the evidence before it. The evidence is that the political system has malfunctioned. The public senses this and the examples are legion.

"The trust between the political system and the public to sustain ambitious policy is close to being severed. If so, Australia faces an unhappy future. This is related to the decline in proper process and the apparent abandonment of the proven techniques of inquiry, debate, consultation and compromise, to carry policy reform. The changes in the media industry are part of the story. In the post 1983-reform age, the media was vital in backing national-interest policies. But that age is passing. With fragmentation of the traditional media and the rise of social media, the new values are fashionable narcissism and much less concern for national-interest policy...

"The political system is not delivering. Australia is living on borrowed time." [159]

In Lightning Ridge, every second Thursday, pension day, there was a sausage sizzle outside the only bank in town, Westpac, for one simple reason: the organisers knew that unemployment and welfare dependency was so rife that virtually everyone in town would show up at the ATM sometime through the day.

On the streets of Sydney, the homeless, the disturbed and the disenfranchised grew more numerous by the day.

The two great men, Gough Whitlam and Malcolm Fraser, died much acclaimed. While both men died convinced of their place in history, the dream of a Great Australia they had both worked so hard to bring about drifted increasingly, perilously close to vanishing point.

****

As winter progressed, the tone of commentary on Islamic State, both domestic and international, changed.

Islamic State was less and less being framed as a terrorist group, and increasingly as a state which used terror as a means of power, and was remaking the always artificial borders of the Middle East. Increasingly,

---

[159] *Triumph and Demise: The Failure of a Labor Generation*, Paul Kelly, Melbourne University Press, 2014.

too, the cognoscenti accepted that it was the West itself, through its own actions, which had created Islamic State; or the circumstances for its rise.

As one of the Arab world's leading journalist Abdul Bari Atwan observed in his 2015 book *Islamic State: The Digital Caliphate*, Islamic State had to be increasingly understood as a nation. Atwan drew a picture of the Islamic State as a well-run organisation which combined bureaucratic efficiency and military expertise with a sophisticated use of information technology. There were Sharia courts, an education council and a command structure.

The jihadists of ISIS might be terrorists according to some but they were both well paid and disciplined, and the atrocities they committed and uploaded on the Internet were part of a coherent strategy.

"Crucifixions, beheadings, the hearts of rape victims cut out and placed upon their chests, mass executions, homosexuals being pushed from high buildings, severed heads impaled on railings or brandished by grinning jihadist children, who have latterly taken to shooting prisoners in the head themselves, these gruesome images of brutal violence are carefully packaged and distributed via Islamic State's media department," Atwan wrote. "As each new atrocity outdoes the last, front-page headlines across the world's media are guaranteed."

Far from being an undisciplined orgy of sadism, ISIS terror had a systematically applied policy that followed well formulated ideas put forward in jihadist literature.

The aim was to wear down the superpowers by constant jihadist threat; and the Islamists were convinced Western democracies had reached a stage of effeminacy which made them unable to sustain battles for a long period of time.

Islamic State succeeded in its aim.

And Australia followed America straight into the trap.

Atwan recorded that Australian authorities were shocked to discover that some 200 of their nationals had joined ISIS, "making the country the biggest per capita exporter of foreign jihadists." [160]

On the domestic front, commentators had initially been reluctant to criticize the Abbott government on the delicate subject of national security, closely linked as it was with national identity and national pride.

By 2015 such caution had been thrown to the winds.

A favourite of journalists Hugh White, Professor of Strategic Studies at the Australian National University in Canberra, said: "Before

---

[160] *Islamic State: The Digital Caliphate*, Abdul Bari Atwan, University of California Press, 2015.

he became Prime Minister, Tony Abbott hardly spoke about national security, but today he talks of little else. Indeed, national security now seems to define and dominate his leadership. That works for him politically, but it carries a risk. To keep national security on the front pages, he has become locked into a spiral of ever-rising risk assessments and increasingly draconian policy responses.

"Already his risk assessments are seriously exaggerated and many of his responses are ill-considered. And it is not clear where this escalating spiral ends, because there is little sign he or his government are likely to find anything else to talk about. Until they, do he has little choice but to keep talking up our vulnerability and ratcheting up his responses. There is a danger he will go too far." [161]

One online commentator on the story, typical of many, claimed the economy was in dire straits and Abbott had nothing else but national security to talk about: "Abbott supported Howard's war in Iraq and Afghanistan which has destabilized the Middle East allowing the proliferation of terror organisations such as Isis and now Abbott seeks to use Terror as a political tool. Leadership is the process of advancing our society not dividing it and on this measure Abbott has failed."

In a lethal spray on the state of the nation which appeared in *The Age* titled "Don't vote for a Political Party vote for a Decent Human Being," journalist Julian Cribb wrote: "Today we have a political system where, in order to prevent terror, our main political parties agree we should smash people who have little or nothing to do with us, in a far-off Asian land, thus creating more terror.

"Our leading politicians prefer a state of perpetual war, where these self-inflicted enemies provide their electoral self-justification. Sure, Islamic State cuts off people's heads, and that's barbaric – but is ripping people (including innocents) apart with high explosives, as Australia does almost every week on your behalf, a superior solution? Is it not also a war crime? Is it likely to bring peace to Australia? Or more death? Why do we put up with these killers at our nation's helm?"[162]

Commentator Nicholas Stuart began his significant piece in *The Canberra Times*, "Tony Abbott makes a hash of Middle East intervention," with a familiar riff on the brutalities of ISIS, the public canings for smoking, imprisonment for failure to pray five times a

---

[161] Tony Abbott preoccupation with national security dangerous, Hugh White, *The Age*, 7 July, 2015.

[162] Don't vote for a Political Party vote for a Decent Human Being, Julian Cribb, *The Age*, 31 August, 2015.

day, the burning alive of a Jordanian pilot, but soon got straight to the point: "Look at the growth of IS. We've heard, time and time again, about how Iraqi forces are 'preparing' an offensive to retake the area just north of the Baghdad and US-trained brigades are involved in this task. But it never happens. And the people we've trained? Our Defence force will only vouch for the fact the units that we've been training could 'potentially participate in operations'. Huh? What have our forces been doing and is this all they have accomplished? Creating 'potential'."

Even the minimalist talk of potential was belied by the sight of a previous unit Australians had been working with, the black-clad counter terrorism service, fleeing towards the capital Baghdad. The so-called training, the so-called humanitarian mission, all at enormous cost to the Australian taxpayer, appeared to be having little impact on the battlefield.

"Meanwhile our pilots are still flying out of a base near the entrance to the Arabian Gulf, which requires the expenditure of huge amounts of time and fuel just to get near their operational area," Stuart wrote. "The Iraqis won't even allow our aircraft to be based in the country we are supposedly helping. And then, once our jets have flown for hours to arrive over the targets they are only allowed to attack targets in Iraq, and not Syria, even though they are the same enemy. This is utter idiocy. The same IS terrorist is, somehow, anathema in and to be destroyed but only when they're fighting Baghdad. This doesn't make sense.

"As we get closer to the scene of the conflict it becomes more and more apparent that the simple moral questions and answers that we in the West engage with are irrelevant or inappropriate in the Middle East. If they are to be resolved these equations will require more sophisticated engagement; they're not amenable to being reduced to simple formulas of good and evil.

"And that's why Abbott is currently flunking... There is an existential struggle currently taking place in the Middle East. Our troops are deployed and yet it's difficult, if not impossible, to see that they have achieved anything at all. The enemy the Prime Minister insisted we had to engage with has become more powerful and stronger since he first urged our involvement.

"Abbott is turning into that most dangerous of creatures – a failure as a war PM." [163]

---

[163] Tony Abbott makes a hash of Middle East intervention, Nicholas Stuart, *The Canberra Times*, 3 August, 2015.

****

For what was perhaps the last time, Alex walked through the main strip of Kings Cross, past shuttered shops, closed clip joints, an almost empty bar.

Darlinghurst Road, as it was infamously known, ran along a long built-over ridge. In the early days of the colony it had featured five windmills, taking advantage of the breezes from the nearby harbour. It was named after Ralph Darling, the governor of NSW between 1824 and 1831. One of its earliest names had been Wind Mill Hill Road; and it had never been more dead than it was in 2015.

Each step he took was like walking across a checkered stage floor, each square lighting up the past; burrowing back into a world now gone.

One of the plaques across which he walked read: "Many Sydney 'identities' who chose artistic and creative lives above money making have lived on this strip of Darlinghurst Road."

Another plaque quoted the words of Lennie Lower, a journalist, columnist and legendary drinker who for many years was hailed as Australia's funniest writer: "I have been slung out of so many flats that all my furniture is now well equipped with wheels."

Dame Mary Gilmore, novelist, poet, activist, feminist, indigenous rights activist, was also a decades long resident of the area; attracted, as were so many other artists and writers, by the demimonde.

Famous Australian painter Norman Lindsay was also well known in the area and a plaque remembered his words: "What's the good of trying to earn a living? Go in for Art."

The site of the now closed Woolworths, built in 1939, had a long and varied history, from a canteen for WW2 soldiers, to the spot where ABC TV was launched by former Prime Minister Robert Menzies in 1958.

Now it was a Neighbourhood Service Centre and library; with a video out the front displaying a bureaucrat's vision of a homeless man being welcomed in, as if, with the accompanying advice: "Organise your parking permit, get a busking permit, ask for graffiti to be removed. Obtain copies of Council reports. Pay your rates. Get it done online."

All with the signature of Sydney Lord Mayor Clover Moore.

"Energising diversity, driving the economy," the platitudes spewing forth from the video came thick and fast. "We have a vision for Sydney 2030. And we're making it happen."

Alex looked at the desolate scene around him.

They were making it happen alright.

There followed a spate of environmental messages, community and footpath gardens, thousands of energy saving street lights, growing community and urban ecology, how to explore Sydney by bike.

The last message that flashed across the screen was: "Creative City Sydney."

You had to be kidding.

As Alex walked away one of the first people he passed was a council worker removing posters from the anti-graffiti anti-poster aluminum light poles, thereby eradicating any signs of genuine creativity.

He passed by 66 Darlinghurst Road, the controversial drug injecting room, and shortly thereafter also passed by 66 Oxford Street, which had a slogan decorating yet another empty shop front: "Sydney City Council. Making Space for Creativity."

Nothing could be further from the truth.

A few metres on yet another council worker was removing yet another lot of posters; you had to give them credit, they were determined to remove any genuine impulse. "What's it like doing that job?" Alex asked. "It's easy," the council worker replied.

****

As Australia passed through the chilly, blustery days of a colder than normal winter the news everywhere was bad; including forecasts for a sharp economic downturn.

Australia's Prime Minister Tony Abbott was in full crusader mode, describing those who went to fight in the Middle East as committing a "modern form of treason" and in one sideshow over the cancellation of Australian citizenship for dual nationals, as a modern form of "banishment."

Commentators described his government as descending into chaos devoid of process or judgment, characterized by abject confusion and rancor, while polls predicted a political wipe out.

Scenes of massacres, news of car bombings, images of homosexuals being thrown off buildings, ever escalating scenes of violence, Islamic State appeared more convinced than ever they were key agents of a coming Apocalypse, The End of Days, and were preparing for full scale war.

In the final month of the Australian winter, August of 2015, came the news that a specialist group of Australians were being trained by Islamic State to commit acts of terror in the West.

Intelligence agencies identified about ten Australian foreign fighters serving with the Anwar al-Awlaki Brigade unit within Islamic State comprised solely of English speaking jihadists.

Foreign Minister Julie Bishop, who increasing numbers of Australians wanted to see as the next Prime Minister, and the sooner the better, said the news was alarming. "I am deeply concerned that Australians are being trained by ISIL to conduct attacks against the West or to encourage people within our communities to engage in terrorist activity," she said. "ISIL has already used Australians in its propaganda videos and it is likely that they will seek to use their English-language ability to spread their poisonous ideology into Australia and other nations." [164]

Also came the news that among an Islamic State hack of the personal details of 1500 officials were eight Australians, including a Victorian Member of Parliament, Defence Department officials and employees of other departments.

Bishop told the Australian parliament: "This is deeply concerning and the subject of investigation by our security and intelligence agencies. The government takes this threat extremely seriously."

While refusing to release the names of those who had died, and warning that the exact figure could not be vouchsafed, the latest government estimates put the number of Australian foreign fighters who had already died in the Middle East at a likely 39.

There had been Australian air strikes nearby Mosul, Sinjar, Tikrit, Rawah, Al Asad, Ramadi and Fallujah. No information was forthcoming to the Australian public on the purposes of the operations or the numbers killed.

Defence officials were known to be concerned over the question of civilian casualties and the resulting propaganda gift to Islamic State. Most public commentary ran along the lines that the airstrikes were ineffective.

The Prime Minister Tony Abbott said: "I don't want to pretend for a second that this campaign at the moment is going perfectly well. We know that the death cult is urging its sympathisers here in Australia to commit acts of terrorist violence. It's critically important that Australia and our partners continue to work very strongly to disrupt, degrade and destroy this death cult."

****

That winter, while visiting the south coast beneath Sydney one cold, dark morning, following the habit of a lifetime, Alex would show up at the earliest opening cafe in the area.

---

[164] Islamic State trains Australians to attack West, Paul Macey, *The Australian*, 14 August, 2015.

He promptly found himself the first on the scene; again. A car which had pulled up at the tobacconist, one of the only other shops which opened at 6am, and ran straight into a traffic hoarding. A woman emerged.

"Do you need help?," he asked.

"My husband's had a heart attack," she shouted back.

The car was old and cheap, as were her clothes. They clearly did not work.

He dialed the emergency number 000.

The surly, hostile attitude from the operator instantly reminded him of a spate of stories on the multiple incompetencies of 000; but she eventually grasped the veracity and urgency of the situation rather than arguing with him over his tone of voice and stepped into professional mode.

The first task was to pull the man from the car and place him on the ground. He was overweight, Australia was in the midst of a so-called obesity crisis, and it was no easy task. And soon enough, thankfully, a marine rescue officer familiar with emergency procedures. An out of uniform policewoman was also quick to lend a hand.

The man was barely breathing.

You need to begin CPR, the ambulance woman said.

The man, who had as it turned out already had a quadruple bypass, turned an awful color. His breaths, which they had been asked to measure, were coming very far apart.

The ambulance and police officers, who he had been very glad to see, took over the scene; applying the paddles several times. Alex stood at a distance, and watched the man's body jerk with the passage of electricity.

One of the police officers asked the man's wife: "Are you alright?"

"Oh, I'm fine," she said and smiled as she watched her husband dying on the street.

Dry eyed, she looked like she would rather be at home, welded to the couch watching soap operas.

The following morning Alex sat down with a group of old men he had a nodding acquaintance with, as was his want, talk to anyone, act as if you belong.

He asked if anyone had known the man who had the heart attack.

"No," came one response.

Then another man, with shoddy clothes, a gut and unkempt beard, relayed that the man from the tobacco shop had hurt his back trying to get the man out of the car and onto the street.

"I'm a good guy," he said. "I would have stolen his wallet."

This was not the Australia of old.

Something had gone terribly wrong.

****

"It's terrible what's happened to this city," he said to the Vietnamese woman making his coffee.

"You not the only one say terrible," she said. "Many people say same. The government, so many rules."

She was referring to the Sydney City Council; its ceaseless regulation of all human and commercial activity.

Alex was sad, he explained, because he had been born here; had some identity with the country.

The city Alex had once treated as his own backyard was lost.

"Maybe it get better in the future," the Vietnamese woman said, handing him his change.

"I don't think so," he replied. "I doubt it very much."

Soon enough, he would not see her again.

And then he passed; again and again, the derelict scenes in the street; and wanted to be long gone. A group of Middle Eastern men drove past in a spanking new Bentley.

They barely noticed the societal collapse they were driving through; more than comfortable inside their own world.

Walking once again by the vacantly fashionable "Building the Future" signs, he knew for certain: this was Paradise Lost, and it was never coming back.

Whatever form the society would take in the future, and there would be considerable chaos and bloodshed before the final outcome, it was not the world he had grown up in, and it was not the world the social engineers had hoodwinked the people into believing it was.

Screwed by the left and screwed by the right.

Jihad within and jihad without. Terror within and terror without.

The freedoms of thought, expression, conduct, enterprise, character which had once been so much a part of Australia had vanished.

In those weeks and months, that held breath when the battle between those trying to trigger an enlightenment and those trying to trigger an apocalypse looked like it could go either way, it was a simple matter of which group of foot soldiers go to the finishing line first. The signs and portents ran every which way.

For some reason a phrase by a Nepalese rough sleeper with whom he had been friendly kept popping into his mind: "You think you the only tiger in the jungle. Not possible."

The fanatical, the fantastical and the theological, all had far too much to do with the present circumstance.

Alex scanned the news and despaired. He read advice to jihadists on the best smart phones and encryption programs; courtesy of

American jihad sites. Increasingly appalled, he read account after account of massacres, tortures, murders, looked at pictures, as millions of people in the West had done, of those about to die.

The 70th anniversary of the dropping of atomic bombs on Hiroshima and Nagasaki came and went. At least 200,000 people had been killed in a blinding flash, and in the injury and radiation poisoning which would follow. In the moral equivalence of massacre, how was that any worse than a lone gunman killing tourists on a Tripoli beach?

Imagine a world where it was impossible to lie?

In those days before, Alex sincerely hoped, an ultimate grace settled upon mankind, a grace that would not be at the behest of any faith, that would not be held within the frame of any belief, there were too many deaths, too much butchery, and in that microcosm of Australia where he had been born, a depressed population, muttering in its own frustrations, abandoned all hope that the wider world would ever make sense and watched football instead.

"There are more things in heaven and on earth, Horatio, than are dreamt of in your philosophy," went the Shakespeare line, while the words "Apocryphal" and "Apocalypse" shimmered in the middle distance.

The world he had known was gone.

"Be happy that you knew it," someone advised, when he expressed his anger at the empty streets, the impoverished state of the country, the hapless state of the media, the gathering strength of the Sharia, the contempt for native spiritualities, the barbarians inside the gate, the horror that had enveloped the world. "Be grateful that you knew it when it was good."

Alex, he would sometimes mutter to himself, was dyslexic across time and space. Tell him to do one thing and he would do another, turn left and he would turn right. He didn't like being told what to think, on spiritual matters or anything else. Nor had most of the people he had ever known.

"Be happy," he thought, "that many of your friends died before they could be stoned to death. Be happy that they weren't faced with the choice, convert or die. Be happy that as apostates they weren't crucified or beheaded. Because they would never have converted. It wasn't in their nature."

Over his lifespan he had seen the wheel turn several times; everything he and that initial little band he had partied with so hard back in the sixties had believed in, all of it had been dumped from the buckets of the Ferris wheel into another land, or lot. The rise of the wowsers. The rise of middle class probity. The rise of the politically correct. The rise of the Christians. The rise of Islamic State. This time around it wasn't just melancholy at the loss of a few souls, or the loss of a scene or demimonde. This time around he grieved for the loss of everything, his home, Australia, a place, the spirits of old, the landscapes that had breathed a timeless spirituality and the inner-city demimondaines which had breathed a licentious thrill, a place where all delinquent, time-sliding souls met before departure; in the once crowded streets which had been so much a part of his youth. A place where they had laughed, genuinely and freely, in delight at each other's physical forms. A place where they could love; and be loved. A place where they had been, for however a brief a time in the firmament, free.

May all beings
All breathing things
All creatures
All individuals
All personalities
May all females
All males
All noble ones
All worldlings
All devas
All humans
All those in the four woeful planes
Be free from enmity and dangers
Be free from mental suffering
Be free from physical suffering
May they take care of themselves happily.

The Chant of Metta.

ABOUT THE AUTHOR

The first money William John Stapleton ever made out of writing was in 1974 when he was co-winner of a short story competition held by what was then Australia's then leading cultural celebration, the Adelaide Arts Festival. He graduated from Macquarie University in Sydney in 1975 with a double major in philosophy and anthropology and did post- graduate work with the Sociology Department at Flinders University. His articles and fiction have appeared in a range of magazines, newspapers and anthologies. Stapleton joined the staff of The Sydney Morning Herald in 1986. In 2004 he moved to The Australian, leaving after 15 years. As a general news reporter in Sydney John Stapleton, or "Stapo" as he was widely known, covered literally thousands of stories: from the funerals of bikies, children and dignitaries to fires, floods, droughts and demonstrations of all kinds. In 2000 he helped found the world's longest running father's show, Dads On The Air. After leaving The Australian at the end of 2009 he established A Sense of Place Publishing while traveling in S.E. Asia. His books include Thailand: Deadly Destination, Terror in Australia: Workers Paradise Lost, Hunting the Famous, and Chaos at the Crossroads: Family Law Reform in Australia.

A collection of John Stapleton's journalism can be found here:
http://thejournalismofjohnstapleton.blogspot.com.au/

www.ingramcontent.com/pod-product-compliance
Lightning Source LLC
Chambersburg PA
CBHW072056020426
42334CB00017B/1524